STUDIES IN CHURC

THE
VENERABLE BEDE
HIS LIFE AND WRITINGS

BY THE

RT. REV. G. F. BROWNE, D.D.

FORMERLY BISHOP OF STEPNEY AND OF BRISTOL
VICE-PRESIDENT OF THE SOCIETY OF ANTIQUARIES

PREFACE

THIS book in its original form was an Essay for the degree of Bachelor in Divinity in the University of Cambridge. It was published in 1879 by the Society for the Promotion of Christian Knowledge, in their series of "The Fathers for English Readers." It has had a steady sale and has been reprinted from time to time. Its main purpose was to deal with the personal and historical parts of Bede's writings.

My five years' tenure of the Professorship of Art and Archæology in the University of Cambridge, 1888–92, resulted from and led to continuous study of the treasures that still remain to us in various parts of these islands from the early ages of Christianity. Several of the books on the History of our Church which I have written since this Essay was published have dealt with some of these treasures and have contained illustrations of them. The two delightful volumes of Bede's Histories with which the Reverend Charles Plummer of Corpus Christi College, Oxford, has enlarged and enriched our knowledge of Bede and his times appeared in 1896. When a fresh reprint of my Essay was called for in 1918, the stereotype plates had been melted down at the instance of the Government. It seemed right to recast and greatly enlarge the book, including in its survey the other parts of Bede's voluminous writings, and giving illustrations of some of the interesting objects described in the text. I have not observed strict uniformity or scientific accuracy in the spelling of Anglo-Saxon names.

G. F. BROWNE.

2 CAMPDEN HOUSE ROAD,
KENSINGTON, W. 8.

CONTENTS

CHAPTER I

THE PERSONAL HISTORY OF BEDE

Aldhelm, Bede, Alcuin—Bede's boyhood—Benedict Biscop—
Bede's Ordination—John of Beverley—A monk's and a
priest's life—Date of Bede's death—The death scene—
Bede's summary of his life—His list of his writings—The
epithet "Venerable"

CHAPTER II

THE CONVERSION OF NORTHUMBRIA

The seven kingdoms—Descent of the kings—Deira and Ber-
nicia—The slave youths in Rome—Pope Gregory's arrange-
ments for the conversion of England—Edwin of Deira—
Importance of York—A Kentish princess—Letters from
Pope Boniface—Paulinus—The Northumbrian House of
Lords—Coifi the archpriest—The British kings Cadfan and
Cadwalla—Defeat and death of Edwin—Apostasy—
Churches built by Paulinus—The West Riding—James the
deacon—Love of music

CHAPTER III

THE RESTORATION OF CHRISTIANITY IN NORTHUMBRIA

Oswald and his brothers—Vision of Columba—Origins of our
Coronation Service—Iona and Aidan—Union of Deira
and Bernicia—Oswald's death—Oswin in Deira—Aidan's
death .

The Venerable Bede

Contents

CHAPTER VIII

THE LIFE OF ST. CUTHBERT

CHAPTER IX

CAEDMON AND WILFRITH

CHAPTER X

THE EPISTLE TO ECGBERT

The Venerable Bede

Contents

THE VENERABLE BEDE

CHAPTER I

THE PERSONAL HISTORY OF BEDE

Aldhelm, Bede, Alcuin—Bede's boyhood—Benedict Biscop—Bede's
Ordination—John of Beverley—A monk's and a priest's life—
Date of Bede's death—The death scene—Bede's summary of his
life—His list of his writings—The epithet "Venerable."

THE early years of the Church in England produced
three great scholars, one after the other, Aldhelm,
Bede, Alcuin. The first was born in or about 635, the
last died in 804. Bede was born about forty years
after Aldhelm, and was a man of thirty-six when
Aldhelm died. Alcuin was born in the year in which
Bede died. Thus the series of great men may be
literally described as continuous.

While the influence of their writings reached far
beyond their own land, the areas of their personal
influence differed very widely. Aldhelm was of the
royal race of the West Saxons, his birth nearly coin-
ciding with the baptism of the first Christian king of
the West Saxons, Cynegils. He was Abbat of the
important monastery of Malmesbury, and on the
division of the bishopric of the West Saxons he became
bishop of the western part, which he covered with

active work. He died at the age of seventy-four,
leaving a widespread personal mark. Bede was a
choir-boy in a newly founded monastery, was ordained
deacon and priest there, lived, wrote, and died there.
In the immediate vicinity of his monastery he was
seen and known and received with much kindness.
Of visits to a distance requiring absence from his cell
at night we only know of two, on one of which occasions
his personal influence had a large effect. Alcuin also
was an inmate of a monastic school almost from
infancy. He became Master of the School of York
in succession to two archbishops of royal race, and
passed thence into the service and friendship of
Charlemagne, in which position his personal influence
and the influence of his letters may fairly be said to
have covered the whole of Europe. He was ordained
deacon early, and never proceeded to the priesthood.

Aldhelm's early training was given at Malmesbury
by an Irish monk, a fugitive from his native land. In
his days, English students had to go over to Ireland to
find learned teachers, and against the need for this
Aldhelm protested vigorously. His more advanced
training came from Abbat Hadrian and Archbishop
Theodore. Thus he had Celtic, Latin, and Greek
elements in his building up in scholarship. Lanfranc
canonised him. Bede was trained by the much-travelled
Benedict Biscop in all that appertained to the monastic
and the priestly life, and he had access to a well-stored
library of manuscripts from Italy and Gaul. Alcuin
was trained by his royal master, Archbishop Ecgbert
of York, and later by Ecgbert's cousin and successor
Albert. These men gathered together a vast library
of ecclesiastical and secular works, probably as great
a library as then existed in the West, and this library

Albert bequeathed to Alcuin, who succeeded him in the mastership of the School of York. Of Ecgbert his first teacher, William of Malmesbury, who wrote a generation after the Norman Conquest, declares that he was an armoury of all the liberal arts, and founded the most noble Library of York. It is needless to say that William fully recognises the unique importance of these three great Englishmen, Aldhelm, Bede, Alcuin.

Of this unique series of English scholars and churchmen, we are now concerned with the middle term, the Venerable Bede. But we shall bear in mind the fact that he is a middle term, and when occasion serves we shall bring in illustrative matter from him who went before and from him who came after.

The Venerable Bede is one of the most striking figures in the history of the English Church. A voluminous and learned Christian writer on many subjects, theological, historical, grammatical, and physical, he sprang from an immediate ancestry of unlettered pagans. The first preacher of Christianity who visited his fathers arrived in the country only fifty years before Bede's birth. Forty years before his birth, the kings of the land were heathens ; one, indeed, was worse than a heathen, for he had been called a Christian and had abjured the faith of Christ. The progress made in those forty years was marvellous. We find kings and people vying with one another in paying honour to Christian bishops and priests ; churches rising in one town and village after another ; large grants of land—grants too profuse, Bede says—for the foundation of monasteries. At the time when Bede was born, we find a Northumbrian noble building the monastery which afterwards received him, employing workmen and manufacturers of glass from Italy, where he studied all the details of the monastic life, in order that his church and all his arrangements might be worthy of his holy purpose. Here, in a monastery built by one who must have passed his boyhood while the land was still pagan, Bede lived and wrote and died but one generation later. In these present times of active missionary enterprise it is difficult to imagine anything more encouraging, and more full of hopeful prophecy, than the final conversion of Northumbria, with its speedy outcome in the person of the Venerable Bede.

The life of Bede was the quiet uneventful life of a monastic student in time of peace. Very little information has been put on record respecting him, probably because there was little to record. The main outlines of his life are all that we know. There is a singular absence of personal allusion in his writings, even where some reference to himself or to his surroundings would have been natural. Thus, to take an instance, in his sermon on the dedication day of the church at Jarrow he makes not the slightest reference to any detail of the building itself. He gives an account of the founder, describes minutely the Temple of Solomon, entering into much curious explanation of the symbolism intended by its dimensions and arrangement, and then raises his hearers at once to the Temple not made with hands.

The Venerable Bede was born in the year of our Lord 673, or possibly a year earlier. The actual place of his birth cannot be determined. He tells us that it was somewhere in the territory assigned about the time of his birth to Benedict Biscop, who founded there the twin monasteries of Wearmouth and Jarrow.

The former of these, the monastery of St. Peter, on the north bank of the river Wear, was built in the year 674, and here Bede was placed at the age of seven years under the charge of the founder, who ruled the monastery as its abbat. Boys in Saxon monasteries did not fare badly. We have a colloquy in which a boy is made to describe his daily food in his monastery. He had worts (*i.e.* kitchen herbs), fish, cheese, butter, beans, and flesh meats. He drank ale when he could get it, and water when he could not wine was too dear.

The sister monastery of St. Paul, at Jarrow, on the south bank of the Tyne, was built by Benedict in the year 682, and Bede was transferred to that establishment under Ceolfrid, its first abbat. Here he remained for the rest of his life, occupying himself in the practical work of the monks, in the priestly office, and in incessant study, literary work, and teaching.

There is a charming account, in the anonymous History of the Abbats of Jarrow which Dr. Giles gives in his fifth volume, of the love of the Psalms and of chanting in which Bede was brought up. He is not mentioned by name, but it is beyond doubt that he is the *unus puerulus*, the one little boy, of the story. We cannot do better than borrow Dr. Plummer's sympathetic rendering of the passage. It was the time of a terrible plague.

" In the monastery over which Ceolfrid presided, all who could read or preach or recite the antiphons and responses were swept away, except the abbot himself and one little lad nourished and taught by him, who is now a priest of the same monastery, and both by word of mouth and by writing commends to all who wish to know them the abbot's worthy deeds.

And the abbot, sad at heart because of this visitation, ordained that, contrary to their former rite, they should, except at vespers and matins, recite their psalms without antiphons. And when this had been done with many tears and lamentations on his part for the space of a week, he could not bear it any longer, but deemed that the psalms, with their antiphons, should be restored according to the order of the regular course ; and all assisting, by means of himself and the aforesaid boy he carried out with no little labour that which he had decreed, until he could either himself train or procure from elsewhere men able to take part in the divine service."

In a striking sermon on the text, " Every one that hath forsaken houses, &c.," preached on the anniversary of Benedict Biscop's death, a sort of Commemoration Sermon, Bede gives a summary of this good man's useful life. A noble by birth, he gave up his place and prospects in the king's household, and went to Rome. There he studied monastic institutions, and was tonsured, and there he determined to spend the rest of his life. Pope Vitalian, however, sent him to England again with Theodore, the great Archbishop of Canterbury whom England owed to the discrimination of that pontiff. King Ecgfrid gave him sites for two monasteries, not taking them—as Bede significantly remarks—from some one else, but giving from his own property. Here Benedict built, as has been said, Monk Wearmouth and Jarrow, the latter about five miles from Wearmouth ; and over these twin establishments he ruled for many years.

Benedict frequently visited the Continent. He never came back empty,—unlike many of those who have made a continental tour, as Bede remarks.

He brought over with him at various times all sorts of treasures for his monasteries. Now a supply of holy books, now the relics of martyrs ; now architects for building his church, now glass-makers for filling and beautifying its windows ; now masters in the art of chanting, keeping them with him a whole year ; now a letter of privileges from the Pope, declaring the monasteries free from visitation. Pictures, too, he brought, representing scenes from Scripture ; intending these not only for ornaments in the church, but also as a means of instruction for those who were not able to read. Indeed, he stored his monasteries so abundantly with things necessary for learning, that the inmates had at hand all the information and assistance they required in the courses of study open to them.

It was necessary to say so much as this of Benedict here, in order to show Bede's surroundings and opportunities. We shall see more of him later on.

How extensive those studies were may be to some extent gathered from a list of the books and treatises which Bede himself wrote. The list[1] is appended by Bede to the Fifth Book of his Ecclesiastical History, and is prefaced by an autobiographical account of the writer, containing, unfortunately, only eighteen or twenty lines. It is concluded by a short sentence of prayerful hope that the Lord Jesus, who had graciously allowed him to partake of the words of wisdom and knowledge, would some time or other take him to the fountain of all knowledge, where he might always appear before His face.

At the age of nineteen, six years before the then canonical age, Bede was ordained Deacon. At the age of thirty he was ordained Priest. At the age of

---

[1] See pages 16–18.

fifty-nine he completed his greatest work, the Ecclesiastical History of the English Race. Four years later he died. In a few brief words he gives a summary account of his life and labours. " I spent all my years in that monastery, ever intent upon the study of the Scriptures. In the intervals between the duties enjoined by the disciplinary rule and the daily care of chanting in the church, I took sweet pleasure in always learning, teaching, or writing." The Bishop who ordained him was John, Bishop of Hexham, who had been educated under Hilda at Whitby. This John is better known as John of Beverley, a pupil of the learned and wise Archbishop Theodore, and it may well be that Bede owed to him much of his learning, especially in the Greek tongue. For Theodore, who was a native of Tarsus in Cilicia, had introduced the knowledge of Greek into England, and fostered it so carefully that in Bede's time there were many who spoke Greek with as much ease as English. The art of chanting Bede learned from a famous adept, John, the Archchanter of St. Peter's at Rome, whom Pope Agatho lent for a year to Benedict Biscop. We are told that multitudes of people from the country round came to Wearmouth to hear John sing.

It is said that Bede declined the office of abbat, not wishing to deprive himself of leisure for study. A glance at the business and necessary occupations of the inmates of a monastery, as gathered from Bede's writings, will show that even without the onerous duties of the abbat, external and domestic, the ordinary priest-monk could not have had very much leisure. The brothers occupied themselves in threshing and winnowing their corn ; in giving milk to the lambs and calves ; in baking, gardening, cooking, and other parts of the less menial work of a large establishment. A considerable part of the day was spent in the observances enjoined by the Rule under which the regular monks lived. The priestly office gave continual work. " The mass-priest must have his missal, his singing-book, his reading-book, his psalter, his manual, his penitential, his numeral. He must have his officiating garments, and must sing from sunrise, with the nine intervals and the nine readings.'' So said an Anglo-Saxon law in later times, and to this considerable amount of work no doubt Bede refers when he speaks of his daily care of chanting in the church. Add to this the preparation and delivery of frequent sermons. When all these duties had been scrupulously performed, then, and only then, had Bede leisure for his reading and teaching, and for the voluminous works which proceeded from his pen. Even in these present times, with all their facilities for literary labour, few lives of fifty-nine years can render so good an account of themselves.

We may reject as undoubtedly erroneous the statement that Bede visited Rome. Some of the monks from Jarrow visited Rome in 701, a year before Bede was priested. It is probable that Pope Sergius may have invited Bede to visit Rome. Some one in the later ages invented the story that he was a Professor in the University of Cambridge, one of the least improbable parts of the story being that the date assigned to his Professorship makes him nine years old at the time. His house was shown between St. John's College and the Round Church (Fuller) ! There is no trustworthy record of any prolonged absence from his monastery. In a letter to a fellow priest on the subject of the vernal equinox, he alludes to a charming visit

he had paid to his correspondent. In the same incidental way we learn that he had stayed with Ecgbert,
at that time Bishop of York. And in a sermon to which
reference has already been made, he reminds his
monastic audience of the experience they all had on
their occasional visits to the world outside, how every
one welcomed them and was eager to house and feed
them. We know also that he visited Lindisfarne, to
read to the monks his history of the lives of the holy
abbats of that monastery. He was afterwards enrolled
in their Book of Life.

If we have little or no detailed information as to
the facts of Bede's life, we have at least a full account
of his death, written by an eye-witness, Cuthbert, to
his friend Cuthwine. And the account is so touchingly
written, it shows us so kind a master, so loving a friend,
so true a Christian, that we may well wish we had some
account of his life from the same hand. We learn from
this letter that Bede died on Wednesday, the eve of
Ascension Day, and he died rather late in the evening,
for we have the account of a good deal which happened
after three o'clock on Wednesday afternoon. Ascension
Day was held to commence at vespers on the preceding
day, and thus Bede lived till Ascension Day, Holy
Thursday, according to the Church's reckoning, and
yet he died on Wednesday according to civil reckoning.
The writer of the touching account of Bede's death
says clearly and formally that Bede lived " up to the
day of the Lord's Ascension, that is, the seventh of the
calends of June." The seventh of the calends of June
is May 26, and thus Ascension Day was May 26. This
was the case in 735 A.D., so that the year 735 fulfils the
necessary conditions. If the meaning could be taken
to be that the date given is the date of the Wednesday

before Ascension Day, the day on which he was taken ill, Ascension Day would be May 27, and that gives 751 as the year of death, which is much too late. It is, however, very difficult to get this meaning from the words.

A different indication of date is given by a manuscript at St. Gall which contains the letter from Cuthbert. It is probably of the eighth century, by far the earliest copy of the letter we possess. It is also the only copy that gives this other date, the " seventh of the Ides of May " instead of the " seventh of the kalends of June," May 9 instead of May 26. Ascension Day did not fall on May 9 in any year between 720 and 799. But in 742 May 9 was the Wednesday before Ascension Day, and it has been argued that Cuthbert was giving the date of the Wednesday, not of the Thursday. This is a forced explanation, as has been pointed out above, and to put the date so late as 742 contradicts the definite statement of the Continuator of the Ecclesiastical History, that Bede died in 735. We know from Bede's letter to Ecgbert, of which we shall see much later on, that in that year Bede was too ill to pay a promised visit to him, and it was probably this illness that carried him off. Further, he closes his own list of his works with his fifty-ninth year, and 742 would leave ten years without any recorded work of his.

It is a curious and interesting coincidence that a like difficulty of precise date occurs in the statement of the final seizure of another of our three greatest men, Alcuin. Indeed it is almost more than curious, for in each case not only Ascension Day but also the seventh of the Ides of May plays an important part. On the night of the Ascension (*nocte Ascensionis*

Domini) he fell fainting on his bed ; on the day of
Pentecost he died. The Annals of Pettau, a monastery
near Salzburg, where we may feel sure that Alcuin's
greatest friend Arno, Archbishop of Salzburg, had all
the facts of Alcuin's last days carefully recorded, tell
us that in 804 Alcuin was struck down on the fifth
day of the week, the eighth of the Ides of May. But
in that year, 804, Ascension Day fell on May 9, so
that Holy Thursday must have been the seventh of
the Ides of May, the day which the St. Gall manuscript
gives as the death day of Bede.

We can now proceed with a summary of Cuthbert's
delightful letter.

From the very slight medical details which are given,
we gather that his death was due to his sedentary
occupations, and to the stooping attitude so constantly
maintained by one who wrote many books in those
days of slow writing. About a fortnight before Easter
in the year in which he died, he was greatly troubled
with shortness of breath, but mercifully without much
pain. He lingered on for some weeks. Throughout the
whole of this time, he gave thanks to God every hour,
day and night, cheerful and always rejoicing. He daily
read lessons to his disciples, and whatever remained of
the day he spent in singing psalms. If a short sleep
interrupted these exercises, he no sooner awoke than he
gave thanks to God with uplifted hands. " I declare
with truth," the faithful Cuthbert exclaims, " I have
never seen with my eyes, nor heard with my ears, any
one so lovingly earnest in giving thanks to the living
God."

He chose a remarkable sentence to chant—remarkable for one whose whole bearing was that of confident
hope—" It is a fearful thing to fall into the hands of

the living God." But it was rather for his pupils' sake that he chose it, for, using it as a text, he urged them to think of their last hour. He also sang some English verses on the same subject, in the Northumbrian dialect, of which the following represents the sense and metre :—

" As to the journey   Ere he goes hence
Each must take,   What to his spirit,
No one is prudent   Of good or of evil,
More than he should be   After the death-day
In considering   Doomed may be."

On one occasion he sang the antiphon, " O King of Glory, Lord of all Power, who didst on this day ascend in triumph above all the Heavens, leave us not desolate, but send to us the promise of the Father, the Spirit of Truth ; Alleluia." At the words, " Leave us not desolate," he burst into tears, and wept for a long time. Then his pupils and he read together. " By turns we read," Cuthbert tells, " and by turns we wept ; nay, we wept always while we read. In such joy we passed the days of Lent." He often repeated the words, " God scourgeth every son whom He receiveth." Besides the lessons to his pupils, and the singing of psalms, he translated into English, during these weeks of prostration, the Gospel of St. John as far as chapter vi. 9, and also some extracts from Bishop Isidore.

On the Tuesday before Ascension Day he was decidedly worse a swelling appeared in his feet. Nevertheless he continued to dictate cheerfully, begging his scribe to write quickly, for he did not know how long he might last, or when it might please his Maker to take him. That night he lay awake, giving thanks alway. The next morning he urged the brethren to finish writing what they had begun, and when that was done, at nine o'clock, they walked in procession with the relics of the Saints—the origin of our "perambulation day"—according to the custom of the time. One stayed with him while the others were thus engaged, and after a time reminded him that there was still a chapter to finish,—would it weary him to be consulted about it ? "Get out your pen and ink," was Bede's reply, "and write fast, it is no trouble to me." So time went on till three in the afternoon. Then the gentle spirit bethought him that he had some things he would like to give to his friends before he died. He bade Cuthbert run quickly and fetch his fellow-priests, that he might distribute the little gifts with which God had endowed him. What a simple picture of the riches of a faithful monk the list presents ! "I have in my chest pepper, napkins, and incense." No gold and silver had he to give, he told them, but with all love and joy he gave them what God had given him. Then he told them that they would see his face no more, and begged them to say masses and prayers for him. They wept ; but he turned their weeping into joy by telling them it was time he returned to Him who made him. He had lived long ; the time of his departure was at hand ; he had a desire to depart and to be with Christ.

Then came the final scene. In the evening his boy-scribe said to him, "One sentence, dear master, is left unfinished." He bade him write quickly. Soon the boy announced that it was finished. "True," the dying man said, "it is finished. Take mine head between thy hands and raise me. Full fain would I sit with my face to my holy oratory, where I was ever

wont to pray, that sitting so I may call on my Father."
And so he sat on the floor of his cell, and chanted
" Glory be to the Father and to the Son and to the
Holy Ghost." And as he breathed the words " the
Holy Ghost " he died.

In his fifty-ninth year, A.D. 731, Bede made a complete list of his writings, as though he felt that his work
was done. With trifling exceptions, they are all in
existence still. Curiously enough one of the most
important of his writings, the Letter to Bishop
Ecgbert, was written three years after the list was
compiled, in the last year of his life.

His preface to the list of writings gives a simple
summary of his quiet, studious, and prayerful life.
He gives the preface and the list as an appendix to the
Ecclesiastical History, but for our purpose it is better
to place it here.

"Thus much," he says, "of the Church History of
Britain,[1] and especially the English race, so far as I
could gather from ancient writings, or tradition, or of
my own knowledge, I, Bede, a servant of Christ and
a priest of the monastery of the blessed Apostles Peter
and Paul at Wearmouth and Jarrow, have, with the
help of the Lord, set down.

" Born in the territory of the same monastery, I
was given at the age of seven to be brought up by the
most reverend Abbat Benedict, and afterwards by
Ceolfrid. Spending all the rest of my life in the
monastery, I gave all my care to meditation on the
Scriptures, and in the intervals of the regular discipline and the daily care of chanting in church, I
found it sweet to be always learning, or teaching, or

[1] Bede uses the plural, Britanniarum, possibly as meaning the
British Isles.

writing. In the nineteenth year of my life I received deacon's orders, and in my thirtieth year priest's orders, in each case by the ministry of the most reverend bishop John, at the request of Abbat Ceolfrid. From the time of my priesthood down to my fifty-ninth year, I have written the following works on Holy Scripture and from the works of the Venerable Fathers with interpretations of their meaning :—

Genesis to the birth of Isaac and the rejection of Ishmael, four books.

On the Tabernacle and its Vessels, and on the Priests' Vestments, three books.

On the first part of Samuel,[1] that is, to the death of Saul, three books.

On the building of the Temple, an allegorical exposition, two books.

On the book of Kings, a book of thirty questions.

On the Proverbs of Solomon, three books.

On the Song of Solomon, seven books.

Excerpts from St. Jerome, on Isaiah, Daniel, part of Jeremiah, and the Twelve Prophets.

On Ezra and Nehemiah, three books.

On the Song of Habakkuk, one book.

[1] This description is in accordance with the arrangement of the Hebrew text; the Septuagint and the Vulgate call the books of Samuel the First and Second Books of Kings. A little lower down in the list of Bede's works, we find mention of thirty questions on the Book of Kings; here the four books of Samuel and Kings are meant; Nothelm, who asked the thirty questions, having described the four books as the Book of Kings, and Bede following him. In the treatise on Habakkuk, mentioned lower down, Bede used an older version than the Vulgate, perhaps because the " very dear sister in Christ," at whose request he wrote the treatise, used the older version. It seems probable that Bede used one or other version according to the circumstances of each case with which he dealt, as a modern writer uses the Psalter or the Authorized Version in quoting the Psalms, according as he prefers the ease of the one or the accuracy of the other.

On the book of the blessed father Tobit, an allegorical exposition, concerning Christ and the Church.

Heads of lections on the Pentateuch of Moses, Joshua, and Judges.

On the books of Kings and Chronicles.

On the book of the blessed father Job.

On the Parables (Proverbs), Ecclesiastes, and the Song of Solomon.

On Isaiah, Ezra, and Nehemiah.

On the gospel of Mark, four books.

On the gospel of Luke, six books.

Two books of Homilies on the Gospel.

On the Apostle [*i.e.* St. Paul], I have carefully transcribed in order all that I have found in St. Augustine's works.

On the Acts of the Apostles, two books.

On each of the seven Catholic Epistles, a book.

On the Revelation of St. John, three books.

Heads of lections on all the New Testament, except the Gospel.

A book of letters to various persons ; one on the Six Ages of the World ; another on the halting places of the children of Israel ; another on Isaiah's words, ' After many days shall they be visited ' ; another on the reason for Leap-year ; and another on the Equinox, according to Anatolius.

The book of the Life and Passion of St. Felix, Confessor, translated into prose from Paulinus's metrical life.

The book of the Life and Passion of St. Anastasius, which was ill translated from the Greek, and worse amended by some unskilled person, I have amended as to the sense.

The Life of the holy father, monk, and bishop, Cuthbert. In heroic verse and also in prose.

The history of the three Abbats of Jarrow wherein I rejoice to serve divine piety, Benedict, Ceolfrid, and Huetbert, two small books.[1]

The Ecclesiastical History of our island and race, five books.

A martyrology of the birthdays of the holy martyrs, in which I have carefully noted all the martyrs I could find, not only on what day they overcame the world, but also in what manner of conflict and under what judge.

A book of Hymns, in various metre or rhythm.

A book of Epigrams, in heroic or elegiac metre.

On the Nature of things and on Times, a book on each.

On Times, a larger book.

A book on Orthography, alphabetically arranged.

A book on the Art of Metre ; a small book on Tropes, *i.e.* on the figures and methods of speech in which Holy Scripture is written."

He concludes his list with this prayer : " To Thee I pray, O gentle Jesus, that he to whom Thou hast granted the enjoyment of draughts of divine knowledge may some time come to Thee, the fount of all wisdom, and in Thy presence ever be."

Some treatises not mentioned in this list are included among Bede's works. Such are his letter to Herefrid " On Thunder," his Penitential, and a short tract on Phlebotomy, full of the curious superstitions prevalent down to recent times as to good and bad stages of the moon for bleeding.

It is evident that the description of Bede given by

---

[1] It is now one book. Near the middle of the book we come to the time when Benedict resigned the abbacy. That may have been the point of division into two books. It reads quite continuously in its present form.

a well-known writer on the Anglo-Saxons is not an exaggeration "He was a phenomenon it is easier to praise than to parallel"; "his works were a kind of cyclopædia of almost all that was then known."

The epithet "Venerable," so constantly applied to Bede, is found, both in his own writings and elsewhere, applied to men of holy life who had not been canonized. Bede frequently calls the founder of Wearmouth and Jarrow "the Venerable Benedict." He is not himself called Venerable in any extant work of a date earlier than the middle of the tenth century. The annalist who continued his Ecclesiastical History for thirty years after his death, calls him Presbyter Beda in making the entry of his death. He is most often called Dominus Beda in early manuscripts of his Homilies, "Sir" being afterwards the title of the priest who had no University degree down to the Reformation, and in some districts considerably later than the Reformation.[1] Writers nearly contemporaneous with him call him Sanctus Beda, Saint Bede, or Holy Bede, and we find Bede himself applying that term to Abbat Benedict Biscop. Other writers of very early date call him Sacerdos Beda, Priest Bede, and Doctor Eximius, the Illustrious Doctor. The title Venerable, as used by Bede himself, did not imply an advanced age, for he writes of the Venerable Easterwine, and Abbat Easterwine died at the age of thirty-six. Thus the epithet as applied to Bede was of comparatively late origin, and had no more personal meaning than the epithets 'judicious,' 'admirable,' applied to Hooker and Crichton. In the middle ages such titles displaced the actual names

---

[1] The Zuinglian clergy in the Engadine are called " Ser " when addressed in the Romauntsch language.

of writers of distinction, and 'the Angelic Doctor,' 'the Seraphic Doctor,' were quoted under those names alone.

Marvellous accounts have been given of the origin of the title Venerable, as applied to Bede. They are scarcely worth repeating, except as showing to what credulity the inventors of wonders were able to appeal. One of these stories assumes that Bede visited Rome. When he was there, he saw on an iron gate the letters PPP. SSS. RRR. FFF. A Roman who observed him standing at the gate examining these letters, called out to him, " What are you looking at, English bull ? " Bede's reply was, " I am looking at what you should be ashamed of," and he read off four Latin lines, the words of which commenced with the twelve letters on the gate.[1] The Romans were so much struck by Bede's readiness and ability that they saluted him as Venerable, a title which the Senate afterwards confirmed ! The letters mean :—

> Pater Patriæ Perditus est
> Sapientia Secum Sublata
> Regnum Romæ Ruit
> Ferro Flamma Fame.

Dr. Giles Englished this as follows :—

> Fallen is the Father of this Folk
> Learning Leaves you Likewise
> Ruined is the Reign of Rome
> By War, Waste, Want.

This seems rather childish. But we learn from a letter of Lull, the Malmesbury monk who succeeded our greatest Missionary Bishop, Boniface of Crediton,

---

[1] This was written on November 8, 1917, when the German forces were over the Tagliamento.

as Archbishop of Mainz in 755, that it was of a type not uncommon then, when literary men occupied their leisure time with little tricks of various kinds with letters and words. In Lull's letter—which contains, by the way, several quotations from Aldhelm, the first Head of Lull's monastery at Malmesbury—we have an enlarged form of the same threat of ills to come, with the explanation :—

RRR	rex romanorum ruit
PPP	pater patriæ profectus est
FFF	ferro frigore fame
MMM	monitum monumentum mortuus est
VVV	victor vitalis veniet
AAA	aurum a nobis aufert.

Yet another form is found in a Würzburg codex of the same century, containing Homilies of Origen :—

Venit Victor Vincens mundum
Rumpit Regnum Romanorum
Fert Famem Frangit romam
Aufert Aurum Argentumque.

The victor comes who conquers the world,
He destroys the kingdom of the Romans,
He brings hunger, he breaks Rome,
He carries off gold and silver.

Another story makes Bede become blind before his death. The boy who led him attempted to play a practical joke upon him. He guided him to a stony place, and told him that a number of people were there, anxious to hear him preach. Bede accordingly addressed a homily to the stones, and at the end of his discourse the stones cried out, " Amen, Venerable Bede." Another version of this

story makes Bede end his sermon with the words,
" Which may God the Father, the Son, and the Holy
Ghost vouchsafe to grant us "   on which angels were
heard to say, " Amen, Venerable Bede."

A third story relates that one of Bede's disciples
was engaged in writing an epitaph on his master,
when he stuck fast for a word. He got as far as
Hac sunt in fossa Bedæ .   ossa, " in this tomb
are the bones of   Bede," and could get no further.
He went to bed to sleep upon the difficulty, and next
morning he found the gap filled by the word Venerabilis,
written no doubt by the hand of an angel, according to
the superstition of the time.

Bede's description of himself would seem to be
" Beda presbyter," for in his Life of St. Cuthbert he
mentions a person whom he describes as " major
Beda presbyter," " the greater Bede the presbyter,"
as if counting himself as the lesser Bede the presbyter.
There were two or three ecclesiastics in later times
called Beda, a fact which may account for some of the
impossible stories related of the Venerable Bede ;
such as the story of his being the teacher of Alcuin.
The supposed connection with Alcuin depends upon
a double coincidence of names.   The Venerable Bede
had a contemporary called Albinus (a name by which
Alcuin was known), and in Charlemagne's time the
famous Alcuin had a contemporary called Beda.   To
this it may be added, that Alcuin was a Northumbrian,
famous for his learning, a student and master of the
Cathedral School of York, which Bede had advised
Ecgbert, Alcuin's teacher, to found, and that in his
time he wrote a letter to the monks of Jarrow, praising
their predecessor Bede as a student and a writer, and
urging them to imitate his good example.

CHAPTER II

THE CONVERSION OF NORTHUMBRIA

The seven kingdoms—Descent of the kings[1]—Deira and Bernicia—
The slave youths in Rome—Pope Gregory's arrangements for the
conversion of England—Edwin of Deira—Importance of York—
A Kentish princess—Letters from Pope Boniface—Paulinus—
The Northumbrian House of Lords—Coifi the archpriest—The
British kings Cadfan and Cadwalla—Defeat and death of Edwin
—Apostasy—Churches built by Paulinus—The West Riding—
James the deacon—Love of music.

WE may now proceed, under Bede's continual guidance,
to consider the interesting story of the conversion of
his own nation to Christianity.

The seven kingdoms of the Anglo-Saxon Heptarchy
were not all founded at or about the same time. The
several parts of Britain were wrested from the British
and Romano-British occupants by successive invasions. Thus Hengist founded the kingdom of Kent
in 449 ; Ælli that of the South Saxons, Sussex, in 447 ;
Cerdic that of the West Saxons in 495 ; Æscwine that
of the East Saxons, Essex, in 527 ; Wuffa that of East
Anglia in 530 ; Creoda that of Mercia, in the Midlands,
at a date not definitely known (he died in 523 at an
advanced age, his grandson Penda, of whom we shall

[1] The genealogies of the royal families of Deira, Mercia, and
Bernicia, so far as they are represented in these pages, will be
found at the end of this chapter. They are abridged from the complete and important lists of the *Anglo-Saxon Bishops, Kings, and
Nobles*, by my valued friend the late W. G. Searle, published by
the Cambridge University Press in 1899.

hear much, being born in 575) ; Ida that of Bernicia in 547 ; Ælle that of Deira in 560, the latest of all. The Mercians, East Anglians, Deirans, and Bernicians were Angles ; Sussex and Essex were Saxon ; the Kentish men were from Jutland.

All of these kings except Ælli of the South Saxons had their pedigree from Woden. The pedigrees of the Northumbrian Ida and Ælle were the longest, thirteen generations in each case. We have in the Anglo-Saxon Chronicle the pedigree of Woden himself, going back so far that if we counted thirty years to a generation his earliest recorded ancestor would be living in our Lord's time.

It is easy to laugh at such claims. But it is evident that the men themselves believed in them ; and it is quite impossible for us in our time to realise the accuracy of oral genealogies preserved by scalds and bards, and constantly recited before keen ears at feasts and drinkings. We have in the recorded history of the kings of Northumbria one or two hints of the care with which the genealogies of men of position were kept. Thus when King Coenred died in 718, the sixth from Ida, he was succeeded by his fourth cousin, who came from another son of Ida. In the next generation, the last of this new line was succeeded by his fourth cousin once removed, who came from yet another son of Ida. With all our accurate manuscript records of the genealogies of the Lady Margaret and Edward IV it is not very easy to keep quite clear at every point of the claims of York and Lancaster. Edward IV and Henry VII were in the same degree of relationship, in descent from Edward III, as Osric and Coenred in descent from Ida.

We naturally begin our consideration of the growth

of Christianity in Bede's Northumbria with the story of its introduction by Edwin, the king of the whole land, Deira and Bernicia. Deira may be taken roughly as Yorkshire and Durham, Bernicia as Northumberland and Scotland up to the Firth of Forth. The boundaries on the west are less easily described. But to begin only with Edwin would be to miss a claim dear to Northumbrians, the claim that to their Northumbrian ancestors the introduction of Christianity to England is due. The story is so well known that it seems almost unnecessary to repeat it. Gregory, once the lay Prætor or Præfect of Rome, and as such Head of the Senate, and afterwards one of the most famous of the Bishops of Rome, visiting the slave market, a year or two before he became pope, was struck by the handsome faces and fine forms of some boys on sale as slaves. He asked of what race they were. He was told that they were Angles. Being inveterately addicted to playing upon words, he replied that they were fit to be made Angels. From what province did they come ? From Deira. Then they must be freed *de irâ—from the wrath*—of God. Who was their king ? Ælla. Then they must be taught to sing Alleluia.

The Saxon homily on Pope Gregory's birthday tells us that the merchants who had the boys for sale were themselves English. The idea of English men taking English boys to Rome to be sold as slaves is at first sight startling, and needs some explanation, which we are fortunately able to give. It should be premised that the demand for slaves had at one time in the history of Rome been so abundantly met, and more than met, by the scores of thousands of captives taken in war, that a slave cost almost nothing, at least in the camp. But for long before the time with which we are dealing, the Roman arms had been less prosperous, and slaves taken by Roman armies had ceased to meet the demand. Property of this character was in great request, and a large number of people were concerned in feeding the Roman market by supplies from various parts of the world. No doubt there had been a regular slave-route from Britain to Rome during the Roman occupation of Britain, when British things and persons were very popular in Rome.

That being premised, if we turn to the earliest history of the occupation of the country north of the Humber by the Angles, we find that Æthelric, the son of Ida who had founded the kingdom of Bernicia in 547, and Ælle who had founded the kingdom of Deira in 560, being ninth cousins, were at war with one another. Æthelric invaded Deira in 588, conquered its first king Ælle, who died at an advanced age, and reigned as king both of Bernicia and of Deira, Ælle's children escaping to the west. Now Gregory's interview with the English slave-masters and slaves was after 586, for it was only then that he returned to Rome after a long sojourn in Constantinople as the representative of the Pope at the court of the Emperor. The presumption is that the boys were captured at the invasion of Deira and carried off to Rome before the war had ended in the death of Ælle. It has been shown elsewhere[1] that it is not improbable that Gregory had heard of some fine specimens of English men as members of an embassy to the court of the emperor Justinian at Constantinople, some years before Gregory himself resided in that city.

Gregory bought some English youths, whether of

---

[1] *Augustine and His Companions*, S.P.C.K., pp. 16, 17.

this group of slaves we do not know, intending to train them in Christianity and send them to teach their pagan fellow-countrymen. As we shall see later, there appears to be a probability, or at least a possibility, that one of them may have been the first missionary sent to Northumbria. Then, in his enthusiastic zeal for missions to the English, he determined to come himself to England. He escaped from Rome, to the grief of the citizens when his departure was discovered. After getting a good distance from the city, he sat under a tree to rest, and began to read. A locust settled on his manuscript. With his wonted method of playing on words, and with the then general belief in omens, he exclaimed, " Locusta ! Loco sta ! Stay at home ! ", and he returned with the messengers sent after him by the Urban Præfect.

After he became Bishop of Rome in 590, he sent one of his own trained priests, Candidus, to take charge of some property of the Roman See at Marseilles. He bade him buy English boys of seventeen or eighteen years of age, who might be trained in monasteries to the service of God. And as all who could be found there—they were evidently to be bought in England—were pagans, a priest was to travel with them, to baptize any who might seem to be dying. The whole arrangement gives a painfully vivid idea of the trade in human flesh. Then, in 595, he set in operation a speedier plan, the mission from Rome of a considerable party of men of position, for the conversion of the English, under Augustine, the prior of the monastery of St. Andrews which Gregory had himself founded on his own family property on the Caelian Hill, and had ruled as abbat. Augustine and his band reached England at the end of 596, or beginning of 597, just

1320 years ago this year (1917). Although the natives
of Deira were the objects of Gregory's first interest,
the Italian mission went to Kent and christianised
that kingdom. Kent was the most accessible of the
kingdoms, and its queen was already a Christian. It
was not till many years later that an attempt was
made to preach the Gospel in Deira.

We can now return to Edwin, the banished son of the
first king of Deira, Ælle. He had been received at the
court of Redwald, the king of the East Angles. The
Bernician king Æthelric, who had expelled him from
Deira in 588 and had reigned over Bernicia and Deira,
had been succeeded by his son Æthelfrith in the
sovereignty of both provinces. Æthelfrith had, curiously enough, married Acha, one of Edwin's sisters.
After reigning from 593 to 616, he appears to have
become uneasy about the intentions of Edwin, now a
strong man in full middle age. He sent messengers to
Redwald, demanding that he should give up his guest
Edwin to him. After consideration, Redwald refused,
and knowing the character of Æthelfrith, which has
come down to us by tradition in very dark colours,
he came upon him with an army before he could get
his forces together, and slew him at the river Idle.
Æthelfrith left a number of sons by Acha, who had
been married before and had a daughter of whom we
shall hear, as we shall of three of her sons by Æthelfrith.

Edwin in his turn kept the sons of Æthelfrith out
of the sovereignty of Bernicia, and reigned over both
provinces with great power. Bede tells us that he was
the greatest of the seven greatest kings of the English,
and had the supremacy over all the kingdoms. This
was the overlordship, known by the title Brytenwalda

or Bretwalda.[1] Bede does not mention that title; we learn it from the Saxon Chronicle, which copies Bede's account of the seven greatest men in dealing with the year 827, and out of compliment to King Alfred (872) adds, "the eighth was Ecgbryht, king of the West Saxons." Bede's account is as follows the first who had this kind of rule was Ælli, king of the South Saxons; the second, Ceaulin, king of the West Saxons; the third, Ethelbert, king of Kent; the fourth, Redwald, king of the East Angles; the fifth, Edwin, who with great power exercised superiority over all the English and British except the kingdom of Kent; the sixth, Oswald, the most Christian king of the Northumbrians; the seventh, Oswy his brother. It is conceivable that if Oswy, the third Northumbrian, had played his cards better, and if succeeding kings had led better lives, the kings of all England might have reigned from York, the seat of the empire of Rome in Britain, the partner of Trèves in the honourable position of the two imperial cities north of the Alps.

Edwin was quite conscious of the importance of his position. His dignity was so great that he had banners carried before him, not only in battle but when he was riding about in peace, visiting cities and vills and districts with his attendants; on such occasions he was also preceded by a standard-bearer. Even when walking about the streets he had carried before him a kind of banner which "the English called Tuuf, and the Romans Tufa," Bede says. The Tufa was one of the Roman insignia, formed of globes of feathers.

In the year of our Lord 625, Edwin wished to

---

[1] The spellings of the six best manuscripts of the Saxon Chronicle are: Bretwalda, Brytenwald, Bretenanwalda, Brytenwealda, Brytenwealda, Brytenweald. Thus all differ except the two which agree.

marry Ethelburga, otherwise called Tate, the sister of
Eadbald, king of Kent. She was a daughter of Ethelbert, the first Christian king. Her brother was willing
that she should marry the king of Northumbria, but
he was not willing that she should marry a pagan.
Edwin gave such assurances respecting religious
matters as overcame Eadbald's scruples. He promised that he would show no hostility to the new
religion ; nay, he would give full permission to Ethelburga to practise the rites of her faith, not only for
herself, but for all who came with her, men and
women, priests and attendants. And he added that
if the new religion proved on careful examination to
be more worthy of God than that which he professed,
he was far from saying that he would not adopt it.

Both the king of Kent and his advisers in ecclesiastical matters must have been forcibly reminded by
this answer of what had occurred in their own land
in the preceding generation. On very similar conditions, King Ethelbert had married Bertha, a
daughter of Charibert, king of the Franks, a Christian. He had allowed her the use of an old Romano-
British church which remained near Canterbury, and
may be said still to remain,—St. Martin's. He had
also allowed her to bring with her a bishop, Liudhard.
Thus, when Augustine landed on the Isle of Thanet,
he found in Kent a pagan king with a Christian wife,
and no doubt Queen Bertha was an important element
in the conversion of the king and kingdom. " The
unbelieving husband shall be saved by the believing
wife." With this example before them, the authorities
of Kent had good reason for trusting their princess
to the Northumbrian king. His conversion would
probably be only a matter of time.

The Archbishop of Canterbury at this time was Justus. He had been a companion and suffragan of Augustine himself, who died twenty years before the events of which we are speaking. He selected the most suitable man he could find as adviser for the princess. This was Paulinus, whom he consecrated bishop on July 21, 625 A.D. The personal staff of the princess being thus completed, she went northwards, and was married at once to King Edwin.

On Easter Day, 626, the king was residing on the banks of the Derwent, in his original kingdom of Deira. Cwichelm, the king of the West Saxons, sent an assassin with a poisoned dagger to kill him. Bede says distinctly that the king's name was Cwichelm, but we know that Cynegils was king of Wessex at this date 626, indeed he reigned from 611 to 643. It is evident, from several notices, that Cwichelm was joint king with Cynegils, but there is considerable confusion as to what his relationship to Cynegils was, brother, or son, or cousin ; indeed, it is not very certain whose son Cynegils himself was. It has been suggested that Cwichelm's aim was to restore the Bretwaldadom to the royal family of the West Saxons, their king Ceaulin having held it before Redwald and Edwin. Ceaulin died in 592, thirty-four years before the attempt on Edwin.

We may more probably look for a less direct explanation. There was some curious connection between the royal families of the West Saxons and the Welsh Britons. The similarity of name between Ceadwalla of the West Saxons, who resigned the kingdom and went to Rome, and Cadwaladr the last of the kings of all the Britons, has led to much confusion, as has also the similarity between the name of the West Saxon Ceadwalla and the name of Cadwaladr's father Cadwallon, Bede's Caedwalla. The most recent book on the British Saints[1] makes Cadwaladr's daughter marry Coenbert, Cwichelm's cousin, a sub-king of Wessex, and become the mother of the West Saxon king Ceadualla. Cadwallon had been brought up with Edwin at the court of his father Cadfan, who was elected king of all the Britons at Chester. Having been friends in youth, in the time of Edwin's exile, they became internecine enemies. Edwin conquered Anglesey from Cadwallon, and Cadwallon eventually killed Edwin in battle, being himself killed in the battle of Catscaul by Oswald.

It is an interesting fact that we have the memorial stone of Edwin's British host and protector, King Cadfan, or Cadvan, or Cataman. It is in the church of Llangadwaladr in Anglesey, the church named after Cadfan's grandson Cadwaladr, who became one of the Welsh saints, having earned as king the nickname Cadomedd, battle-shunner. The inscription on the stone is not very legible ; it is an unusually valuable example of early lettering, and its Latin spelling is curious. It is also an apt example of the high esteem in which Welshmen held themselves. It runs thus :—

" *Catamanus rex sapientisimus opinatisimus omnium regum.*"

King Cataman, the wisest and most renowned of all kings. (See Plate 1.)

This king Cadvan is not to be taken as the saint of that name. The saint was of a high Armorican family. He led a large number of his fellow-country-men to Wales in the fifth century, probably under

---

[1] Baring-Gould and Fisher, 4 vols., 1908.

pressure of the Franks who were establishing their position in Gaul under Clovis. St. Cadfan founded the church called from him Llangadfan, and is commemorated at Towyn in the remarkable church dedicated to him there.

The attempt on Edwin's life, whatever its cause and purpose may have been, very nearly succeeded. He was seriously wounded, and was only saved by the interposition first of his chief and favourite minister, Lulla, and then of a faithful soldier, Forthere, both of whom were slain by the assassin's dagger. The same night a daughter was born to him, the first-fruits of his marriage with Ethelburga. Paulinus declared that Christian prayers had obtained a safe and easy deliverance for the queen from the great pain and peril of childbirth. In gratitude for this and for his own deliverance, Edwin gave the infant to Paulinus to be made a Christian, and on the following Whitsunday she and twelve others of the king's connections were baptized. She was Eanflæd, and she married Oswy, the king of Bernicia and Deira.

Edwin had also promised that if he should succeed in his war against the king of Wessex, he would cast off his idols and serve Christ. The hoped-for success came, and the king returned to fulfil his promise. He at once abandoned the worship of idols, but he hesitated long before he would receive the sacraments of the Christian faith. He went through a course of careful instruction by Paulinus, and he then conferred with the wisest of his own advisers. Bede describes him as a man of the utmost sagacity, a character which the facts recorded of him completely justify. He sat often and long alone, debating with himself in silence whether he should take the great step.

At this crisis a letter reached him from Pope Boniface. The Pope urged him to become a Christian, and sent him the blessing of his protector Peter, a shirt, with a golden ornament, and a garment of Ancyra. The letter, which Bede has preserved, is a powerful one, stating the case against idols in a vigorous manner. Boniface wrote at the same time to Ethelburga, pressing her to be instant with the king, in season and out of season. Though a celibate himself, the Pope showed a full appreciation of the power of the weapon he thus brought to bear upon the king. He bade her write and tell him of her success, as soon as possible, when an opportunity of sending a letter by messenger occurred. And he showed some discrimination in the presents he sent to the queen. In addition to the blessing of Peter, he sent her a silver mirror, and an ivory comb inlaid with gold.

Still the king held out ; not, as it would seem, from any spirit of obstinacy, but because he wished to be sure about what he was doing. Such a convert is worth waiting for. Paulinus got a little tired of waiting, and determined to make a startling appeal to the king's superstition. Bede says that we may suppose the knowledge which enabled him to make this appeal to have been conveyed in a vision. Another explanation will occur to the reader.

Some years before this time, Edwin had been in exile at the court of Redwald of East Anglia. Messengers arrived, as we have seen, from the king who had exiled him, demanding that he should be given up. As Edwin sat alone one stormy night, awaiting in the utmost anxiety the decision of Redwald and his ministers, a stranger came to him, a man with a strange face, clad in a strange garb. He asked Edwin what

he would do for one who could promise him safety for
the present, the throne of his kingdom in the future,
and, beyond the future, such salvation as neither he
nor his fathers had dreamed of. Edwin was full of
promises. He had been wandering, a vagabond, for
many years. He would do anything such a man told
him to do. The stranger then pressed his hand on
his head, and said, " When this sign comes to thee,
remember thy promises and perform them."

Years rolled on. To Edwin, freed long ago from
his fears at Redwald's court, king now of Deira and
Bernicia both, sitting as we left him in constant
thought and doubt, Paulinus one day came. He
pressed his hand on the king's head. " Knowest
thou that sign ? " Edwin fell at his feet ; declared
that he must and would become a Christian ; begged
only for a little time, that he might if possible bring
over the great men of the kingdom with him. To
this Paulinus consented, and a great council was
held. Bede's account of it makes us long for a fuller
report.

The king asked each magnate in turn what he
thought of the new doctrines and the new worship.
The chief priest, Coifi, was the first to answer. Coifi
may be taken as the type of a cunning priest without
convictions, one who serves at the altar that the altar
may serve him. " He was anxious that the new
doctrines should be made clearly known to them, for
he had come to the conclusion that there was no reality
in that which he had so far professed. No one had
been more diligent than he in the worship of the gods,
and yet many had more of the king's favour, more of
worldly prosperity, than he with all his care for the
gods. Had those same gods been good for anything

at all, they would, of course, have ensured his promotion to a position of pre-eminence. If the king liked the new religion better, after looking into it, by all means let it be adopted." It is only fair to say that Coifi appeared in a much more favourable light in a second speech and in eventual action.

The next speaker was a man of very different mould. It would be well if in all councils in this land there were men with thoughts so just and expressions so happy. He is a type of the thinking layman. " What came before life, and what comes after, all is mystery. The life of each man, that is all that each man knows." An apt simile occurred to him, beautiful in its simplicity. It may well have been that he drew it at the moment of speaking from an actual event ; for we have been told that long time had elapsed since July, 626, and the king and magnates were baptized at Easter, 627, so that the council was held in winter. This was the simile. " The king and his chief captains and ministers are sitting in council on a dark winter's day ; rain and snow without ; within, a bright fire in their midst. Suddenly a little bird flies in, a sparrow, in at one door and then out at another. Where it came from none can say, nor whither it has gone. So is the life of man. Clear enough itself, but before it, and after the end thereof, darkness ; it may be, storm. If the new doctrine will tell us anything of these mysteries, the before and the after, it is the religion that is wanted." Others supported this view.

Then Coifi became more worthy of himself. He begged that Paulinus might be heard. Paulinus was heard, and was listened to attentively. There were few such orators as he, who could convert a township in a sermon. And nature had given him a form fit for an orator. A certain abbat of Peartaneu,[1] a man of singular veracity, Deda by name, told Bede that he had talked with an aged man who was baptized by Paulinus in Trent stream, in the presence of King Edwin. The old man described the eloquent missionary bishop as tall of stature ; stooping slightly ; with black hair, thin face, nose slender and aquiline, aspect reverend and majestic. This was the man who was brought in to expound before the chief priest of the faith he had come to overthrow, the precepts and the promises of the faith he preached. And this was the result. " I have long known, O king, that there was nothing in our religion ; for the more I sought for truth in it the less I found it. And here I freely confess that in this new preaching I find the truth which there I could not find. It gives us life, salvation, and happiness eternal. Let us make haste to abjure and to burn the altars we have consecrated to such poor purpose." All reason for further delay had now disappeared. The king's decision was made. He gave Paulinus licence to preach publicly. He made the announcement that he had himself abandoned idolatry, and that he accepted the faith of Christ. Then he asked Coifi who should set about the destruction of the idols. This was a more serious question for the king than for Coifi. The king had once believed, and he trembled. Coifi had not believed, and he did not tremble. " None so fit as I. I taught the people to worship them. I will destroy them." So he called for a spear and a stallion charger, forbidden things both for a pagan priest, and he galloped up Goodmanham[2] lane, and rode

---

[1] Partency, in Lincolnshire. This was a cell to Bardney.
[2] Near Market Weighton in Yorkshire. Called in Bede's time Godmundingham.

full tilt at the temple door. The people thought him mad ; but he pierced the door with his spear, and called on those with him to finish the work of destruction. Then they burned the temple, with its idols and all that was contained within its precincts.

The king and his chiefs were baptized at York on Easter Day, April 12, 627, in the wooden church which Edwin had built in honour of St. Peter. The spring of water which it enclosed is still in existence under the minster, as are considerable portions of the walls of stone which followed. Though there had been a British bishop of York, this is the first church on record of the series which has reached its climax in the present glorious Minster. The king at once commenced a church of stone of larger dimensions, enclosing the original oratory, but before the church was finished he was killed in battle at Hethfeld,[1] by an army of Britons and pagan Mercians, A.D. 633. The Christian Britons were led by Cadwallon (Caedualla), the friend of Edwin's youth and the son of his protector Cadvan. The pagan Mercians were led by their king Penda, of whom we shall hear more. Edwin's first wife, married when he was in exile, was Quenberga, the daughter of the Mercian king Cearl, Penda's predecessor. As in the case of our modern times, dynastic intermarriages did not prevent national wars. In those days they did not save the lives of individual princes. Edwin was forty-seven years of age at the time of his death, and had reigned seventeen years, having spent many years in exile.

So long as the king lived after his baptism, that is, for six years, the work of conversion went on rapidly. Osfrid and Eadfrid, the sons born to Edwin by Quen-

[1] Hatfeld, in Yorkshire.

berga during his exile, were baptized, and Iffi, the young son of Osfrid, and many noble and illustrious persons. Bede tells us of a visit of thirty-six days, paid by Paulinus to the king and queen at one of their country seats, during the whole of which time the bishop catechized and baptized. The people flocked from all the neighbouring villages and hamlets to hear him. As soon as they had heard him, they believed. As soon as they believed, he baptized them in the river Glen,[1] which ran by. This was in Bernicia. In Deira, we have records of his being often with the king at his seat at Catterick. There, in like manner, he catechized and baptized, the Swale being his laver of regeneration ; for in the early infancy of the Church, Bede remarks, oratories and fonts could not be made. We may ask, why ? It would seem that Paulinus, in his great power as a persuasive orator, forgot or neglected the less marked but more useful function of an organizer and establisher. Had Bede been able to say that after a time this severe personal work became less necessary on the part of Paulinus, because oratories and fonts were established, and here and there, in an ever-increasing number of places, priests were found, each the centre of a body of true believers and acting as a missionary to the pagans around, we should not have had to record the apostasy of the land on the death of the king. It is related of Edwin, that wherever he found a good spring of water near a frequented road, he had a post fixed at the place with a brass dish chained to it for the use of travellers ; and so strict was his administration of justice that the dishes remained uninjured. We can but regret that he did not establish in like manner

1 At Yeverin, in Glendale.

supplies of the water of life for his subjects travelling to another world.

Bede does tell us of one church built in Deira by Paulinus. This was in a district recently taken from the Romano-Britons of the kingdom of Rheged, at whose court Taliessin barded and sang. The district was called Campodonum, probably in the region of Huddersfield. The pagans who slew Edwin burned the church and all the town (vill) it served. The church was evidently of wood, for the altar, Bede says, was saved because it was of stone. The later kings replaced the vill of Campodonum by a residence for themselves in the region of Loidis (Leeds). The stone altar of Campodonum was taken to the neighbouring monastery in Elmet wood, and in Bede's time was still preserved there by the very reverend abbat and priest Thridwulf. The name of the district Elmete is still in use.

It may be remembered that the people of these two regions of the old Romano-British kingdom of Rheged retain two characteristics, one from their Roman origin, the other from the British. They are correct non-aspirators, as the Romans were, not putting an *h* in wrong places, and they sing in parts naturally, as did the Britons and as do the British-Welsh.

Paulinus had also built a church, and this a beautiful stone church, in a region south of the Humber, after converting Blecca, the præfect of the city of Lincoln. The walls of this church stood in Bede's time, but the roof had fallen in. It was in this church that Paulinus performed a remarkable ceremony in the year 627. Alone, he consecrated Honorius to the archbishopric of Canterbury. There was no other bishop of England to join in the consecration. London had long ceased to have a bishop, and the pagan Londoners did not receive a bishop till some time after this. The Burgundian Felix did not come to Dunwich till 630. Besides Canterbury, there was only one see in that province, Rochester, whose bishop Romanus had gone on an embassy to the Pope and was drowned in this same year 627.

This visit to the province of Lindissi (Lindsey),[1] on which Edwin accompanied him, had one happy result. To it we owe the personal description of Paulinus given on page 37. The description accords well with our idea of a fine specimen of a member of a British royal family. The Cambrian Annals tell that the baptizing in the Swale was done by Run, or Rum, son of Urien or Urbgen, king of the British kingdom of Rheged. As nothing is said of any inability on the part of Paulinus to make himself understood by the English or by the people of the Yorkshire dales, who must still have been in considerable part British in speech, it is worth mentioning as a suggestion that Paulinus may have been one of the captives carried off to Rome and there trained in Christianity, and that to him British Gaelic was a native and Anglo-Saxon an early acquired language.

One thing it appears Paulinus did of an intentionally permanent character. He set up crosses at Easingwold, a few miles north of York, which were in existence in Norman times. The boundaries of an estate there were then described as running up to the crosses of Paulinus. Dewsbury, also, claims to have some stone memorial from his time; as does Whalley also. We must remember Paulinus's crosses when we notice a remark of Bede relating to Bernicia.

[1] The name of the people of Lindissi was Lindisfaras. This is not infrequently confused with Lindisfarnenses, the people of Holy Isle.

On the death of Edwin, Cadwalla, king of the Britons who still made head against the Northumbrian English from the mountain-fastnesses of the north-west to which they had retired, and Penda, king of the Mercians, proceeded to make a great slaughter of the Northumbrians, especially of those who were Christians. Cadwalla's object was to destroy all the English, and though a Christian, he was not more likely to spare the Christian Northumbrians than was his pagan ally. For even in those early times of Christianity in this island, the *odium theologicum* raged, and there was hatred between the English, who were in communion with the Canterbury mission, and the Britons, who had refused to make terms with Augustine. It will be necessary to speak in more detail hereafter on this subject (*see* Chapter V). For the present, it is enough to say that the Christians of Northumbria were not likely to fare better with their conqueror on the ground of his being a Christian too. The people abjured Christianity as lightly as many of them had taken it up. Paulinus fled before the storm and returned to Canterbury, taking with him Ethelburga and some of her children. He was made Bishop of Rochester, and there he remained till his death. Christianity almost entirely disappeared from Northumbria. Osric, Edwin's cousin, succeeded to the throne of Deira. He had been converted and baptized by Paulinus, but he went with the stream and abjured the faith. In Bernicia, the rightful heir, Eanfrid, whom Edwin had deprived, became king. He had lived in exile among the Christians in Caledonia, and had been baptized by them ; but he, too, abjured the faith when he came to the throne.

It is evident that Paulinus had made two mistakes.

He had promised temporal rewards, prosperity and success against their enemies, to those whom he converted, and when a tide of misfortune set in, the hollowness of conversion on such terms was shown. And, as has been said, he had established nothing. He left no nucleus from which the light might shine forth again when the storm was past. A day's preaching converted hundreds   he baptized them and left them. A day's defeat swept them all away.

There is one bright spot in the dark picture. James the Deacon had been a companion of Augustine. He was the sweet singer of the party when they first arrived in Kent, when they made so great an impression on the king by the processional chant with which they approached him. He had gone to the north with Paulinus, and he did not fly. He remained for some time in York, and then went to the neighbourhood of Catterick, where the village of Akeborough[1] took its name from him, as Bede informs us. Here he did what he could by teaching and baptizing, and he lived to see times of peace restored, when he taught to the new generation of Christians the Roman or Canterbury method of singing. He was the only sign of an establishment left by Paulinus. Akeborough still exists, and retains its name in the form Aikbar, which the Yorkshire people call Yakbur, as they no doubt pronounced the original Jacobiburgus, Jacobur, or Jacbur. It is a small farm house, and close by is the little stream in which James baptized his converts. At Hauxwell, on the higher ground in the immediate neighbourhood, there is in the churchyard an Anglo-Saxon cross with very simple interlacing work and a panel which has borne an

[1] Jacobi burgus, Jacob's (*i.e.* James's) town.

inscription, one letter of which, the initial of the name Gacobi or Jacobi, could be read thirty years ago. Fifty years before that, the curate of the parish and the then well known Sister Dora made a tracing of the inscription, which read *Hæc est crux sancti Gacobi.* (This is the cross of the Holy James.) James probably had a well of pure drinking water on this higher ground, and the village took its name from James's well, Yaucswell, with the broad pronunciation of the *a.* The Irish or Anglo-Saxon G stood for J and was pronounced as Y. (See Plate 2.)

The condition of the Church in Northumbria was worse than that of the church which Paulinus had built in Lincoln, of which Bede tells—" Its walls stand in our time, but the roof is fallen in." Indeed the account given by Stephen Eddi, the biographer of Bishop Wilfrith, of the condition of the fabric of the metropolitan church of York, is as apt a commentary as could have been written upon the state of things which prevailed after the flight of Paulinus. When Wilfrith was made bishop, he found the church of the oratory[1] in ruins. The timbers of the roof were perishing, and did not keep out the weather ; the windows were without protection, the rain pouring in and the birds of the air flying in and out ; the walls were bare, and defiled with all manner of abominations.

As Paulinus had so much to do with the beginnings of Christianity among the races which first drew the attention of Gregory to the English, we must summarize his proceedings on the death of Edwin, following, as always, Bede's faithful record.

---

[1] The first York Minster was so called because King Edwin built it round the oratory at which he had been baptized.

He followed the example of the Italian prelates who had fled from London and Rochester on an outbreak of paganism on the death of the first Christian king of the Londoners. He fled to Kent by sea, taking with him Ethelburga, whom he had some years before brought from Kent by the same route. They were guided by Bassus, a most valiant soldier of Edwin's. The little Eanflæd was with them, and a son and grandson of Edwin who died in infancy. Some rich possessions of Edwin were brought to Canterbury and kept there, among them a large gold cross and a chalice of gold.

After the flight of Paulinus he received from the Pope a present of the pallium, constituting him Archbishop of York, and licence to consecrate the Archbishop of Canterbury if a vacancy came in his time. Honorius, whom Paulinus had consecrated, also received the pall, with a corresponding licence to consecrate an Archbishop of York. The Pope, like a wise man, accepted accomplished facts. Paulinus became Bishop of Rochester, and there he left on his death the useless pall, which had arrived too late to make him Archbishop of York. The sixth Bishop of York in succession to him was the first Archbishop, just a hundred years after his flight.

We have spoken of James the Deacon as the sweet singer, and we know the attractive power of the singing of the arch-cantor whom Biscop imported. It is evident that the Northumbrians were greatly interested in church music, and it is certain that like other Anglo-Saxons they were fond of music, whether ecclesiastical or secular. The Britons were, no doubt, as their descendants are, naturally inclined to good singing ; we may suppose that the " Leeds Choir " is a lineal descendant from the choirs in Elmete Wood. We do not hear complaints of the voices of our Anglo-Saxon ancestors, as we do of the voices of Germans and Gauls. John the Deacon declares in his Life of Pope Gregory the Great—we may wonder, by the way, whether the Angle youths who captivated Gregory had as one special charm very musical voices —that when the Germans or the Gauls tried to sing the Gregorian chant with its " delicate modulations," their barbarous and bibulous throats produced a rattle like wagons crashing down steps, so that the feelings of the congregation were rasped and stunned instead of being smoothed. In Charlemagne's time the Franks were great offenders in the roughness of their singing in church. They could not manage to enunciate the words when they came to the inflections and trills and runs, the " curls " as they appear to have been called ; they broke them up in their throats, rather than expressed them. In England much pains was taken in guarding against such faults. A Council of the English Church held in 747, twelve years after the death of Bede, himself a skilful singer, made a decree which might with advantage be enforced among us in this twentieth century. Priests must not gabble or chatter the service in church after the fashion of secular poets, lest they destroy or confuse the rhythm and clearness of the sacred words ; they must follow a simple and holy melody, after the manner of the Church ; and if anyone is not able so to sing, he must read clearly what it is his business to say.

DEIRA

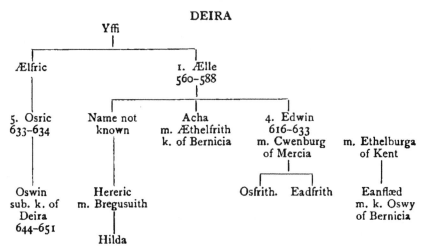

2. Æthelric and 3. Æthelfrith are placed under Bernicia, being kings of
Bernicia and Deira

MERCIA

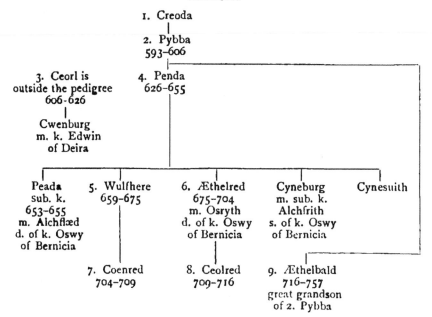

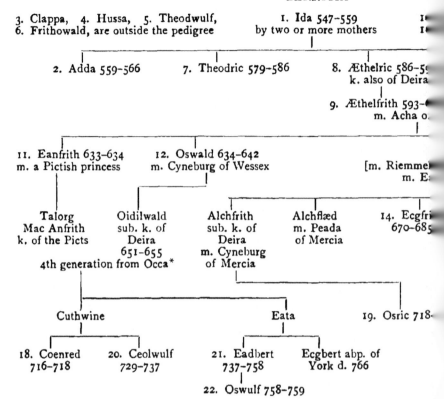

3. Clappa,   4. Hussa,   5. Theodwulf,   1. Ida 547-559   I
6. Frithowald, are outside the pedigree   by two or more mothers   I

2. Adda 559-566   7. Theodric 579-586   8. Æthelric 586-5
                                                        k. also of Deira

                                                      9. Æthelfrith 593-
                                                        m. Acha o

11. Eanfrith 633-634   12. Oswald 634-642   [m. Riemme
m. a Pictish princess   m. Cyneburg of Wessex   m. E

Talorg   Oidilwald   Alchfrith   Alchflæd   14. Ecgfri
Mac Anfrith   sub. k. of   sub. k. of   m. Peada   670-68
k. of the Picts Deira   Deira   of Mercia
                 651-655   m. Cyneburg
4th generation from Occa*   of Mercia

Cuthwine   Eata   19. Osric 718-

18. Coenred   20. Ceolwulf   21. Eadbert   Ecgbert abp. of
716-718   729-737   737-758   York d. 766

                                  22. Oswulf 758-759

CHAPTER III

Oswald and his brothers—Vision of Columba—Origins of our Coronation service—Iona and Aidan—Union of Deira and Bernicia—Oswald's death—Oswin in Deira—Aidan's death.

THE two apostate kings, Osric of Deira and Eanfrid of Bernicia, were both slain by Cadwalla in the year following Edwin's death. This year was so full of misery to the Northumbrians, and the apostasy of the kings seemed so dreadful to the Christian historians who followed, that by common consent, as Bede informs us, the year was counted as part of the reign of Oswald, the next king, and Osric and Eanfrid were omitted from the list of kings. Oswald was the brother of Eanfrid, and was a very earnest Christian. He determined to attack Cadwalla, in the year 635, and collected an army at a spot not far from Hexham and the Roman wall, called by the English Hefenfeld. When all was ready, he had a large wooden cross made and set up, supporting it with his own hands while the earth was being thrown into the hole in which it was fixed, and he and all his army knelt and prayed for success. Cadwalla was routed and slain, and Oswald became king. Not unnaturally, the cross was endowed by the people with miraculous power. Bede tells us that in his time small chips of wood were cut from it and steeped in water, and the water thus hallowed cured both man and beast. Bede, it may be remarked in passing, was a firm believer in miracles, on which point some information will be found in Chapter XV. The monks of Hexham built a church on the spot after Oswald's death, with good reason, as Bede observes, for until Oswald set up that cross there had been no sign of the Christian faith set up in all Bernicia—no church, no cross, no altar. We have seen that this was not true of Deira.

Oswald at once set about restoring Christianity among his subjects ; but he neither sought for the return of Paulinus, nor applied to Canterbury for assistance. He had been brought up among the Scots, and to the friends and teachers of his exile he turned for assistance in his worthy object. They sent him a monk from Iona, a man whose disposition was not suited to the work ; he returned, and reported at a council of the brethren of Iona, that he had not been able to do any good ; the English were an uncivilized race, stubborn and barbarous. After some anxious debate had taken place as to what should be done, a gentle voice was heard. It was that of a young monk, Aidan by name, who wished to say something on the matter. The others gave audience while he spoke as follows to the unsuccessful missioner. " It seems to me, brother, that you were too hard with your ignorant hearers. The apostolic precept enjoins that we should give first the milk of easy doctrines, till such time as they are fit to receive deeper truths and perform higher duties." All present were struck with the idea that Aidan would be the right man to send, and happily for Northumbria he was willing to go. He was consecrated bishop, and he selected Lindisfarne as his see.

Bede does not explain why he did not choose York, which had been the see of Paulinus. It may have been because Paulinus was still living, at Rochester, where he died A.D. 644, so that there might, perhaps, be doubt as to the vacancy of the see ; or, it may have been that Oswald and Aidan were anxious to have nothing to do with the Canterbury mission, and another Bishop of York would have reminded them too much of the former failure, and might have been of evil omen. But most probably the king would have it so because he wished to have his ecclesiastical centre in his own hereditary kingdom of Bernicia, and the bishop would have it so because his Scottish home was an island, the holy isle of Hy, which we call Iona by a curious mistake. There was no consonant in the Gaelic name, nor in the Latin name *Ioua insula*, the isle of I or Hy. An early mediæval scribe miscopied *Ioua* and wrote it *Iona*, and Iona it has remained.

Aidan set about his work in a systematic manner. He at once obtained from the king a class of twelve English boys, to be trained for the priesthood. We trace the after-career of one only of these, but it is easy to imagine how much good the others may have done. This one was Eata, Abbat of Melrose, and eventually selected as Abbat, and Bishop, of Lindisfarne, under circumstances which made that position one of peculiar difficulty. If his abbacy lasted ten years, he was still at Lindisfarne when Bede was born. He was a true disciple of Aidan, as Bede's character of him shows, "a man most reverend and most gentle." Aidan also spent much of the money which he received from wealthy persons in ransoming those who had been unjustly sold as slaves, and many of these ransomed slaves he taught and trained,

ordaining them finally to the priesthood. By means
of his Theological College, recruited in these and other
ways, he supplied Northumbria with priests.

The circumstances of the time were, for some years
at least, highly favourable to ·the spread of Christianity. Oswald was a successful sovereign. He
united under his firm rule the four nationalities which
his kingdom in its fullest extent contained,—Angles,
Britons, Picts, and Scots ; for the northern boundary
of Northumbria was often pushed far into what we
now call Scotland. He also effected a real union
between Deira and Bernicia, till then too often at
variance. Thus, wherever Aidan's emissaries went,
they found peace. The king was as humble as he
was successful. There is a pretty Easter story told
of his unselfishness. One Easter Day he was sitting
down to dinner. Royal dainties filled a silver dish
before him. Aidan was his priest, and hands were
already raised to bless the bread when the almoner
came in, " the king's minister," as Bede describes
him, " to whom the care of the poor had been assigned."
How delightful to think of a Secretary of State for the
Care of the Poor ! Those early people have a good
deal to teach us. He told the king that the streets were
crowded with people begging bread. The king ordered
the whole dinner to be taken out to them, and when
they had eaten, he cut up the silver dish, and divided
the pieces among them. Aidan was overjoyed on
witnessing this pious act, and taking the king by the
right hand exclaimed, " May this hand never decay ! "
And so it would seem it fell out ; for when Oswald was
slain in battle, his right hand and arm were cut off,
and Bede himself saw them still fresh, enclosed in a
silver case, at Bamborough. The arm of Oswald came

into the possession of the Abbey of Peterborough. King Stephen saw it there.

The king took an active part in helping on Aidan's work, applying himself industriously to build and extend the Church of Christ in his kingdom. Aidan had not learned to speak the English tongue with ease, while, on the other hand, the king, who had been brought up in Caledonia, understood the bishop's Scottish language well. When Aidan preached, it was delightful, Bede reports, to see and hear the king interpreting to his captains and ministers the word of God from his mouth.

Oswald's mother was sister to the thoughtful and good King Edwin, and we may not unfairly add him to the long list of famous men who have owed to their mothers much more than their natural life.

The king was killed in a great battle at Maserfeld,[1] on August 5, 642, in the thirty-eighth year of his reign. He was slain by the same king who had killed Edwin, the pagan Penda, king of the Mercian English, who were still a pagan people. The spot where his body fell became the scene of many striking stories of miracles, some account of which will be given later. Bede attributes the wonder-working power of the place to the intercessions of Oswald in behalf of those who resorted to it in faith. He remarks, that it should be no matter of surprise that Oswald's prayers in the heavenly kingdom proved so efficacious, for while governing his temporal kingdom he was instant in prayer, and took more pains about the kingdom that is eternal. The reader is probably familiar with the

---

[1] There is a Merserfield near Winwick, in Lancashire. Oswestry, *sc.* Oswald's tree, has been suggested as the scene of the battle. Oswald's head was found in the same tomb with Bede's bones in 1104, at Durham.

conventional representation of an Anglo-Saxon king, sitting on the throne with his hands either pressed together or held apart, in either case pointed towards heaven. Oswald may have been the original of this representation, for so constantly was he praying or giving thanks to God, that whenever he sat he held his hands turned upwards on his knees. Though he died on the field of battle, he died in prayer, and this fact passed into a proverb. Unfortunately Bede leaves us only the Latin form, which has a certain proverbial rhythm, but is doubtless far inferior in character and spirit to the English original :—

> God have mercy upon their souls !
> Quoth Oswald as he fell to the ground.

The church of Winwick claims in a remarkable— indeed unique—manner to have been a spot much favoured by Oswald. There runs round the exterior of the church a Latin inscription in large capitals its first words are—" Hic locus, Oswalde, quondam placuit tibi valde " (" This place was very dear to thee of yore, Oswald ").

There is preserved at this church the central boss and the arms of what has been a very noble Anglo-Saxon cross, of unusual size. This and the arm of a cross preserved in the crypt at Lastingham are probably the largest that we now possess. Panels on the arm at Winwick have reference to the death of Oswald. Plate 3 shows a panel which represents his dismemberment.[1]

We cannot part with Oswald without looking into

[1] The Vicar of Winwick, the Reverend M. L. Smith, has kindly sent a photograph of this panel. I had figured it roughly but correctly thirty years ago, in a paper read before the Lancashire and Cheshire Antiquarian Society.

a matter of great interest, involving a suggestion that Oswald and Aidan have left their mark upon our Coronation Service. We have to leave Bede for our facts in this case, and turn to Adamnan's Life of St. Columba. Adamnan was the ninth Abbat of Iona, of the same royal Irish race as Columba. He was abbat from 679 to 704, and was the instructor of a learned Anglo-Saxon prince, Aldfrith, who succeeded to the throne of Northumbria in 685 as we shall see. He visited King Aldfrith on more than one occasion. During his visit in 688 he spent some time at Jarrow, and was there converted by Abbat Ceolfrid to the method of reckoning Easter adopted at the synod of Whitby, of which we shall hear. Bede no doubt saw him on that occasion, of which he gives a description. He has high praise for Adamnan, evidently well deserved. Ceolfrid himself wrote an account of Adamnan's visit which Bede has preserved for us in the long letter on the Easter question written to Naiton, king of the Picts, in 710. There can be little doubt, if any, that Bede compiled the letter, but in it Ceolfrid speaks in the first person. He tells Naiton that he discovered wonderful wisdom, humility, and religion in Adamnan's words and behaviour.

Oswald, we must remember, had lived in Iona, and there had learned the magic charm of the records of Columba's sayings and doings.

Adamnan tells us in the first chapter of his Life of St. Columba that his predecessor Failbe told him an interesting fact, which he had heard from the mouth of King Oswald himself when the king was relating the circumstances to Seghine, the abbat of his time. The day before his great fight with the Britons, who had overrun Northumbria after the defeat and death of Edwin, Oswald was lying in his tent, wearied with the work of marking out his camp. He slept. Columba appeared to him in a vision. He announced himself to Oswald by name, and addressed him as the Lord addressed Joshua the son of Nun before he crossed Jordan, " Be strong and play the man ; I am with thee, as I was with Moses." He added the charge to go out that night and fight, his enemy Catlon (Cadwalla) would be delivered into his hands. Those words, " Be strong and play the man," were copied into the Anglo-Saxon forms for the coronation of kings, and they form the anthem in our own Coronation Service.

We can now turn to Adamnan's record of the form of service used by Columba at the coronation of the first independent king of the Irish settlers on the west coast of the country we call Scotland.[1] Up to Columba's time their lords had been subject to the superior king of the people who had remained in Ireland. Adamnan got the account from a Life of Columba written by a previous abbat. We may safely presume that it had come down to them direct from Columba.

It is evident that Columba had to make up his mind on two important points. There was a vacancy. Which of two brothers should he advise them to take ? And should he declare that the one chosen was to be an independent sovereign, or keep up a succession of inferior lords ? To him thus doubting, there came a vision of the night. An angel presented to him a crystal codex, a form for the coronation of kings, and bade him read it. There he found the name of the brother he was to appoint. The crystal codex was

[1] See page 88.

presumably a book with crystals worked into the binding, a very favourite practice in times rather later than that, or possibly with a cover of crystal.

Then Adamnan gives us the account of the ordination of the king, ordination being the term used. From this we learn that in the year 574 there was (1) a set form for the ordination of kings, (2) a sermon, apparently added by Columba, (3) the imposition of hands, (4) an address of exhortation, that the sceptre might not pass out of the hands of the king and his descendants, and (5) presumably the king seated, almost certainly on some special stone, holding in his hand a sceptre, and (6) the solemn blessing of the king when ordained.

There is now no imposition of hands in our Coronation Service, but an Anglo-Saxon form has a prayer for " this thy servant who by the imposition of our hands is this day constituted queen." The exhortation to good rule, in order that the sceptre might not depart from the sovereign and his descendants, was taken word for word into the Anglo-Saxon forms, though we have it not. All the rest we have, direct from Columba, with Columba's words in the vision to Oswald, incorporated no doubt when Oswald was crowned by Aidan. It is quite probable that Oswald and Aidan had seen a Columban coronation at Iona ; we may take it as certain that from Iona they took their form. From Oswald's coronation it came down to King George V.

When Oswald was slain, the old dual arrangement came into force again. His brother Oswy succeeded him, having as his partner in the kingdom King Oswin, a son of the apostate Osric. Oswin ruled in Deira, and was a happy contrast to his father. He was tall and of a graceful figure, courteous and agreeable in manner. He was liberal to all, high and low, and by his noble qualities of body and mind he won the love of all. Chief of his many charms was the grace of humility. There is a touching story of Aidan's conviction that he was too good to live, a story which gives us a valuable insight into the characters of the two men, and reflects great credit on the king. Oswin had given Aidan a very fine horse for any journey in which speed was necessary, and for assistance in crossing rivers ; for on ordinary occasions Aidan travelled on foot. One day Aidan met a beggar, who asked an alms. Having nothing else to give, he gave him the horse with its royal trappings. The king heard of this, and when next they met, he asked the bishop as they went in to dinner why he had given that horse, fit for a king, to a beggar. Were there not plenty of other horses in the king's possession, of less value or of different breed, any one of which he might have given to the beggar instead of the one which the king had specially selected for the bishop's own use ? Surely, the bishop replied, the son of a mare was not more dear to the king than that son of God whose needs he had relieved ! They went in to dinner, and the bishop sat down. But the king did not sit. He had just returned from hunting, and he stood before the fire warming himself, chafing, we may suppose, at the bishop's reckless almsgiving, and at the rebuke he had received. Suddenly his mood changed. He ungirt his sword and threw himself at the bishop's feet, entreating him to be reconciled. From that time forward, he penitently declared, he would never mention the matter again, nor would he ever again question any gift which the bishop might make to the sons of God from the king's possessions. Aidan was frightened by such humility. He sprang from his seat and raised the king, assuring him of complete reconciliation, and begging him to cast off his sadness and take his meal with cheerfulness. The king recovered his spirits, but the bishop grew more and more sad, till at last he burst into tears. His attendant priest asked him in the Scottish language, which the king and his ministers did not understand, why he wept. " Because I feel sure he is not long for this life. So humble a king I never saw. This people is not worthy of such a king." And in all too short a time this presentiment was shown to be just. Oswy quarrelled with Oswin, and led an army against him. Oswin collected an army, but found he was not strong enough to face his brother king ; so with characteristic resignation he disbanded his forces, and with one attendant, a trusty soldier, Tondhere, retired to the dwelling of a friend, Earl Hunwald. Hunwald betrayed him to Oswy, and the humble king and the faithful soldier were slain together at Ingethlinum, on August 20, 642. The monastery of Gilling, near Richmond, was built here soon after, that prayers might be offered for the king who was slain and for the king who slew him. We have a small inscribed stone of those times bearing the names of Oswin and Tondhere.

On the twelfth day after the murder of Oswin, Aidan followed the friend he had loved so well. He left behind him a most salutary example of self-denial and untiring labour. It was the highest commendation of his doctrine, Bede says, that he taught no otherwise than as he and his followers lived. Whenever he met any on his journeys, rich or poor, if they were heathen, he exhorted them to embrace the true faith, if Christians, he sought to strengthen them in the faith, and to quicken them to almsgiving and other good works. He and all his companions, whether shorn monks or laymen, spent the time which was not occupied in active work, in reading the Scriptures and learning psalms, " so different," Bede says, " from the slothfulness of our times." If he was invited to eat with the king, he went with one clerk only, or two, and as soon as he had made a slight repast, he hastened to return to his reading or writing. In his time, many religious men and women were induced by his example to fast always till three o'clock on Wednesdays and Fridays, except during the fifty days following Easter. Bede's praise of him is unbounded, save only on the vexed question of the rule for the determination of Easter (*see* Chapter IV). He summarizes the good bishop's character as follows " Love of peace and charity ; self-denial and humility ; a mind superior to anger and avarice ; despising pride and vain-glory ; industrious in keeping and teaching the heavenly commandments ; diligent in reading and in vigil ; reproving the haughty and powerful with the authority becoming a priest, and as tender in comforting the afflicted." And even on the one subject on which men of Bede's views differed from men of Aidan's views, and differed with a hatred which even in these days it is not easy to imagine or comprehend, Bede wrote of him with a charity worthy of all imitation. "Although he observed not the true time of celebrating Easter, yet the object he had in view in all that he said, did, or preached, was the same as ours, that is, the redemption of mankind through the

Passion, Resurrection, and Ascension of the Man Jesus Christ, the mediator between God and Man." Who could wish for a kindlier hand to write his epitaph !

The details of Aidan's death afford a singular illustration of the primitive simplicity of his life. He was at one of the king's country houses when his end drew near. This was a favourite resort of his, for there was a church there, and he had also a sleeping-place, so that he could make it a centre for excursions through the neighbouring district. He did this also at other of the king's houses, having nothing of his own but a church and a few fields near it. When his companions saw how ill he was, they made a sort of tent for him, apparently a lean-to, attached to the west wall of the church. And there he died, leaning on a beam placed as a buttress for the support of the wall. Bede relates that when the village and church were burned some years later by Penda of Mercia, whose course of evil-doing seems unending as we read chapter after chapter of the history, the beam was not burned. The church was rebuilt, and the beam was restored to its place as a buttress, and again the church was burned and again the beam was not burned ; yea, though the fire blazed through the holes by which it was fastened to the church, yet was not the beam burned. After this second preservation, the beam was stored as a relic in the renovated church, and Bede tells us that in his time it worked miracles. Aidan's church establishment in Northumbria proved as tenacious of existence as the buttress on which he died.

His death was only thirty years before the birth of Bede. He was succeeded by another Scotic prelate, Finan, who did indeed enter into his labours.

CHAPTER IV

CHRISTIANITY IN NORTHUMBRIA TO THE TIME OF BEDE

King Oswy—Christianity in Mercia—Penda slain—Date of the Easter Feast—The Conference of Whitby—Wilfrith—Colman—Migration to Ireland—Alchfrith—His memorial cross at Bewcastle—Runic inscriptions.

Two years after Aidan's death, his work bore fruit far beyond the bounds of Northumbria. The pagan Penda of Mercia was still living, and he had made his son king of the Middle Angles. This son, Peada, was anxious to marry the daughter of Oswy of Northumbria. Oswy refused to give him Ælflæd unless he promised to become a Christian. He heard the Christian preachers, and their arguments were supported by the friendly persuasions of his brother-in-law Alchfrith, son of Oswy, who had married a daughter of Penda, Cyniburga. He was so completely won over that he declared he must become a Christian whether he obtained Elfleda[1] or not. Accordingly he came with his earls and soldiers, and was baptized at a village near the Roman wall, by Finan, the successor of Aidan. This, Bede says, was a noted village of the kings, called At the Wall. It is probably represented now by Benwell, the name Ben-

---

[1] This is a more usual spelling than Ælflæd. The Anglo-Saxon personal names appear under various forms, chiefly because Bede latinises them.

well being taken to mean the Head of the Wall. He then returned to his own kingdom with four priests, one a Scot, Diuma, the others English : Cedd, Adda, and Betti. The priests had great success among the Middle Angles, and even among the Mercians ; for to the honour of Penda, murderous old pagan as he was, it is recorded that he was quite willing to allow his son's preachers to come into Mercia, if any Mercians wanted to hear them. And we cannot but feel respect for him when we read that he heartily despised such professing Christians as he saw living evil lives,—" base wretches, not to do what the God they believe in tells them." The four priests mentioned above were the direct means of converting to Christianity the Middle Angles, the Mercians, the East Saxons, and, to speak generally, a great part of England, exclusive of Northumbria and Kent and the extreme south and south-west.

At length Penda was slain ; and as a sort of compensation for all the harm he had done to Northumbria and its Christianity through many long years, his death proved to be an important epoch in Christian progress in the kingdom. In the year 655, twenty years only before the birth of Bede, King Oswy had determined to put an end, if possible, to the continual harass caused by Penda's hostility. He had accordingly offered to Penda a large amount of property if he would let Northumbria alone. Penda refused the offer of a part of the land, and set himself to work to take the whole, and to extirpate the Northumbrian English. Oswy, when he heard of the refusal, exclaimed that he would offer his gifts to a king who would accept them, the Lord his God. He bound himself by a vow to give to God twelve

farms for building monasteries, and to dedicate his
infant daughter to perpetual virginity, if he proved
victorious against Penda.   With much inferior forces
he and his son Alchfrith, the sub-king of Deira, met
the enemy of their house on the banks of the river
Vinwed,[1] in the district of Loidis (Leeds), and there
they slew Penda, and broke the strength of Mercia.
This battle was fought on the 15th of November,
much later in the year than the other battles of which
we have spoken, and the flooded state of the river
aided greatly in the destruction of the pagans.   Oswy
carried out his vow.   He gave six portions of land in
Deira and six in Bernicia, each containing ten families,
according to the old English method of reckoning the
extent of land.   In these, as Bede says, war was to
cease ; monks were to engage in the warfare that is
spiritual, and were to pray for the peace of the land.
This foundation of monasteries on a large scale naturally gave a great impetus to the monastic movement.
The little Ælflæd was sent to her relative Hilda, at that
time abbess of Heruteu, *i.e.* " the island of the stag,"
now known as Hartlepool.   Two years later, Hilda
obtained a possession of ten families on the Yorkshire
coast, at Streoneshalch, where she founded the
monastery afterwards so well known as the abbey of
Whitby.   Here Ælflæd lived for sixty years.   Only
ten years or so before Oswy's vow, there was so great
a dearth of monasteries in the land, that many who
wished to enter the monastic life were obliged to go to
the Franks or the Gauls.

It appears that Aidan had not built a church at
Lindisfarne.   Finan commenced one immediately

[1] Supposed by Camden to be the Aire, in Yorkshire.   More probably the Went or Wynt, south of the Aire.

upon his succession to the bishopric, building it of hewn oak, and thatching it with reeds, after the manner of the Scots, Bede says. A later bishop, Eadbert, took off the thatch, and covered the roof and walls with lead. In Finan's time the controversy about the true time of keeping Easter, already alluded to, began to assume considerable dimensions. The question in its full detail need not now be entered into, but some of its main features are easily intelligible, and must be stated here.

Our rule for determining which Sunday in any year is to be kept as Easter Day is stated in the " Tables and Rules " prefixed to the Book of Common Prayer, as follows : Easter Day, on which the rest of the movable Feasts and Holy-days depend, is always the First Sunday after the Full Moon which happens upon or next after the twenty-first day of March ; and if that Full Moon happens upon a Sunday, Easter Day is the Sunday after. This very precise rule is stated in a net form, and is best thus stated. It fixes the attention upon the full moon. The early discussions turned upon the preceding new moon, fourteen days before. It comes of course to the same thing, but the rule is less briefly stated if it employs the new moon as the test.

Two points of this rule are quite definite ; (1) Easter Day is always to be a Sunday ; and (2) if the vernal full moon falls on a Sunday, Easter Day is not that Sunday, it is the Sunday after. Both of these points are the fixed result of early controversies. The third point is that the full moon is to be the full moon on the 21st of March, if that day is full moon ; if it is not full moon, then the full moon next after the 21st. In no case is Easter Day to be before or on the vernal equinox, the 21st of March.

Easter Day commemorates the Resurrection of our Lord. That event is generally understood to have occurred on the third day from the Passover, *i.e.* the third day from the 14th day of the month Nisan. The month Nisan commenced with the new moon of the vernal equinox, and thus the Passover, the 14th day of the month, fell on the day of the full moon, and the Resurrection Day on the third day after. Easter Day, however, does not represent that third day. In the earliest times of Christianity, the Paschal Feast combined the commemoration of the Passion and of the Resurrection, and its commencement—our Easter Day—coincided rather with the Passion than with the third day.

The greater part of the earliest Christians said that the Feast must commence on a Lord's Day, and not on the 14th day of the moon if that was not a Lord's Day. The others persisted that the actual 14th day of the moon must be treated as the anniversary, whatever day of the week it might be. These latter were called Quartodecimans, from the Latin word meaning Fourteenth ; and as it happened that some of the early Quartodecimans held erroneous views on some points of doctrine, Quarto-decimanism became stamped as a heresy. The observance of the Sunday next after the actual day fixed by the change of the moon became the orthodox and Catholic custom. This our rule expresses.

The British Church, of which some account is given in Chapter V, was accused of being Quartodeciman. They were not Quartodecimans in the old and accepted meaning of that word ; but their opponents could claim to call them Quartodecimans, because they kept Easter Day on the fourteenth day of the moon if that fell on a Sunday, whereas the Church of the West waited till the next Sunday, as do we. The Britons kept Easter Day always on the Lord's-day, not on the week-day determined by the old rule for the determination of the Passover. But they did not agree with the Church of the West in their rule to decide which new moon to take as the basis of their calculations. The Britons said that theirs was the old rule, from which the Church of the West had departed.

It had been arranged at the Council of Nicæa, A.D. 325, that the Patriarch of Alexandria should obtain the assistance of Egyptian astronomers, and should announce to the Christian world each year what was the true day of Easter. The announcement was made in a formal letter addressed by the Patriarch to the Bishop of Rome, and a manuscript containing a most interesting series of these letters, written by Athanasius, was found early in last century by the late Archdeacon Tattam in the convent of St. Mary Deipara, in the desert of Nitria. The letters have been published, under the name of " The Festal Epistles of Athanasius." The Patriarch Athanasius, it may be mentioned, calls himself Pope in these letters. Some changes were made later, and the British Christians certainly had something to say for themselves when they argued that it was hard to charge them with error when they had kept to the old rule throughout. It would seem that after the withdrawal of the Roman forces early in the fifth century, the British Church was not kept informed of ecclesiastical changes outside.

The Alexandrian rule had not permanently regulated the incidence of Easter Day. The Alexandrians held that the selection of the vernal new moon was limited to the period March 8 to April 5, both inclusive, the altered Western style took the period March 5 to April 3, both inclusive. While that made a great difference between the two Easter Days in some years, it much more frequently made no difference at all. If a new moon came on March 5 or March 6, the West took it as the vernal new moon and March 19 or 20 as the vernal full moon ; Alexandria waited for the next full moon. If a new moon came on April 4 or April 5 Alexandria took it as the vernal new moon and April 18 or 19 as the Easter full moon ; the West had had its vernal new moon on March 7 or 8, and its Easter full moon on March 21 or 22. If a new moon came on any of the days from March 8 and April 3, both inclusive, the Alexandrian rule and the Western rule gave the same day for Easter Day. In the infrequent cases of a new moon at the earlier or the later extremity of date, their Easter Days differed by about a month. To take a particular case, in 417 A.D. there was a new moon on March 6. This was taken to be the Paschal Moon in Rome. Fourteen days brought the full moon on March 20. That was a Tuesday in 417. Five days more gave March 25 as Easter Day. On March 25 the Eastern Church was deep in the Lenten fast. Alexandria had rejected the new moon of March 6 as being too early, and was waiting for the next new moon on April 3, which would give them April 22 for Easter Sunday. Our present rule would have agreed with Alexandria against Rome, for we take March 7 as the first possible day for the Paschal moon to begin, March 21 being the earliest day we recognize for the Paschal full moon.

It has been said above that the controversy on this subject assumed considerable dimensions in the time of Finan. Bede says that so long as Aidan lived, the question was allowed to remain dormant, the universal respect in which he was held making every one unwilling to raise an objection to any part of his proceedings. " His time of keeping Easter was patiently tolerated by all men. They knew that he could not act in a manner contrary to the custom of those who sent him to Northumbria, and they saw that he industriously laboured to practise all works of faith, piety, and love." Here is a happy example of toleration. At the same time there is no evidence of any great amount of feeling against Aidan's practice. James the Deacon, the sweet singer, had maintained the Canterbury practice, which was that of Rome ; but his influence could be but small compared with that of the king and of Aidan, both of whom were accustomed to the Scotic rule of Easter, which was the same as that of the British. During Finan's episcopacy, two or three circumstances combined to throw more weight into the Canterbury or Roman scale. A Scottish monk and saint, Ronan, who had been trained on the Continent, held a disputation with Finan, alleging that the Scots were at variance with the universal Church in their rule for keeping Easter. He made no impression upon Finan, who seems to have spoken his mind rather freely, " being of a hot and violent temper." But the disputation called a good deal of attention to the subject. Queen Eanfleda, too, had seen the Canterbury rule observed in Kent, and she had with her a Kentish priest, Romanus, who followed that rule. Thus it fell out on one occasion, that when the king was enjoying the Easter feast, his enjoyment was spoiled by the absence of his consort's countenance, she and her damsels being still deep in the Lenten fast. The queen, we are told, was keeping Palm Sunday on the day which the king called Easter Day. This was therefore the day of full moon, for the British allowed that day as Easter Day, while the others said (as we do) that Easter Day is the Sunday not *on* but *next after* the full moon. The full moon was on a Sunday in the years 645, 647, 648, and 651. The year 651 suits Bede's narrative. The reason for our rule is, that if the full moon falls on a Sunday, to keep that day as Easter Day is to begin to keep Easter before the full moon has actually come.[1] Then, in the year 661, yet another Scot succeeded Finan, Colman by name, and the controversy broke out with violence. Oswy kept the old Easter, but his son Alchfrith, as well as the queen, kept the new. Alchfrith had come under the influence of Wilfrith, a Northumbrian born, but trained at Lyon and an enthusiastic Romanizer ; and, as Bede says, he rightly thought that Wilfrith's doctrine ought to be preferred to all the traditions of the Scots. Bede lets us have a peep behind the scenes which shows us the vigour of Alchfrith's convictions. He tells us that Alchfrith gave Wilfrith the monastery of Ripon, with land containing forty families. This he had a short time before given to those who followed the practice of the Scots ; but, inasmuch as, " being left to their choice," they quitted the place rather than abandon their practice, he made it over to Wilfrith.

With such influences at work, the controversy soon came to a head. A synod was held in 664 at the monastery of Streoneshalch, or the Bay of the Lighthouse, now Whitby. King Oswy presided. He him-

---

[1] For example, if the full moon actually came at 11 a.m. on a Sunday, and that day was kept as Easter Day, several hours of the feast would be kept before the arrival of the full moon.

self followed the Scotic practice, but, as became a president, he held an independent course in the synod. His son Alchfrith was there, a vigorous partisan of the Catholic custom, as its supporters called the Canterbury, *i.e.* the Roman, way. James the Deacon—the perennial James—is said by Bede to have been there, though it was now nearly seventy years since he sang his processional hymn in the isle of Thanet. He was on the Catholic side, of course ; so was Romanus, the Kentish priest of Queen Eanfleda ; so was Agilbert, bishop of Dorchester among the West Saxons, who was at the time paying a long visit to his friends, Alchfrith the prince and Wilfrith the Abbat of Ripon. Agilbert's priest Agatho was there on the same side, and Wilfrith. On the other side were Colman, bishop of Lindisfarne, with his Scottish clerks ; the Abbess Hilda and her train ; and the venerable bishop Chad, the brother of Cedd of whom we have spoken above. To the honour of every one, it is reported by the Catholic part that Chad was the interpreter for both sides,—a most vigilant interpreter, Bede assures us.

The king made a short opening speech. "They all expected the same kingdom of Heaven ; they ought not to differ in the celebration of the mysteries of the kingdom. What they had to do was to inquire which was the true tradition. That once determined, all should follow it." Then he called on his Bishop, Colman, to speak. Colman "kept what he had received from his fathers. They in turn had received it by tradition from the blessed Evangelist St. John, the disciple whom Jesus loved." He spoke at some length, but this was the pith of his discourse.

The king called on Agilbert. Whether as a happy device or as a matter of real necessity, Agilbert

pleaded the want of sufficient familiarity with the
English tongue. Might his disciple Wilfrith speak for
him ?   The synod assented, and thus the keenest
partisan of the Catholic way, the most powerful
speaker in the assembly, was put in the forefront of
the discussion, a place to which his own position could
not have entitled him. Bede gives his speech, and the
retorts of Colman and Wilfrith's replies, in a form
which renders it probable that we have a report more
or less verbatim.

Wilfrith informed his hearers that the Easter which
the Catholic party observed was "that which he had
himself seen observed by all in Rome,—Rome where
St. Peter and St. Paul lived, taught, suffered, and were
buried." We should note that statement of the double
claim of Rome to priority ; not that it was the see of
St. Peter, it was the place where the twin chiefs lay.
He had seen the same kept in Italy and France when
he travelled through those countries. He found that
in Africa, Asia, Egypt, Greece, in all parts of the world
where there was a Church of Christ, the same Easter
was kept by all nations and languages ; except, indeed,
Colman and his complices the Picts and Britons, who
in remote islands—and only in parts even of them—
opposed the universe.

Here Colman broke in with a repetition of his
argument.   " Could he and his be thus accused of folly
and obstinacy, when they did as did St. John, who
laid his head on his Lord's bosom ? "

Then Wilfrith proceeded to demolish Colman's argument. If Colman relied—he retorted—upon authority, for his statements respecting the methods of St.
John and St. Peter, he must have access to sources of
information which had since been closed to the student

of the New Testament and of ecclesiastical history. Wilfrith asserted—and one assertion was as good as another—that St. John followed literally the Jewish rule, and, as a concession to Jewish converts, kept Easter on the day next but one after the day of Passover, whether week-day or not. As parallels to this proceeding, Wilfrith quoted St. Paul's circumcision of Timothy, his offerings in the Temple, his shaving his head with Aquila and Priscilla. But when St. Peter preached at Rome, Wilfrith continued, he taught men to wait till the Lord's-day between the fifteenth and the twenty-first day of the moon. Thus Colman followed neither the practice of St. John nor that of St. Peter ; for he did not keep Easter on a week-day, and his Easter Day was the Lord's-day between the fourteenth and the twentieth day of the moon, so that the Easter feast actually began sometimes on the evening of the thirteenth day of the moon, which was certainly earlier than our Lord ate the Passover. Wilfrith further urged that by excluding the twenty-first day of the moon, the British contravened the Jewish Law. Thus the unfortunate men were shown to agree neither with St. John nor with St. Peter, neither with the Law nor with the Gospel.

Colman fell back upon authorities of a more recent date. " Did the holy Anatolius, so much commended in Church history, act contrary to the Law and the Gospel in teaching that Easter was to be celebrated from the fourteenth to the twentieth ? Did their most reverend Father Columba, and his successors, act contrary to the Law and the Gospel,—men whose holiness was attested by miracles and signs following ? "

Wilfrith denied that they agreed with Anatolius,

whose cycle of nineteen years[1] was unknown to the British or neglected by them. As for their Columba and his followers, of whom Colman asserted that their faithfulness was attested by miracles, he might answer in the words of the Scripture, that there were many who would say in the day of judgment, " Lord, have we not prophesied in thy name, and in thy name cast out devils, and done many mighty works ? " to whom the Lord would reply, " I never knew you." We may suppose that murmurs were heard at this audacious and unseemly retort. At any rate, Wilfrith qualified what he had said, but after a fashion which resembled some retractions in a more modern assembly. " Far be it from him to say so of their fathers,"—not because they did not deserve it, but—" because it was more just to believe good than evil of persons one does not know." And then he spoke of the pious intentions with which no doubt in their rustic simplicity they loved God. But he had another blow in store for Colman and Columba. " What though that Columba of theirs—nay, of ours, too, if he was a servant of Christ," he interposed, mindful, perhaps, of former murmurs, but guarding himself against any positive recognition of any virtue in Columba—" what though that Columba of theirs was powerful in miracles and was a holy man, was he to be preferred to the most blessed prince of the Apostles, St. Peter, to whom the Lord gave the keys of the kingdom of Heaven ? "

The king had now made up his mind, if indeed it was only now that he had done so. He brought the discussion to an end. " Is it true, Colman, that our

---

[1] After nineteen years the sun and moon hold nearly the same relative position ; more nearly still after five nineteens, ninety-five years.

Lord gave to Peter the keys of the kingdom of Heaven ? " " It is true, O king." " Can you show that any such power was given to your Columba ? " " None," Colman answered. " Do you both agree that these words were principally addressed to St. Peter, and that the keys of Heaven were given to him by the Lord ? " With unwonted oneness, Colman and Wilfrith replied, " We do."

Then the king delivered his opinion. Stephen Eddi says on the authority of Wilfrith that he delivered it with a smile, *subridens*. The whole assembly ratified it, both those who sat and those who stood— a valuable hint perhaps that there was a popular element in the synod. " I also say that he is the door-keeper. Him will I not contradict, lest when I come to the gates of the kingdom of Heaven there be none to open them, he who hath the keys being my enemy."

The result of the synod was that the great majority of the worsted party throughout the country went over with the king. Colman, however, went back to the Scots, being determined not to abandon his traditional practice. There was also a further difficulty in the way of an agreement, for he and his had a form of tonsure different from that of the Italian party. The Britons, with the Easterns, tonsured the front of the head, in a crescent form. The Catholic party tonsured the top of the head, leaving a ring of hair to represent the crown of thorns. This they called the tonsure of St. Peter, and being in want of a bad name to call the other by, they called it the tonsure of Simon Magus. From the time of the synod of Whitby, however, these differences ceased in England, and Christians were one in practice as in faith.

It is an important fact that Stephen Eddi, Wilfrith's

chaplain and intimate friend, writing Wilfrith's life after the bishop had passed away, omits all mention of the Petrine origin of the accepted rule, and makes his master base his claim on the canon of the Council of Nicæa. It would appear that Wilfrith had realised the non-historical nature of his argument, and that Eddi represents his mature opinion.

Bede has a very interesting chapter in connection with the departure of Bishop Colman from Northumbria. Colman took away with him from Lindisfarne all the Scots he had gathered round him in the island monastery and thirty of the English students there, all alike trained in monastic discipline. He left a certain number of brethren in his church. He went first to Hii, that is, Iona, and thence to a small island to the west of Ireland, called by the Scots, that is, the native Irish, Inisboufinde, a Gaelic word meaning the island of the white heifer; the Gaelic of to-day would differ only slightly from that form. Here he built a monastery and placed in it all his monks of both nations. This introduces a highly characteristic touch. The two nations did not agree. The English monks remained at the monastery throughout the year, working in the summer to provide stores for the winter season. The Irish monks wandered about during the summer over districts known to them, and on their return to the monastery they claimed to live on the stores gathered by the English. Colman felt he must put an end to the standing discussion, and he bought a place on the mainland of Ireland called Mageo. He left the Irish monks in the island off the west coast and placed the English at Mageo, where a succession of English monks was kept up under excellent discipline and grew larger and larger till the time when Bede wrote. Mageo is now spelled as pronounced, Mayo. It was known as Mayo of the English.

Colman was succeeded in the bishopric of Lindisfarne by Tuda, a bishop of Irish consecration, who had stood on Wilfrith's side at Whitby. He was carried off by the great plague in his first year, and was succeeded by Eata, the English Abbat of Lindisfarne, one of the twelve Northumbrian boys whom Aidan had received to be trained at Lindisfarne. He was the Abbat of Melrose also.

We have seen that Oswy had the assistance of his son Alchfrith in his final and successful fight with the pagan Penda, who had been such a scourge to Bernicia and Deira. We have seen, too, how amicably they worked together in a controversy affecting the Church of the land as gravely as Penda's action had affected the State, although Alchfrith had come over to the new view while his father had stood by the old. Alchfrith was ever active in the cause of the Christian faith. He was a main mover in the conversion of Peada. His rule as sub-king of Deira promised good things. The promise was not to be fulfilled. After the Synod of Whitby, acting as king of Deira, he sent his friend Wilfrith to Paris to be consecrated to the bishopric of his capital city of York. Wilfrith spent an inordinate time in Gaul, and Oswy, acting as over-lord, appointed Ceadda (Chad) to York. From that time Bede ceases to mention Alchfrith. Ælfwine, another son of Oswy, acts as sub-king with his brother Ecgfrith. The same is true of Eddi, the chaplain, friend, and biographer of Wilfrith. Exactly when he is describing a scene in which Alchfrith would have revelled, when Wilfrith was reciting at Ripon the ancient British

sacred sites which he had sought out and had received
as gifts from " the kings," Eddi tells us that the new
King Ecgfrith and his brother Ælfwine—not his
brother Alchfrith—were the kings present. It would
have been only decent to say how much Alchfrith
would have valued this recovery and the splendid
ceremony of the dedication of the great church at his
own much-loved Ripon. Something tragic must have
happened. It would seem that the father and son had
come to open quarrel, and Alchfrith had been slain.
Possibly there had been a recurrence of the cruel sort
of murder which had removed Oswin. But the probability is that the Oswy party regarded Alchfrith as an
evil-doer beyond the pale even in those days. The
most famous of our national memorials, the great
cross-shaft at Bewcastle in Cumberland, bears the
name of Alchfrith, as son of Oswy, and the name of
Cyniburga his Mercian wife, and a prayer for his soul
with a reference to some serious sin. The inscriptions
on the shaft are numerous. They are in the early
Anglian runes and some of them are disputed, among
them the names of Wulfhere the king of the Mercians,
Alchfrith's brother-in-law, and Cynesthwitha, his
wife's sister, and the date in the form of " the first
year of Ecgfrith the king of this realm." That is the
proper method of dating at that period. It gives the
date 670 A.D., which fits well into the story. It also
explains the erection of a noble monument, the finest
the nation possesses, in memory of one whose evil-
doing had been such that the contemporary historian,
Eddi, and the historian of the next generation, Bede,
could not write his name on their page after the
perpetration of the deed, whatever it was. The
" first year of Ecgfrith " meant that Oswy was dead

and out of the way, and suggests that Ecgfrith did not take the view of the enormity of Alchfrith's conduct which the historians took. There may be something in the fact, for such it seems to be, that if Alchfrith had lived he would have succeeded Oswy as his oldest son, older than Ecgfrith and much more prominent. A representation of the side of the shaft which contains the longest of the inscriptions and gives a representation of Alchfrith himself is shown on Plate 4.[1] The figure above Alchfrith is Our Lord, with the inscription " ✠ GESSUS KRISTTUS " above the head. Above that again the Baptist, and above that the broken socket from which the cross-head, also inscribed with runes, was blown in the time of " Belted Will Howard," about 1615. On the runes at Ruthwell, see page 178.

Bede, writing of times only ten years before his own birth, takes occasion to remark upon the extreme frugality of the Scottish bishops who had ruled in Northumbria—Aidan, Finan, and Colman. When Colman and his party left Lindisfarne, those who followed found no money, only cattle, and scarcely house-room enough for the party which had left. The king had never been accustomed to bring a large retinue with him when he came to perform his devotions in the church   he brought five or six companions at the outside, to spare the bishop expense, and if they accepted food, they were satisfied with the plain fare of the ecclesiastics. The result of so good an example of self-denial and frugality on the part of the bishop and his clergy was that the religious habit was held in great veneration. All persons joyfully received a monk, or one of the clergy, as God's servant. Those

[1] On the whole subject of the remarkable monument, see *The Ancient Cross Shafts at Bewcastle and Ruthwell* (Cambridge University Press), by Bishop G. F. Browne.

who met such ran to them, bowing, and begged to be signed with the hand or blessed with the mouth. On Sundays the people flocked eagerly to church and monastery, to hear the word of God. If a priest came into a village, the inhabitants crowded round him to hear the word of life. In those days, Bede remarks, apparently with a sad glance to his own times, in those days the clergy had no other aim than to preach, to baptize, to visit the sick, to undertake the cure of souls.

Such is the description which Bede gives of the state of Christianity in Northumbria, a very few years before his birth. It remains only to record that even so late as this—and we have now come to the year 665—the East Saxons relapsed once more into paganism, believing that a pestilence which devastated their country was due to the wrath of the gods they had neglected and abjured. And the year after, Archbishop Theodore came to Canterbury, and with him the knowledge and teaching power which prepared the way for Bede and made such a phenomenon possible. The interval between Theodore's arrival and Bede's commencement of his career as a student and writer is covered by the life of St. Cuthbert, the details of which will be found in Chapter VIII.

CHAPTER V

THE BRITISH CHRISTIANS

First introduction of Christianity into Britain—Tertullian's evidence
—Council of Arles—Orthodoxy of the Britons—Departure of the
Romans—The Britons and Augustine—Picts and Scots—Flight
of Roman bishops—The Welsh Church—Summary of conversion
of the several kingdoms.

HAVING now completed under Bede's guidance the story of the conversion of both branches of the Northumbrian English to Christianity, it seems necessary to say something of the British Christians, one branch of whom, under their king Cadwalla, have made a tragic appearance on our pages.

We are naturally carried back to the very earliest times in the known history of our land, which commences a few years before the birth of Jesus Christ.

School chronologies used to give A.D. 596 as the date of the " introduction of Christianity into this island by Augustine," but Christianity had been known and practised here very long before Augustine's time. There were British Christians, and in large numbers too, four hundred years before Augustine came to Christianize the Angles and Saxons.

No one can say, with any approach to certainty, by whom Christianity was first brought to Britain. The connection between Rome and this island was so close in the latter years of St. Paul's life, that there is much reason to suppose that the new religion became known here very early, probably by some chance means. It has been said that St. Paul himself visited Britain, in the interval between the end of the Acts of the Apostles and his second captivity and death. An ecclesiastical historian (Theodoret) asserted that St. Paul carried out during that interval his intention of visiting Spain,[1] and that he proceeded further to the islands scattered in the sea. Theodoret wrote more than a hundred and fifty years before Augustine's time. Clement of Rome, a contemporary of St. Paul, says that the Apostle went to the extreme limits of the West ; and we may remember that a Roman poet described Britain as the " furthest island of the West." The great historian of the early Church, Eusebius, writing about the year 320, says decidedly that some of the Apostles crossed the sea to the British Isles.

The information we derive from secular sources as to the means of communication between Britain and Rome renders it highly probable that some attempt would be made to Christianize the island in Apostolic times. Britain was then governed by Roman viceroys, and was no doubt a frequent topic of conversation among the Prætorian soldiers with whom St. Paul lived for some time. The sons of British princes were sent to Rome, both as hostages for the good conduct of their fathers and for purposes of education. Seneca, the brother of the Gallio of the Acts, had large possessions in Britain. The poet Martial, who went to Rome about the year of St. Paul's death, sings the praises of a British matron Claudia Rufina, wife of Pudens, and asserts that his verses were sung in Britain. It is natural to

---

[1] Romans xv. 24.

identify Martial's British Pudens and Claudia, living in Rome, with St. Paul's Christian Pudens and Claudia, also living in Rome (2 Tim. iv. 21) at the very time when Martial went there. Pomponia Græcina, whose husband commanded in Britain A.D. 43–52, was accused at Rome A.D. 57 of " foreign superstition," and this has been held to mean Christianity. Other links between early Britain and Christianity might be added. On the face of it, the belief that Christianity was introduced into Britain from Rome through Gaul in the earliest years of the Christian Church is the reverse of unreasonable. But it is probable that it came in an informal way, from the talk of soldiers and of traders. If any of the great apostolic missionaries had been concerned in its introduction, the British Christians must—one would suppose—have had some tradition to that effect, and considering how closely Britain was connected with Rome, the early Roman writers must have referred to what would have been almost a domestic fact.

The tradition that the Apostles divided the world among themselves by lot has no historical authority. According to that tradition, Britain fell to the lot of Simon Zelotes, who thereupon came to the island and introduced Christianity. A more persistent tradition, though of later origin, assigns Joseph of Arimathæa as the founder of the Church here, adding that he was sent by Philip, who preached in the land of the Franks. Joseph and his eleven companions are said to have settled at Avalon, and the " Twelve Hides " of Glastonbury are said to represent the parcels of land which the then king gave to the twelve missionaries. The English bishops claimed for their Church precedence over some Churches at the Council of Basle (A.D. 1431) as having been founded by Joseph ; and Queen Elizabeth and Archbishop Parker claimed the same origin for the Church. We should not claim it now.

Passing by these traditions and suppositions, it is certain that Tertullian (about A.D. 200) described the spread of Christianity in the island as so wide that parts which the Roman armies could not reach had been subdued to Christ, and that British bishops were present at the Council of Arles, held in the year 314. The Emperor Constantine the Great, and also Athanasius, testified to the orthodoxy[1] of the British Church between A.D. 325 and A.D. 350. About three-quarters of a century later, the great Pelagian heresy, respecting man's dependence on the grace of God, was commenced by a British Christian, Pelagius being the Greek equivalent for Morgan.

The departure of the Romans, who carried off the flower of the population in their armies, and the arrival of the Saxons, effected the ruin of the Britons, and all but obliterated the British Church. According to Bede's account—and we have no account which contradicts it—the Britons eventually deserved their fate. They had found courage to drive off the northern enemies who had invaded them as soon as the Romans retired, though at first they had been so terrified as to allow the Picts and Scots to drag them off Severus's wall with hooks, and so make a way over that useless barrier. But when the invaders had been after a time sent out of the land again, the

---

[1] Constantine named the Britons among the Churches which were exemplary and orthodox in their time of keeping Easter. This is a curious fact, considering the contempt which the orthodox poured upon the British view later on. The orthodox had developed their view and the British had not.

Britons became too prosperous. There was a remarkable plenty of the fruits of the earth, such as
had never been known before, and the people waxed
idle and wanton in consequence. Vice spread rapidly
among them. Bede's traditions informed him that
cruelty, the hatred of truth, and the love of lying,
were rampant ; so much so that any one who was a
little more inclined to the truth than his neighbours
was hated and destroyed as a "subverter of Britain."
And this was not confined to the laity. The clergy
indulged themselves in drunkenness, quarrelsome-
ness, and so on. At length a pestilence came upon
them and slew the greater part of them, and then
their northern enemies attacked them again, and they
invited the Saxons to come to their aid. We know
what that led to. Bede gives none of the details
which we learn from other sources, and only tells in
general terms of the cruelty of the Saxons. The
priests were slain at the altar ; prelates and people
were destroyed with fire and the sword ; many who
had fled to the mountains were seized, and murdered
in heaps ; others were more successful, and con-
trived to find refuge in the mountainous parts on the
west of the island, Cornwall, Wales, and Cumberland.[1] There they kept up the succession of bishops
—indeed, the sees of St. David's, Lampeter, and
St. Asaph's were founded during this period of distress—and when Augustine came to Christianize the
Saxons, one of the most important questions he had
to refer to Pope Gregory was, what was he to do
with the British bishops ?

It should have been quite possible for Augustine's

[1] They formed practically three separate churches, those of
Cornwall, Wales, and Cumbria.

mission and the British Church they found on their arrival to differ on some points of practice,[1] and yet to agree in the main and be friendly disposed. But unfortunately Augustine acted injudiciously in the matter of his dealings with them. He treated them, as we gather from the accounts of those who took his side, as inferiors, and as having failed in their duty towards the Saxon invaders, whom they had not attempted to convert from heathenism.[2] They should have been treated with great consideration by the Italians, as the survivors of an early and interesting Christian Church which the Saxons had ruined ; while the argument that they had not converted the Saxons was not worth much, for they had been compelled to fly before the conquering invaders, who were not likely to listen to the teaching of despised fugitives.

And it was not true that the Britons had made no attempt to maintain their profession of Christianity among the Saxons. They had stood their ground manfully,—more manfully, indeed, than the Italian mission did when the time of like trial came. Bishop Theonas, probably of Lincoln, and Bishop Thadioc, of York, had fled from their sees only a very few years before Augustine's arrival.

Augustine had two interviews with the British bishops. The first was held at the furthest point westward which the protection of the King of Kent made it safe for Augustine to reach. Geographical and racial and political considerations point to the spot where a great Roman road crosses the upper

[1] The only points specified were the date of Easter in exceptional years, and some detail—we do not quite know what—in the ceremony of Baptism.

[2] St. Patrick went from Roman Britain to convert Ireland, and it was a British bishop, Ninian, who converted the Southern Picts.

waters of the Thames, where the ancient town of Cricklade now stands, conveniently near the great British fortress of Malmesbury. This was the one place, convenient to the Britons, where the Kentish deputation and the British representatives stood on ground safe for each. Political considerations weigh heavily against the place which used to be regarded as probable, namely Aust, near the English end of the great ferry across the Severn.

The second interview was short and unsuccessful. The native bishops[1] had consulted an aged man as to the course they should pursue with regard to Augustine's overtures. He advised them, that if on their next visiting him he rose to meet them and greeted them kindly, they should come to terms with him. If, on the other hand, Augustine remained seated, they should at once leave him, and break off communication with him ; for if he treated them haughtily while they were still independent, he could not be trusted to treat them properly if they became in any sense his suffragans. Augustine did remain seated, and his visitors took the advice they had received, and refused to make any agreement with him. They parted with high words, on Augustine's side at least, and one result was, that the Canterbury mission was viewed with jealousy and dislike by the native Christians. To so great a length was this carried, that in the time of Laurentius, Augustine's successor, a certain Scotic prelate, Dagan by name, passing through Canterbury, refused to eat in the same house with the Italian Christians.

The mention of a Scotic prelate calls for some

---

[1] The bishops had with them many very learned men, chiefly from the monastery of Bangor. This was Bangor ys Coed, Bangor by the wood, not the present Cathedral City of Bangor.

explanation. As in Northumbria we have to deal with two districts and two kingdoms with one race, Deira and Bernicia of the Angles, so in the part of the island north of Northumbria, we have to deal with two districts and two kingdoms but with two races, the Picts and the Scots. Instead of lying north and south, as Bernicia and Deira, the Picts were to the east and the Scots to the west. The Picts settled to the east of the great central ridge, in Gaelic *Drum*, which forms the backbone of the country we now call Scotland. Inverness was their capital. The Scots occupied the country to the west of the Drum, Argyleshire and those parts. They were Irish people, and the Irish were then called Scots. The name Scots accompanied the Irish settlers to the west of the Drum, and thence the land came to be called the land of the Scots. After the union of the two races under Kenneth MacAlpine, the whole of Caledonia came to be called Scotland as it is now. The Picts were converted or, as some say, reconverted to Christianity under Columba. Scotic seems a better name than Scottish to indicate the national Church which centred round Iona.

Augustine and his party achieved but a very small part of the work they had been sent to do. The little kingdom of Kent, with its king at Canterbury and its sub-king at Rochester, was their only permanent conquest. They had, indeed, converted London, then the capital of the East-Saxon kingdom, but their bishop of London fled from his see when a popular tumult was raised against him, and never returned. The cause of the tumult is worth mentioning, as an indication of the barbarous character of the times. Bishop Mellitus of London, afterwards of Canterbury, was in the act of administering the Holy Eucharist when the sons of the king came in from hunting, tired and hungry. They demanded some of the white bread and of the wine, but Mellitus refused, informing them that they must first be baptized. The king's sons in their anger raised the tumult before which Mellitus fled, and for many years there was no bishop of London. In a similar manner Justus, the first Bishop of Rochester, fled before a popular tumult. And even Augustine's immediate successor, Laurentius, was on the eve of flight when a so-called miracle stopped him. When Ethelbert, the first Christian king of Kent, died, his son succeeded him, and in accordance with the ancient practice of his race, made arrangements to take as his wife the young widow of the late king his father. Laurentius protested against this, and the king was very angry with him. The anti-Christian party fanned the flame, and Laurentius determined to fly. The night before his flight he slept for safety in a church near Canterbury, and the next morning he appeared before the king in great bodily distress, having—so he said—been soundly scourged by St. Peter during the night. The king was so much impressed by this unheard-of punishment that he made friends with Laurentius, perhaps fearing that his own turn would come next. Paulinus, as we have seen already, fled before an outburst of Saxon paganism. Thus the Italians learned, in one place after another, what it was to have to fly before the Saxons, as the British Christians had done.

In the Fourth Book of his Ecclesiastical History, Bede records a similar case of a Christian bishop abandoning his position, and flying to a safe place. King Ecgfrith of Northumbria led an army against his neighbours the Picts, contrary to the earnest advice of Cuthbert, and the Picts by a feigned flight drew him and his forces into the recesses of the hill country, and slew them there. Taking heart from this success, they recovered the lands which the English had taken from them in former times. The British, too, following their example, shook off the English yoke in the north-west. Thereupon the English Bishop Trumwine, who had been appointed bishop over the Picts and was settled at the monastery of Abercorn, fled with his companions and took refuge at Whitby, where he spent the rest of his life. Bede narrates this without any remark which suggests a criticism of Trumwine's conduct.

We may remark here that the scourging of Laurentius, and its effect upon the king, was reproduced afterwards in Northumbria. We have the story from Stephen Eddi, Wilfrith's companion and biographer, not from Bede, who wrote a little later. When Wilfrith was deposed and cast into prison, the queen took possession of his chrismary, which was well filled with relics, and kept it in her room, or hung it in her carriage when she made a journey. After a time, the king and she in the course of a royal progress through the cities and castles and towns of the kingdom, came to the monastery of Coldingham, over which the late king's sister, Æbba, presided.[1] They rested there for a time, and during the night the queen was seized by a demon and soundly flogged, like Pilate's wife, Eddi says, so that she was found the next morning in a dying state. Æbba went to tell the king of the dreadful thing that had happened,

---

[1] For the state of morals at Coldingham under its royal abbess, see p. 287.

and gave him her mind freely on the subject, as Eddi tells. He had deposed Wilfrith, had treated contemptuously the orders from Rome, and finally had shut up the holy bishop in prison no wonder the queen was flogged. He must release the bishop ; if he could not replace him in the bishopric, he must give him free leave to go where he would ; and the queen must give him back the chrismary she had taken from his neck. The king hearkened to the abbess, Wilfrith was released, the relics were restored to him, the queen was healed and was flogged no more.

The British Church continued to exist in Wales for many centuries, and it exists there still. While other British communities came to terms with the Italian party in the Anglo-Saxon Church after the synod of Whitby, A.D. 664, and agreed to abandon the traditional rule for the determination of Easter, and other details in which they were at variance with the usages introduced by the Italian mission, the bishops in Wales still held themselves independent of the See of Canterbury. The earliest consecration of a Welsh bishop by an English archbishop of which we have evidence was in 1092. At that time Thomas, Archbishop of York, was acting during the vacancy caused by the death of Lanfranc. He consecrated Hervè le Breton to the see of Bangor in 1092. That the connection with the English Church had become close and real then may be gathered from the fact that, when the see of Ely was created in 1109, Hervè was selected as its first bishop. In 1107, Urban was consecrated on August 11 as Bishop of Llandaff by Anselm of Canterbury, Gerard of York, and six bishops of the two provinces. In 1115, Bernard was consecrated to St. David's on December 26 by Ralph of Canterbury; and in 1143 the remaining Welsh diocese had its Bishop Gilbert consecrated at Lambeth by Theobald of Canterbury.

The very ancient Church of the Welsh was only finally brought into the English Church when the Welsh State was absorbed at the end of the thirteenth century. It still remained a church, within a church, though in every sense an integral part of the National Church of England as a whole. Whether it is so to remain, or is to be cut out and utterly spoiled of its ancient endowments, of which in these crowded times it has made such noble use, may come to be decided by a Parliament very different from that which is now, at the end of 1917, managing our affairs. Our public men are being taught now both that an end is coming to factious mischief of that class, and that a people tried as we are being tried are much more likely to create than to destroy, when questions of national means for the furtherance of national religion are to the fore.

It has been remarked in the course of this chapter that Augustine's mission did but a small part of the work they had come to do. The following summary of the means by which the various English kingdoms were converted will show how small a part of the island they succeeded in christianizing.

Kent alone was Christianized permanently by Augustine and his band.

Redwald, king of the East Angles, was baptized in Kent, and thus owed his Christianity to Augustine's mission. But he and his relapsed into heathenism, and Sigebert, the succeeding king of the East Angles, who is said to have been the first to establish schools in those parts, having been educated in Gaul, procured the reconversion of his kingdom by the missionary labours of Felix, a Burgundian prelate, from whom Felixstowe and probably Flixton derive their names.

The East Saxons were christianized by Augustine's mission, but, as we have seen, they relapsed into heathenism. The Italian bishop of London, Mellitus, fled from his see and left it unoccupied for many years, when Cedd, the brother of St. Chad, became bishop of London, and Sigebert, the king of the East Saxons—not the East Anglian Sigebert,—was baptized by Finan, the Scotic successor of Aidan in Northumbria. The East Saxons once more relapsed, and their final conversion was at length accomplished by Jaruman of Lichfield, of the Scotic succession of bishops, A.D. 664.

Northumbria, as we have seen, was christianized by Augustine's mission, relapsed, and was reconverted by Aidan, of the Scotic Church.

The West Saxons were christianized by Birinus, an Italian prelate who came over independently of the Canterbury mission, and apparently after the demonstration of the want of success of that mission. The Pope advised him to seek consecration in Italy, and not from Honorius, Augustine's successor, and he was accordingly consecrated before leaving for England by Asterius of Milan, at that time living at Genoa. The Canterbury mission seems to have been treated as a failure by Rome, for after Augustine's death no pall was sent to his successors till the conversion of Northumbria.

The South Saxons, to preach to whom the Canterbury mission had but to cross the boundary between Kent and Sussex, were christianized by the Northumbrian Wilfrith, a keen Romanizer, but brought up in the Scotic Church.

The Middle Angles and Mercians received Christianity from Northumbria, after Oswald had re-established it there by the aid of the Scotic Aidan.

Thus it would appear that the little kingdom of Kent, with its bishoprics of Canterbury and Rochester, was the only part of this island permanently converted by Augustine and his band. By far the larger portion of the island was christianized by means of the Scotic Church with its centre at Iona, whose knowledge of Christianity could be traced through Ireland to its nucleus in the British Church, one branch of which Augustine so unfortunately offended.

Besides the time of keeping Easter, and the tonsure, and some question of baptism, the British Church had other usages which differed from those introduced by Augustine, and by the sage advice of Pope Gregory, Augustine retained some of them for use in England. The lessons read from Scripture at Ordination were apparently peculiar to the British Church. The practice of anointing the hands of deacons, priests, and bishops, at Ordination, was another peculiar rite, and was retained in the Anglo-Saxon Church. This being so, it is probable that other practices peculiar to the Anglo-Saxon Church were in like manner retained from the British use, though we have not the same historical ground for the supposition   such were the prayer at giving the stole to deacons, the delivering the Gospels to deacons, the rite of investing priests with the stole. A version of the Holy Scriptures which differed from other known versions must have been in use in the British Church, if early quotations from Scripture are to be taken as made correctly and not from memory.

Portions of buildings almost certainly used as

churches in British times still remain. These are found in the Castle of Dover, at Richborough and Reculver, probably at Lyminge in Kent, and at Brixworth in Northamptonshire. Parts of the old British church of St. Martin's, Canterbury, are incorporated in the present church. Considerable remains of St. Pancras Church exist at Canterbury. A few sepulchral monuments of the same early date have been discovered, and a considerable number of pieces of pottery and other remains bearing Christian symbols.

CHAPTER VI

Bede's Preface—His view of the advantage of history—King
Alfred's opinion — King Ceolwulf — "Volume," "book,"
"codex"—Sources of the History—Orosius—Range of the
History—The Romans—The walls in Britain from sea to sea—
The Picts and Scots—The Jutes, Saxons, and Angles—Hengist
and Horsa—The Cat Stane—The explanation of the Walls—
Pelagianism—Gildas—Bede's care for accuracy—The British
Isles in Bede's time—Five languages in the Isles—The Scots
from Ireland—The first arrival of the Picts of Caledonia.

BEDE's greatest work was the *Ecclesiastical History of
the English People.* It appears that Bede had written
it at Jarrow, and the king of Northumbria, Ceolwulf,
had heard of it and had requested Bede to let him
see it. Ceolwulf was of a studious disposition, and
eventually gave up the sovereignty and became a
monk. Bede tells in the first words of the Preface,
which he addressed to the king, that he had very
gladly acceded to the king's request. He had sent the
manuscript to Ceolwulf to be read and approved, and
after examination the king had returned it. Bede
then put any final touches that were needed, and
sent it once more to the king, to be transcribed, and
studied at his leisure by Ceolwulf.

It is worth while to form some idea of how long it
would take to carry out the work of transcribing the
whole of the five books of the Ecclesiastical History.
Experiment shows that with our modern fluid ink
and steel-nib pens, a very facile hand, pressing only

just hard enough on the paper to make a legible mark, could form each letter of the History separately, in smaller size than the early mediæval lettering, without any pause, in six hundred hours, working very nimbly the whole time. To make each letter thick and black, with no fine strokes, would cost at least three times as long. That is probably an underestimate. To do the work with anything of the nature of a pigment would of course take longer still. And it must be borne in mind that most of it could only be done in daylight.

As it was now to be as we should say published, Bede thought it right to preface it with a statement of the sources from which he had obtained this great mass of information. He compliments the king on his desire to know the facts of the past, especially the past of his own race. As this was the reason why King Alfred selected Bede's Ecclesiastical History of the English as one of the four books to be translated into English for the men of his time, Bede's words pay a prophetic compliment to King Alfred which he well deserves. There is a double advantage in history, Bede points out, and we can well imagine that this passage clenched King Alfred's determination to have the whole work put into English. If our history tells us of the good actions of good men, the attentive hearer—observe how Bede shows naturally that the people of his time, speaking generally, could not read, and that the copies of his book would be at most very few—the attentive hearer would be moved to imitate that which is good. On the other hand, if the history tells evil things of evil people, the religious and pious hearer or reader—here he comes to a class some of whom could see and read the history in the monastery or the king's dwelling—the hearer or reader would be moved to shun that which is noxious and perverse, and do that which is good in the sight of God. Therefore it no doubt was that King Ceolwulf desired to have this History, for his own sake and for the sake of those over whom he had been set by God to reign.

Bede concluded his Preface with an appeal to the reader not to impute to him any error which may be discovered in the work, for he had, as the true law of history is, laboured sincerely to collect simply all that common report held, for the information of those that should come after. And he ended with an earnest appeal for the prayers of the readers for his manifold infirmities both of mind and body.

The actual manuscript of the History Bede calls a "volume." This properly means a roll. He generally uses the word *liber*, the ordinary word for a book consisting of leaves, *folia*, stitched together, the word *liber*, meaning "bark," or "rind," from the material used in very early times. For a manuscript of the whole of the Scriptures he uses the word *codex* (*caudex*), literally a flat piece of wood sawn into thin slices like leaves. This gives exactly the idea of solid substance which the vast codex hereinafter described as the Codex Amiatinus gives to those who are fortunate enough to behold it.

From the beginning of the volume to the time when the English nation received the faith of Christ, he tells us that he had gathered his facts from the writings of those who had gone before, the compendious History of Orosius playing a large part here. From that date to his own time he had obtained his information from those who best knew all that was known in the several kingdoms. He applied in the first place to Albinus, the Abbat of Canterbury, for exact information respecting the history of Christianity in that part of the island. Albinus had been a pupil of Archbishop Theodore and of Abbat Hadrian, and from them he had learned, in that accurate way in which men with few or no books do learn what they hear, the true account of what had been done in their time. Theodore was the great consolidator of the English Church, and thus the history of the most important period of its existence was made known to Bede almost at first hand. For the earlier history of the Church in Kent, Albinus referred to the records in his keeping, and he sent Nothelm, a priest of London, to search the archives in Rome, where Nothelm found some valuable letters of Gregory and other popes which Bede incorporated in his History. Daniel, bishop of the West Saxons (the south-west part of the island, west of Sussex), sent him a written account of the commencement of Christianity in that district, as also in Sussex and the Isle of Wight. The monks of Læstingau (Lastingham) gave him information respecting the missionary labours of Cedd and his brother Ceadda among the Mercians in the centre of England. From the same source he learned the details of the revival of Christianity in Essex, whose capital was London, many years after it had been expelled by paganism in Augustine's old age. Abbat Esius was his authority for the eastern counties, where also a good deal was learned from tradition. Bishop Cunebert and other persons of good credit told him the story of the province of Lindsey (Lincolnshire). As to his own province, Northumbria, he had the faithful testimony of innumerable persons of repute.

The Ecclesiastical History of the English gives us, speaking generally, all that we know of the christianizing of the Jutes and the Angles and the Saxons. As we have seen, Stephen Eddi, a contemporary of Bede, is our authority for much of the life and doings of Wilfrith, with their bearing on the very interesting and important question of the relations of the Church of the English, as its founder Gregory calls it, to the Roman Church, again to employ Gregory's own phrase. And, as also we have seen, another contemporary of Bede, Adamnan, tells us some very interesting facts in connection with Oswald, king and saint, from which we have traced an influence upon ceremonies of our own time. But there the help of other Church historians of the time begins and ends. All else comes from Bede. For the commencement of his History, down to the coming of Augustine (A.D. 596), he was indebted to the writings of earlier historians.

An almost exact half of the First Book of the History gives a summary of events in Britain down to the time of the coming of Augustine. This summary is skilfully compiled. It begins with Julius Cæsar and his operations in Britain, and tells of Claudius and his successes here, and Vespasian whom Claudius sent after his return to Rome. It tells the story of Lucius, a king of the Britons, asking Eleutherus, the Bishop of Rome, to send Christian teachers here, A.D. 156. Bede's next statement gives us an account of the building of "the *vallum* of Severus," A.D. 189. Next comes the persecution by Diocletian, A.D. 286, and the charming account of the martyrdom of St. Alban. Constantine's call from Britain to the empire of Rome, and the Arian heresy, come next. Gratian, Arcadius, and Honorius, lead us up to the time of the Pelagian heresy. With the year 383 we are brought to the first mention of the inroads of the Picts and Scots, whom he describes as vehemently cruel, and the appeal to Rome for a return of the Roman soldiery who had left the island defenceless. Bede mentions incidentally that there were in his time abundant evidences of their long rule in Britain, nearly 470 years from Julius Cæsar, cities, temples, bridges, paved roads, besides the Wall of Severus. A legion was sent, with the advice that the Britons should themselves build another wall, from the Forth to the Clyde, which they did, using turf in its construction because they had no one capable of so great a work as building it of stone. Abundant remains of it were to be seen in Bede's time. It started two miles from Abercorn and ran to Alcluith, that is, Dumbarton. Its starting-place on the Forth is called by Bede in its Pictish form Peanfahel, in its English form Penneltun, presumably meaning the head of the wall, like Benwell on the Wall of Hadrian. If, as seems probable, Kinnell on the Forth represents the Head of the Wall, we have an apt illustration of the use of k in place of p or b, which makes (Malcolm) ' Canmore ' the same word as ' Pen(mæn)maur,' and turns ' quatuor ' into ' petwar ' and ' quinque ' into ' pump.'

After this, Bede tells, yet another legion was sent, which built a great stone wall from sea to sea, not far from " the rampart of Severus." This wall was eight feet thick and twelve feet high, as anyone could see in Bede's time. It was built at public and private expense, the Britons giving help in the work. The legion built towers on the sea coast, south of the wall, where their ships were, because it was feared the barbarians would break through there. Then they left, after giving all manner of good advice about courage and resistance, and never came back again. The Picts and Scots, having learned that the Romans had said a final farewell, naturally broke through afresh and perpetrated great cruelties.

In 446 the wretched remains of the Britons sent to the Roman commander Ætius an appeal known as the groans of the Britons. " The barbarians drive us into the sea, the sea drives us back to the barbarians ; either we are slain or we drown." Ætius had his hands more than full with the intolerable ravages of the Huns under Attila. The Britons recovered their courage and things went well again ; they went from success to luxury, from luxury to crime of every worst kind. Their northern enemies overran Britain again, and at length the Britons under Vortigern invited the Saxons from beyond the seas to come over and protect them. The result was fatal to the Britons. Three of the most powerful races of Germany came over to Britain, Jutes, Saxons, and Angles, and by degrees drove the Britons out of most parts of the land to seek shelter in the mountainous parts of the West. They made a good fight for it here and there. One of the two original leaders, Horsa, was killed in a battle in east Kent, where a monument bearing his name was still in existence in Bede's time. This fact of a monument— no doubt of stone—bearing Horsa's name, is direct evidence of a family or tribal custom, and is therefore in favour—so far as it goes—of the explanation usually given to the very remarkable inscription on the great boulder stone at Kirkliston, called the Cat Stane, that is, the Battle Stone. The inscription is :—" In oc tvmvlo iacit Vetta f(ilius) Victi." A very close examination with eye and finger and lens seems to make it clear that if any further letters were meant to be added the intention was never carried out. Bede tells us that Hengist and Horsa were sons of Victigilsus, *who was son of Vitta and grandson of Vecta.* It is a most remarkable coincidence of recurrent family names if this stone and Horsa's inscriptional stone have no sort of kinship. It is quite true that we do not know of the formula *In hoc tumulo,* or the word *jacet* being used for pagan burials in this island, but they are customary in the British inscriptions and no doubt came from Romano-British times. It is easy to conceive an alliance of an early Saxon leader with the enfeebled Britons against the hated Picts, and the British burial of their ally in the large enclosed cemetery in which the Cat Stane stands. Bede informs us that the Saxon visitors did repel the Picts.

Bede's account of the three walls across the land from east to west is ingenious but very far from correct. He lived not far from two of them, and he had evidently seen the third, the wall built of stacked peat and turf. Gildas, whom he naturally follows in telling of the sad times of the Ruin of Britain, was not a well-informed guide. Indeed, with all our greater knowledge of the facts of the Roman occupation, the explanation of the times and purpose of the walls has only come in the lifetime of very many of us. The turf wall from Forth to Clyde was built under Antoninus Pius, about A.D. 140, by his representative Lollius Urbicus. It was built to relieve the pressure on the great wall which Hadrian had built from Tyne to Solway, and to protect the people north of Hadrian's Wall against the barbarians still further north. Antoninus was the adopted heir and the successor of Hadrian ; he was thus a wall-builder by adoption and

continuous policy. Hadrian's Wall was built about
A.D. 121. It is still astonishingly complete in many
parts, the greatest monument we possess. Bede, as we
have seen, attributes this enormous piece of work to
the very latest of the Roman forces here, and describes
it as not far from the *vallum* of Severus. There is no
evidence that Severus made this *vallum*. Bede's whole
system of dates here is wrong. The Emperor Severus
was here in A.D. 208, when he repaired Hadrian's Wall,
and two years later the turf wall of Antoninus, dying
at York in 211.

This vallum has been the subject of much discussion. It lies south of the great stone wall, very close
to it in places, in some places three-quarters of a mile
away. It is not continuous. It is not carried through
to the coast. The fosse has earthworks on each side
of it, north and south. This curious fact has been used
to explain the existence of the vallum.[1] The principal
quarries for the stone of the wall are naturally on the
south side of the wall. The trench was dug and the
vallum was made a rampart against hostile attack
from the north while the stone was being excavated
and the troops were resting at night. When all was
finished, the earthworks were made on the south side
of the trench, so that the protectors of the wall against
the north would have a parallel protection against
rebellion or treachery on their rear.

The Saxons soon joined forces with the Picts and
ravaged the whole land of the Britons, until at last
Ambrosius, a sole survivor of the Romans, and of
the royal race, put heart into the Britons and won the
great victory of Mount Badon, A.D. 476. Then Bede

---

[1] *Per lineam valli,* by George Neilson, Glasgow. Wm. Hodge and
Son, 1891.

goes back half a century and tells of the Pelagian heresy breaking out, invented by a British Morgan, the equivalent of the Greek Pelagius (sea-born). And Germanus, Bishop of Auxerre, and Lupus, of Troyes, came over to combat the heresy, which they did with great success. After careful individual teaching they called a great popular assembly, men, wives, and children, and held a disputation, the people acting as spectator and judge; in the end they shouted down the heretics and scarce kept their hands off them. This was about A.D. 429.

The Britons are said by their own historian Gildas, Bede writes, to have gone from bad to worse. He is throughout this part of his History quoting the book on The Ruin of Britain, which Gildas wrote about the year 544. All rules of truth and justice were so completely subverted that the memory of the existence of such virtues had disappeared, except among the very few. Ambrosius is the only Briton named by Gildas of whom he speaks well. The most unmentionable evil which Gildas in his tearful history relates is this,—the Britons never preached the faith of Christ to the Saxon and Anglian inhabitants of the land, and so in the goodness of God Gregory was moved by divine inspiration to send Augustine to preach the word to the English.

Gildas did not live to see this. The most recent investigations make him die at the age of ninety-four in the year 570, one of six children of a Briton of royal blood, five of whom, including Gildas, became Welsh Saints. Their father was a great-nephew of the hero Ambrosius, the Welsh Emrys, whose fortress of Dinas Emrys is near Beddgelert.

From the first mention of Pope Gregory, Bede's

History follows the fortunes of the Angles and Saxons to his own time, and is our one continuous authority for their doings.

Some idea of the care with which Bede compiled his books may be gathered from the account he has left of the composition of his Life of St. Cuthbert, Bishop of Lindisfarne. He informs his readers in a preface that he had not presumed to write any of the deeds of so great a man without minute investigation. He obtained his information from those who had known the beginning, the middle, and the end of Cuthbert's life, and to establish the truth of what he wrote, he gave the names of those from whom he learned various parts of the story. When the life was written, he still kept it back from publication in order that he might submit portions of it to the criticism of one of the brethren of Jarrow, Herefrid the priest, and of others who had known Cuthbert intimately. The book, amended in accordance with the suggestions of these competent persons, was sent to the monks of Lindisfarne, at whose request it had been undertaken by Bede. During two days it was read in the presence of the elder brethren there, Bede himself being present. They found that not any one part of it needed alteration, and they decided by common consent that it was to be accepted and read without hesitation, and to be copied for publication. The Bishop of Lindisfarne, and apparently some of the brethren, suggested in conversation certain additions, which Bede describes as equally important with what he had already written. He reminded them, however, that the work as it stood had been very carefully considered and finished, and he did not think it convenient and right to insert new matter.

The opening chapter of the Ecclesiastical History is full of interest, since it contains a description of England and Ireland as they were in Bede's time. Britain excelled in grain and in trees, and in pasture for cattle. In some parts of the island vines grew. Land fowl and water fowl abounded. The rivers were full of fish, especially the greatest plenty of salmon and eels. It is well to give the most honourable interpretation we lawfully can to Bede's name, *isicius*, for this most plentiful of British fishes. Salmon is the most probable of the possible meanings. Ducange's synonyms would suggest pike and shad as competitors. The Anglo-Saxon evidence given by Dr. Plummer is strongly in favour of salmon. Those of us who have fished salmon with Gaelic gilles may say the same for the Gaelic evidence. The fish *isicius* was famous in Latin culinary art, as giving its name to a favourite dish, the recipe for which is as follows : cook the fish, lay it in vinegar or wine, and sprinkle over it a powder of aromatic spices. Isidore, from whom Bede learned so much, though we have no means of knowing whether he studied Isidore's Origins as a cookery-book, tells us in his rather laboured way that the fish *isocen* was the original material of this dish and gave to it its name, but any kind of fish could be used for making *isicium*.

Seals, he proceeds, and porpoises, were very frequently taken, and whales too. Pearl-mussels were found, containing pearls of different colours, ruby, purple, violet, and green, besides the ordinary white pearl. There was a superabundance of shellfish (cockles) from which scarlet dye was made of so excellent a character that neither the sun nor rain made it fade, and it became more and more brilliant

with age. There were saline springs and hot springs,
and baths were arranged at these places for both sexes.
Bede accounts for the hot springs by a dictum of St.
Basil, that water grows hot even to scalding when
running over certain metals. The last word of modern
science on this subject is that radium is the creator of
the internal heat of large masses of rock, whether you
tunnel in horizontally or go vertically downwards
toward the fabled fires of the centre of the world.
Bede no doubt had in mind the waters of Bath, where
radium has now been found. There were mines of
copper, iron, lead, and silver, with plenty of jet,
bright and sparkling, of which Bede remarks that
when rubbed it holds fast anything to which it is
applied as amber does. He adds that when heated it
drives away serpents. Probably it does, when it is hot
enough.

Bede speaks of Britain as having been at one time
more rich in great towns than it was in his time. It
had formerly, he says, twenty-eight noble cities, besides
innumerable castles, all furnished with strong walls,
towers, gates, and locks. We cannot learn what these
twenty-eight cities were, but it is only reasonable to
suppose that they were the twenty-eight episcopal sees
of which Bede tells, seven in the province of York,
seven in the province of Caerleon, and fourteen in the
province of London.

In the north-country home of Bede the nights were
short in summer. He writes as if this were equally
the case in all parts of the island. The reason,
he says, is that Britain lies nearly under the North
Pole ; and, therefore, the sun has not a long night
journey under the earth to reach the Eastern
parts again. The nights were sometimes so light

that at midnight men could not say whether the evening twilight was still abiding or the morning twilight coming on.

The climate of Ireland far surpassed that of England. Snow scarcely ever lay there three days. The winter was so mild that the Irish never made hay in the summer for winter provender, or built stables for their horses. There were no snakes. Attempts were frequently made to take snakes over from Britain, but as soon as Irish air reached the ship, they died. Indeed so specific a remedy against snakes was anything Irish, that a drink made from the scrapings of the leaves of books that had been in Ireland cured their bite. Ireland was rich in milk and honey ; there were plenty of vines ; fish and fowl abounded ; and the island was remarkable for deer and goats.

Five languages prevailed in Britain in Bede's time. Divine truth was studied in the language of the English, the Britons, the Scots, the Picts, and the Latins, the last being made common to all by the special study of the Scriptures, not that it was still the spoken language of any race in the island. The Britons at first had the island to themselves, Bede tells us. After a time, some Picts from Scythia,[1] sailing in long ships, were blown to the coast of Ireland, then occupied by the Scots. The Scots assured the strangers that they could find them no room in Ireland, but, they said, they could give them some excellent advice. There was an island to the north-east which they often saw in clear weather. They had better go and take possession, and if any one opposed them, the Scots would help them. It was an easy way of getting rid of troublesome visitors, and it succeeded. The Picts

[1] Probably a distant part of Scandinavia.

in time made good their hold upon North Britain. Nothing is said of any previous inhabitants, and as the next thing the Picts wanted was wives, there were perhaps no inhabitants. The Scots, whose advice had proved so excellent, were requested to provide the Picts with permanent advisers in the shape of wives. They consented, but only on a condition which strikes us as curious, namely, that if ever there was any doubt about the succession to the throne, they should take a female line of the royal family in preference to a male line. Bede says that this custom prevailed among the Picts in his time. A similar rule exists in some savage nations in our own day, the reason with them being, that the child of a woman of royal race must have some royal blood in its veins, whoever the father may be.

This curious rule of royal descent among the Picts has naturally worked out curiously in special cases. Eanfrith, for instance, the brother of Oswald and Oswy, fled to the Picts when Oswald fled to the Scots (Irish) of Iona. He married a Pictish princess and had a son Talorg who was called MacAinfrit after him. When Oswy's son Ecgfrith very foolishly and with fatal results invaded the territory of the Picts in Forfarshire, the Pictish king who defeated and slew him was his cousin on the father's side, through the Pictish marriage of Eanfrith. In another case the rule led to the union of the Picts and Scots under one sovereign. Kenneth, known as MacAlpine, succeeded by paternal descent to the kingship of the Scots on the west side of North Britain, and succeeded also to the kingship of the Picts on the east side of North Britain by maternal descent from a Pictish princess. He became thus the first king of a combined Caledonia, which came to be called Scotland, and he transferred the seat of government to Scone.

That, however, is anticipating events which came long after Bede had passed away. He completed the story of the occupation of North Britain by invaders with an account of the passing over to the west coast of a large party of Scots, that is, Irishmen, from Ireland. He describes them as Dalreudins. We know them as Dalriads. It was they for whom, as we have seen in the story of Oswald, Columba erected a kingdom independent of the kingship of the bulk of the Dalriads who had remained in Hibernia, thus unconsciously paving the way to a kingdom of all Scotland.

CHAPTER VII

THE LIVES OF THE ABBATS

Benedict Biscop—The tombs of the Apostles—Alchfrith—Visit to
Rome—Theodore of Tarsus—Biscop at Canterbury—Further
visits to Rome—King Ecgfrith—Foundation of Wearmouth—
Visit to Gaul—Wilfrith's dedication of the church at Ripon—
Recovery of British Holy Sites—Alchfrith again—Pictures of
saints—The Vision of Drythelm—The Revelation of St. Peter—
Foundation of Jarrow—Dedication stone—Privileges from the
Pope—Pictures at Jarrow—Death scene of Biscop—Bede's age
at that time—Abbat Easterwine—Abbat Ceolfrith—The Codex
Amiatinus—Alcuin's recollections of Wearmouth—A pretty
saying of Bede.

BEING for the most part concerned with the past
history of the Church, the earlier books of the
Ecclesiastical History do not enter very much into
the personal details we should have found so interesting. But the later books give us much of this detail,
and there are some among the writings of Bede which
from the nature of the subject throw still more light
upon the manners of the time, chiefly as regards the
ecclesiastical life. These are especially the Life of
St. Cuthbert and the Lives of the earliest Abbats of
Wearmouth and Jarrow. We have already seen that
Bede gives in one of his homilies some details[1] of the
life of Benedict Biscop, the founder and first abbat of
these two monasteries. In the Life he gives fuller
information. Benedict was of a noble family of Northumbria, of the Angles, as Bede puts it, and worthy of

[1] Page 6.

the society of Angels, a pun copied from Pope Gregory. He was a minister of King Oswy, and had received from him a grant of land suitable to his station, according to the custom of those times. We see another reference to this custom in Bede's letter to Archbishop Ecgbert, where he laments that the kings had been so profuse in their grants for the establishment of monasteries, that they had no lands left to give to the sons of nobles, who either were compelled to leave their country, or led idle and dissolute lives at home.

At the early age of twenty-five, Biscop resigned his office, apparently a military command, and with it the donative he had held. In obedience to a desire he had long felt, he went to Rome to visit the tombs of the apostles. Those were, no doubt, the tombs of St. Peter and St. Paul, of which Eusebius says, that St. Peter's tomb was to be seen on the Vatican, St. Paul's on the Ostian Way. He then returned to England and passed some time in meditating upon all that he had seen, especially upon the charms of the ecclesiastical life ; and we are told that he urged his views upon such persons as he could persuade to hear him. The son of King Oswy, Alchfrith, became anxious to visit the holy places in Rome, and arranged with Biscop that they should go together. Oswy, however, made Alchfrith stay at home, but Biscop carried out the intended journey and remained in Rome for some months. He then went to the monks in the island of Lérins, and received the tonsure. After spending two years there, he was " overcome by love of the Apostle St. Peter," and returned to Rome, the arrival of a trading vessel enabling him to leave the island.

He reached Rome at a fortunate crisis. The kings of Kent and Northumbria had requested[1] Pope Vitalian to send them a suitable man as Archbishop of Canterbury, the archbishop elect having died of the plague in Rome. Vitalian selected, after more than one failure, Theodore of Tarsus in Cilicia, a man of great learning, skilled in the Latin and Greek languages. Abbat Hadrian, another man of much learning, an African, who had refused the Pope's offer of the vacant archbishopric, was given to Theodore as a counsellor and assistant, and Vitalian added Biscop to the party. These three selections show that Vitalian possessed great insight into character, and knew what was good for England under the conditions then existing. Theodore was an Eastern, not a Western, and he was not even in full orders. He had to wait long, though he was nearer seventy than sixty years old, till the marks of his Eastern tonsure had disappeared, and the hair had grown across the front of the head, so as to allow of the Western tonsure, to represent the crown of thorns. Notwithstanding his advanced age, his minor orders, and his Eastern training, Vitalian determined that Theodore was the right man. And throughout an extraordinarily active life as archbishop for more than twenty years, Theodore much more than justified the choice. Before his time, England was a missionary station ; he left it an established Church.

Of Biscop we are told that Vitalian saw he would become a man of wisdom, industry, piety, and nobleness. He therefore commanded him to give up the idea of living far from his country in the service of Christ. He set before him, as Bede says, the prospect of a higher usefulness. He appointed him to convey to

[1] So Vitalian seems to have understood them.

England that teacher of truth whom the country so earnestly desired, and to act as his interpreter and guide both on the way and after their arrival in Kent. Biscop cheerfully agreed to this course, and going to Canterbury with Theodore, he became abbat of the monastery there, and taught till Hadrian came to take his place as abbat and head of the educational staff. In this useful work he spent two years. The candle thus lighted by Theodore and Biscop burned with more and more brilliance in England for nearly a hundred and fifty years, till the dark times of the Danish invasions.

Again, for a third time, he went to Rome. His object was to purchase books of sacred literature and relics of martyrs. Besides those which he bought, he received some as presents from friends. At Vienne, also, purchases had been made for him, and he came home by way of that town to add them to his store. His first intention was to visit the King of Wessex (the district to the west of Sussex), who had been a useful friend to him ; but hearing that this king was dead, he came to Northumbria, where Ecgfrith had been king for three years. His enthusiasm for the monastic life, and the wonders he had to show in manuscripts and relics, so wrought upon Ecgfrith that he made him a large grant of land out of his own property and bade him build a monastery. This was commenced at the mouth of the river Wear, on the north side of the river, in the year 674 after Christ.

A year after the foundation of Monk Wearmouth, the indefatigable Biscop crossed the seas to Gaul to look for masons able to build a church of stone after the Roman style, for which he had a great love. He brought the workmen back with him, and so much energy was given to the task that within a year from the foundations being laid the roof was on and masses were celebrated. When the church was nearly finished, he sent messengers to Gaul, being too busy, no doubt, in superintending the building to find time to go himself, and hired workers in glass to fill the windows of the church, cloisters, and dining-rooms. Bede informs us that the art of making glass was up to that time unknown in Britain, and adds that the Gallic workmen remained long enough to teach the English people their handicraft, which was well fitted for many ecclesiastical uses.

We have no detailed account of the consecration of the abbey church. But it will not be out of place to give here the description of Wilfrith's consecration of his church at Ripon, as we find it in Eddi's contemporary Life of Wilfrith. The church was built of polished stone, from the foundations in the ground up to the roof ; it was ornamented with numerous pillars and porches ; within, it was adorned with silver and gold and purple. When all was ready, Wilfrith invited the most Christian kings Ecgfrith and Ælfwine, the abbats, prefects, lieutenants, and all persons of position. After Solomon's example, they consecrated the church and the prayers of the people uttered therein ; they dedicated the altar with its bases, put on it a purple cloth inwoven with gold, and the people communicated. Then Wilfrith stood before the altar with his face to the people, and read out in a clear voice a list of the lands which the kings had given for their souls, gifts ratified that day by the consent and subscription of the bishops and all the chief men ; he read also a list of the various holy places, now restored, which the British clergy had deserted when they fled before the sword of the

Angles,—" before the sword of our race," as Wilfrith had to put it. The gifts of the kings were large, including lands in various places whose names were recited. When this address was ended, the kings and people commenced a great feast, which lasted through three days and three nights. Wilfrith added to the possessions of the church a marvel of beauty unheard of before those times, namely, a manuscript of the Four Gospels written on parchment richly illuminated, and enclosed in cases of pure gold adorned with gems. Bede says, as we have seen, that the art of making glass was unknown in England till the time when Biscop introduced workmen into Northumbria ; but Wilfrith had before that time used glass abundantly at Ripon, and had also glazed the windows of the dilapidated church he found at York.

We have seen that Wilfrith, in performing the consecration of the great church at Ripon, part of the crypt of which lies below the floor of the nave of the present cathedral church, recited among the possessions of the abbey the holy places which had been consecrated to the service of God in the flourishing times of the British Church. It is impossible not to regret that Wilfrith left no record, so far as we know, of the dedications of these sites. The antiquarian instinct was overpowered by the strong party feeling which could not recognise the British saints to whom presumably the ruined churches and the desecrated sleeping-places of the Britons were dedicated. In Cornwall, Wales, Scotland, Ireland, we have the old dedications, not on record only but in daily use. England is a sad blank in this respect.

It will have been noticed also that Eddi says the kings Ecgfrith and Ælfwine, two brothers, had given lands. This looks like independent royal action on the part of Ælfwine as king of Deira, and on the part of Ecgfrith as king of Bernicia. More probably Ælfwine's gifts of lands in Deira was ratified by the signature of the over-king of the whole of Deira and Bernicia.

It should be noted, too, that Eddi avoids reference to the fact that Ecgfrith's younger brother is now joint king in place of the oldest of the three brothers, Alchfrith. This omission is the more remarkable because of the firm friendship which had bound together Wilfrith and Alchfrith, especially in Church matters. It is one of the many unexpressed suggestions on the part of the two historians, Eddi and Bede, that some tragedy of an unusual character had put an end to King Alchfrith's career of usefulness in State and Church. We can imagine how greatly he would have enjoyed the splendid ceremony at Ripon Minster.

A silence on the part of Bede even more striking than this, in regard to matters of extreme importance in connection with this same Wilfrith, is described at the end of Chapter IX.

Biscop further obtained from Gaul everything that was necessary for the service of the church, such as vestments and sacred vessels, because these could not be procured in England. Some of the things which he thought necessary for the full perfection of his church and monastery were not to be found even in Gaul, and in order to supply these he set out a fourth time for Rome, as soon as he had thoroughly established the rules of the monastery and had brought everything into working order. On this occasion he collected many pictures of sacred subjects, and secured the services of the arch-chanter of St. Peter's in Rome, John, the Abbat of St. Martin's, who not only taught the monks how to sing the services in the Roman fashion, but left at Wearmouth considerable manuscript information as to the ceremonies proper to various festivals. We have a most interesting list of the pictures. First, there were likenesses of the Virgin Mary and the twelve Apostles, to be placed on boards fixed across the nave from side to side. Next came pictures of scenes from ecclesiastical history, for the south wall of the nave ; and then pictures from the Revelation of St. John, for the north wall. Thus, as Bede says, every one who entered the church, whether he could read or not, could see, wherever he turned his eyes, the countenances of Christ and His saints ; he could dwell upon the blessings of the Incarnation ; he could examine his heart closely, having before his eyes the perils of the last judgment. This last use of the pictures will suggest to the recollection of readers the grotesque frescoes seen in so many village churches in these days of the removal of whitewash, the huge gaping dragon's mouth full of flames, representing the place of torment, with busy demons hurling in the souls of men.

A matter of extraordinary interest must be mentioned here. We have seen that Bede tells of a series of pictures of scenes from the Revelation of St. John. In the vision of the other world vouchsafed to Drythelm, an account of which is now to be given, it will be seen that there are details which have no connection with anything related or suggested in the Revelation of St. John. In recent investigations in Egypt, some portions of the apocryphal Revelation of St. Peter have been found among collections of papyri of very early date. The Revelation of Peter, lost through all these centuries, is found to be the source of the most remarkable parts of the vision, Bede's Latin version agreeing word for word with the Greek original of the papyri. Drythelm was a Northumbrian, from the district then called Cunningham, and he became a monk at Melrose, where King Aldfrith used to visit him. It was there that he told at very full length the marvellous series of scenes in his vision, related in the twelfth chapter of the Fifth Book of the Ecclesiastical History. It is reasonable to suppose that Biscop's pictures at Monk Wearmouth were the inspiration of the vision.

Drythelm had apparently died in the middle of the night. He came to himself in the morning. He saw during the period of his trance the places of torment and of happiness. There were degrees of torment. First a broad valley full of men's souls ; one side was piercingly cold, the other was a flaming and unquenchable fire. The unhappy souls, unable to endure the cutting cold, leaped into the flames ; and then, unable to endure the flames, leaped back into the snow and hail. Thus the valley was filled with human souls flying always in restless agony from one side to the other. It is a striking picture. The second place of torment was a vast pit, from which from time to time great clouds of dusky flame sprang up, blazing for a while, and then falling back into the abyss. These clouds of flame were full of souls, carried up like sparks, and sinking again with the flames. Had Bede lived now in that same country of coal and iron, he could have seen, whenever he looked forth at night, apt illustrations of this part of the vision. As the dead man stood there, the air became horrid with demoniac laughter and shrieks of tortured souls. Demons were seen dragging men's souls to the pit of fire and plunging in with them, descending deeper and deeper, till the jeers of the torturers could no longer be distinguished from the shrieks of the victims. Among these victims were a tonsured priest, a layman, and a woman ; and the words seem to imply that they were persons whom the entranced man recognised. The remainder of the vision will be found in the chapter on Bede's Homilies at page 248.

It may be worth while to add that the vision produced a lasting impression on Drythelm. Bede had the story from an intimate friend of the man, who told him further that all his life Drythelm lived in the full and clear consciousness of what he had seen. His home being near a river, he was wont to walk into the water up to his waist, and at times up to his neck, and to stand there saying his prayers, now and again dipping completely under water. When he came out, he never changed or dried his clothes. In the winter he would stand in the river while the pieces of broken ice dashed against him, and when one called to him from the bank, "I wonder, brother Drythelm, that you can endure such cold !" he would reply, " I, at least, have seen severer cold than this." And when one said to him, "I wonder how you can endure such austere fasting !" he would reply, " I, at least, have seen severer austerity than this."

Biscop obtained for his monastery a letter of privileges from the Pope. This secured the institution from interference from without. Bede expressly says that this letter was obtained not only with the consent of the king but by his earnest wish. And we find by a further reference at a later period of Bede's History, that the validity of the letter depended upon its confirmation by English authority. He relates that in the

time of Abbat Ceolfrith, when further property had
been acquired for the monastery of Jarrow, a letter of
privileges was obtained from Pope Sergius similar
to that which. Pope Agatho had granted to Biscop.
This, he adds, was brought back to Britain, and
being exhibited before a synod, was confirmed by the
signatures of the bishops present and of King Aldfrith,
as the former letter was confirmed by the king and
bishops of the time.

King Ecgfrith was much struck by the zeal and
piety of Biscop, whom Bede frequently calls Venerable, little supposing that by that title he would
himself be known in after ages throughout the Christian world. The king would appear, also, to have
formed a high opinion of the advantages of the
monastic life. He made an additional grant of a
considerable amount of land, and stipulated that
another monastery should be built on it, as a sister
establishment to the monastery of Wearmouth. Within
a year the new monastery was built, and Biscop sent
as its head his most strenuous assistant and companion in travel, Ceolfrith, with a party of seventeen
monks. He then appointed Easterwine to act as abbat
of Wearmouth, and himself set out on a fifth journey
to Rome, about A.D. 685. As usual, he came back loaded
with all manner of valuable ecclesiastical possessions.
There were large numbers of manuscripts and of
holy pictures. Some of the latter, representing scenes
in our Lord's life, he hung round a church he had
built at Wearmouth in honour of the Virgin Mary.
Others were employed for adorning the church and
monastery at Jarrow. Bede describes these last as
arranged with the utmost skill, so as to show the
harmony of the Old and New Testament. Thus two

pictures were hung side by side, one showing Isaac
bearing the wood for the sacrifice of himself, the
other showing Our Lord bearing His cross. Another
pair of pictures in juxtaposition showed the serpent
lifted up by Moses in the wilderness, and the Son
of Man lifted up on the cross.

It is singularly fortunate that we have the dedication stone of this church. It is in two separate pieces,
as though they had been let into the wall of the church
on either side of some central object. The sundial at
Kirkdale Church near Lastingham[1] has been let into
the wall above the south door, and on either side of it
is an inscription which has for us exceeding—indeed
unique—interest, recording that that church was rebuilt
in the days of Edward the king and Tosti the earl,
that is, immediately before the Norman Conquest.
As there is a sundial on the Bewcastle Cross, erected
in the first year of King Ecgfrith, there may have
been a sundial between the two parts of the dedication
stone at Jarrow, dated in the fifteenth year of the
same King Ecgfrith. The inscription, see Plate 6,
runs thus :—

> " Dedicatio basilicae
> sci Pauli VIII K̄l Mai
> anno XV Ecfridi reg
> Ceolfridi abb eiusdem
> q' eccles do auctore
> conditoris anno IIII."

" *The dedication of the basilica[2] of St. Paul on the
ninth of the Calends of May in the fifteenth year of King
Ecfrid and the fourth year of Ceolfrid the Abbat and
under God the builder of the same church.*"

[1] See Plate 5.   [2] See page 170.

The date is 685, Ecgfrith's first year being 670. As he was killed in an aggressive invasion of the Picts of Forfar in the year 685, he did not live long after the completion of the church which was built on the site given by him. It will be noticed that Benedict Biscop's name is not mentioned. He was in Rome at the time, only returning after the disaster to Ecgfrith, which ended the supremacy of Northumbria over the Picts.

Biscop knew how to make the most of his opportunities when on his travels. We find him bringing from Rome two royal robes or palls, made entirely of silk and worked in an incomparable manner. These he sold to the king and his councillors for an important piece of land on the south side of the mouth of the Wear. The price paid may remind us that, four hundred years before, a Roman emperor had refused his wife a silk dress. He also brought a manuscript collection of geographical writings, of beautiful workmanship, which he sold to the same king, Aldfrith of Northumbria, for a considerably larger piece of land on the river Fresca.

A life of such activity and usefulness was closed by a peaceful death. Bede's account of the illness and death is written very much in the spirit in which his own disciple came in time to write the story of his death in its turn. Biscop was stricken with palsy, which for three years crept from one part of his body to another, beginning at the lower extremities. His colleague in the Abbey of Wearmouth, Easterwine's successor Sigfrid, was taken ill about the same time with a wasting disease. When neither of the abbats could visit the other, both having lost the use of their limbs, the monks carried Sigfrid to Benedict and laid him so that the two loving friends could give each other the kiss of peace. Bede says that they were so weak that, though their heads were laid on the same pillow, they could not of themselves turn so that their lips should meet, and the brethren had to guide their heads before they could perform the parting act of Christian love. It is a subject worthy of the skill and imagination of the best of the painters of old, and there are painters even now who might do justice to it.

There were three points on which the dying abbat laid great stress in his practical injunctions to his monks. One was the strict maintenance of the Rule which he had given them. He assured them that its several regulations were not devised by himself or of his own will. He had seen in his large experience on the Continent seventeen monasteries whose rules he preferred to all others, and from these seventeen he had copied the statutes which he imposed upon his twin monasteries. Another point was the magnificent library he had collected. This library, most abundant in all that was necessary for instruction in sacred matters, he would have kept entire ; no neglect was to be allowed, no division or dispersion. The last point was, the succession to the abbacy ; and here we have a suggestive hint of the prevalence of an evil of which Bede wrote strongly to Bishop Ecgbert some years later. He urged the brethren not to elect any one as abbat by reason of his birth. He would have no claims of next of kin. He was particularly anxious that they should not elect his own brother ; he would rather his monastery became a wilderness than have this man to succeed him, for they all knew that he did not walk in the way of truth. Apparently he feared that a claim something like that of hereditary succession might be set up. That the fear was no visionary one may be seen from later ecclesiastical history, when benefices of various kinds, even bishoprics, were handed down from father to son ; and the evils arising from this practice had no doubt much to do with the enforcement of celibacy among the clergy. In Biscop's own time the hereditary descent of an abbey was no unknown thing ; thus the Abbess of Wetadun persuaded Bishop John of Hexham to cure her daughter after the flesh, whom she designed to make abbess after her. Not only would Biscop not have a hereditary abbat, he would not have an abbat brought in from another monastery. It may be remembered that the Abbat of Westminster who surrendered his abbey to Henry VIII was the first abbat for 300 years who had not been a monk of Westminster. The duty of the brethren was, in accordance with the Rule of Abbat Benedict the Great, in accordance with their own statutes, to inquire carefully who of themselves was best fitted for the post, and, after due election, to have him confirmed as abbat by the bishop's benediction. This rule had, of course, much to recommend it. But in monastic as in collegiate life there comes a time when the election of a head from outside is necessary to the well-being of the institution.

When Benedict grew worse he was unable to sleep at night, and his solace was to have the Book of Job and other parts of Scripture read to him. He became so weak that he could not rise to pray, and could not depend upon himself to say the words of the daily Psalms. He therefore summoned to his cell a party of the brothers at each of the canonical hours, and dividing them into two choirs, made them sing the appointed psalms antiphonally, joining in himself whenever he felt his voice strong enough. On the night of his death he received the Eucharistic Sacrament as a viaticum. He died while a portion of the Gospel was being read by a priest. It was remarked as an omen of good, that the brethren who were engaged in the church in singing the Psalter through while he was *in extremis*, had reached Psalm 82 (our 83), headed " Lord, who is like unto Thee ? " a sure token, as they believed, that all the enemies of his soul were overcome by the power of the Lord.

At the time of Biscop's death, Bede was about sixteen years old. He had been an inmate of the monastery at Wearmouth for one year, and had spent eight years at Jarrow. Thus he writes of what he had himself seen and known, in his account of Benedict and of the three or four abbats who succeeded him. His account of Easterwine, abbat in Biscop's lifetime, is especially vivid, and we may suppose that the charming combination of physical strength and kindly courtesy, for which Easterwine was distinguished, took firm hold of the ready sympathy and memory of a growing boy. Here is a delightful picture of him as Bede draws him, when he entered upon the joint abbacy at the early age of thirty-one, to be carried off by a pestilence after five years of gentle and powerful rule. He was a young man of great strength and sweet speech ; high-spirited and generous ; pleasant to look upon. Humility was a marked feature in his character. He was cousin on the father's side to Abbat Benedict, and had been a chief officer of the king, but Bede remarks that he never from his first entrance as a monk expected that any deference should be paid him, or that the abbat should show him any

favour as a near relative. He found pleasure in threshing and winnowing, milking the ewes and kine, working in the bakehouse, the garden, and the kitchen.
When he was promoted to the abbacy, he made it his
principle to remain unchanged in his manner to the
brethren.   When necessity arose, he inflicted the
punishments laid down in the Rule under which they
lived ; but he held that prevention was better than
punishment, and endeavoured to make the brethren
feel unwilling to bring a cloud of pain over his open
countenance.   When he went out to look after the
business of the monastery, if he came upon any of
the brethren at work, he would join them for a time,
taking the plough-tail or the smith's hammer.   He
had the same food as the brethren, and in the same
room, which Bede notes apparently as an unusual
arrangement.   He slept in the common dormitory,
where he had slept when he was only " priest Easterwine," and even when death was known to be coming
on, he retained his pallet almost to the last, being
removed to a more private room only five days before
his death.   From this room he came out but once
alive, and on that occasion he sat in the open air and
called up all the brethren one by one, and gave them
the kiss of peace, they the while weeping bitterly over
the impending loss of such a friend and ruler.

Ceolfrith has been mentioned as the first abbat
of Jarrow, the abbat who took Bede with him from
Wearmouth.   A year before Biscop's death, Ceolfrith
had been associated with him in the joint abbacy of
the two monasteries, and he ruled as sole abbat after
that event for twenty-seven years.   During this long
tenure of office, Bede grew to man's estate, was
ordained deacon and priest, studied and wrote.   He

was about forty-three when Ceolfrith died, and it is probable that if the story of his refusing the abbacy is correct, the occasion was the vacancy caused by Ceolfrith's resignation. Bede's portrait of this abbat's work is drawn from life. He built many oratories in the monastery. He largely increased the sacred vessels and vestments. He doubled the libraries of the two monasteries,—little fear of his needing Benedict's warning against dissipating the books. He gave to each of the monasteries a complete Bible of the new translation, as Bede describes Jerome's work, Benedict having brought from Rome one of the old translation. He found money to add to the land which Benedict had received in exchange for the book of geography mentioned above, and for the money and land he obtained an estate more conveniently situated, half the size of the original endowment of Jarrow, at the village of Sambuce, perhaps Sandoc. He also gave to Jarrow a considerable estate at Dalton. He showed incomparable skill in saying prayers and in chanting ; great energy in punishing those who deserved it, with moderation towards weaker vessels ; and an abstinence unusual among rulers—so Bede says —in eating and drinking and in the manner of dress.

After twenty-seven or twenty-eight years spent thus, he found that his charge had greatly increased, and his powers of administration, weakened by age, were no longer equal to the task. He therefore announced his resignation of the abbacy. Among the reasons for his resignation, Bede mentions one which did Ceolfrith great honour, and might be adopted by some in the present day whose means are sufficient to enable them to resign their offices to more vigorous hands. He felt that he was now unfitted, owing to the infirmities of old age, for impressing upon the brethren the due forms of spiritual exercise by precept and by example. Within three days of the announcement of his intention to resign, he set out from the monastery, in spite of the tears and supplications of the brethren, who entreated him not to deprive them of his presence and rule. Nothing could stop him. Two motives urged him to immediate departure. One was the fear lest he should die before he could reach Rome,—Rome which he had visited in his youth with Abbat Benedict, Rome where he wished to end his life. He feared lest any of his friends or of the nobles of the country who held him in much honour, should delay his departure if the knowledge of his intention became generally known. The other motive was a curious one. He was afraid that some one might give him money, which he would have no opportunity of repaying without considerable loss of time and interference with his journey. For, Bede explains, whenever any one gave him anything or did him any favour, he invariably made a return fully equivalent, either at once or after a due interval.

The leave-taking was very solemn. Bede describes it in a manner which leaves little or no doubt that he was himself an actor in the scene. At first dawn on one of the early days of June, when the season for travel had fairly commenced, mass was sung in the church of the blessed Virgin Mary and in the church of St. Peter. Those present communicated. Then all the brethren of Wearmouth and some of those from Jarrow assembled in St. Peter's. Ceolfrith lighted the incense for the last time in the accustomed place, said a prayer at the altar, and gave the blessing, standing on the steps of the altar with the censer in his hands. Litanies were sung, interrupted by the sobs of the brethren. Then they passed out into the oratory of St. Laurence, which was in the dormitory opposite the door of the church. There Ceolfrith said his last farewell. He charged them to let brotherly love continue, and to correct the faults of the erring. He forgave all against whom he had aught, and prayed pardon of all who had aught against him, if he had ever administered his office with undue severity. The whole company went down to the banks of the Wear, where the ferryboat lay. They knelt and received from him the kiss of peace. He prayed, and entered the boat with the companions of his journey. The deacons of the church went with him in the boat, bearing lighted tapers and the golden cross. Arrived at the other side of the Wear, he adored the cross ; then mounted his horse and rode away. It is evident that he was making for some port of departure further south. The anonymous Life of Ceolfrith, which tells us some very interesting personal details, tells us that he was to take ship in the Humber, that the whole month from June 4 to July 4 was occupied by the land journey from the Wear to the Humber and the delay before starting for the sea, and that before his ship reached its appointed port it was driven to shore in three different provinces, in all of which he was most honourably received. He left in the two monasteries not less than six hundred brethren.

Ceolfrith's fear lest he should die before he could reach Rome was justified by the event. Some delay was caused by their having to wait for a ship on the English coast. During this interval the new abbat, Huetbert, announced to him in person his election to the vacant office, which Ceolfrith approved and Bishop

Acca of Hexham confirmed. He reached Langres, only to die there, on the 25th of September, 716, and he was buried in the monastery of the twin martyrs, one mile from the town on the south side. He was in his seventy-fifth year when he died, and though so advanced in age, and suffering from illness, he persisted to the last in maintaining the rigour of the Rule which he had so long administered. Every day of his hundred and fourteen days' journey from Wearmouth to Langres he observed the canonical hours of prayer, and twice daily he chanted the Psalter. Even when he was so ill that he could not ride on horseback, but was carried in a litter, he sang mass every morning. Indeed there were only four days on which he did not sing mass—one when he was on the seas, and three when he was dying.

Here the remark must be made, how fortunate it is that we have still in existence remains connected with the persons of our history. In some senses the personal relics of St. Cuthbert, to be described in a later chapter, are the most remarkable. But on a larger view none of the cases is so striking, or of such importance, as the personal relic of Abbat Ceolfrith now in the great Library of Florence.

Ceolfrith took with him on his last journey towards Rome one of the pandects, manuscripts of the whole Bible, Old and New Testaments, of which we know that there were three at Wearmouth. This was to be his choice gift to the Pope. When he died, nothing was heard of the pandect, so far as Bede's record goes. It passed out of history for 1170 years, to appear again in 1886. But the anonymous Life again comes in with personal information. Some of the brethren returned to Northumbria to report the fact and details of the death. Others completed the journey to Rome with the gifts for the Pope, among which was the pandect of Jerome's translation from the Hebrew and the Greek.

There is in the Laurenziana at Florence a huge manuscript of the whole Bible, so large and heavy that it is drawn out of its safe on a shelf and thus lodged on a stretcher to be carried by two men. It had an inscription telling of its being taken as a gift to Rome by Peter, an abbat from the distant lands of the Lombards, who desired to lay his body in Rome, *Petrus Langobardorum extremis de finibus abbas.* It had been long in a monastery on the Monte Amiata, and thence was known as Codex Amiatinus. It is of the highest possible value in testing the various readings of the earliest Latin Bibles.

A little more than thirty years ago, de Rossi found that with the exception of the second letter, the *e* in *Petrus*, the whole of the *Petrus Langobardorum* was written over an erasure. The erasure had left here and there small fragments of the original letters, the second letter *e* being not erased. De Rossi read the words as *Ceolfridus Britonum*; but this present writer pointed out that on various grounds that was scarcely admissible, and *Ceolfridus Anglorum* must have been the words. De Rossi examined the text again, and found the top of the *l* of *Anglorum*. Thus the reading was settled as *Ceolfridus Anglorum extremis de finibus abbas*, and the vast and priceless Codex Amiatinus proved to be that one of the Wearmouth pandects which Ceolfrith took with him when he went to Rome to die.[1] Once more the anonymous

---

[1] On the remains of another of these pandects see my *Boniface of Crediton*, pp. 130-9, and *Recollections of a Bishop*, p. 185.

Life steps in. It gives us in a debased form six lines of the inscription which it tells was written at the beginning :—

" Corpus ad eximii merits venerabile Petri
    Dedicat ecclesiæ quem caput alta fides.
  Ceolfridus Anglorum extimis de finibus abbas,"
                    etc.

The anonymous Life has a statement which perhaps gives us a hint as to the use of the codex as a gift by this Peter, a Lombard abbat. The anonymous author tells us that when Ceolfrith at last landed in Gaul he was specially honoured by the king, Helwric. This king gave him letters to the authorities of all parts of his kingdom, directing them to pass him on free from charge and expense. Besides this, the king gave him letters to Liutprand, the king of the Lombards. No doubt the Wearmouth monks carried this letter to the Lombard king, and it is conceivable that in this way the name of the Lombard abbat who had passed them on and not improbably accompanied them to Rome was inserted at that date in place of the unfamiliar name of Ceolfrith, an abbat who did not make personal appearance there. Indeed it may have been a direct forgery, perpetrated then. No such king of the Gauls as Helwric is known. The sole nominal king at the time, the last but one of the Merovingians fading away, was Chilperic, and that presumably was Helwric. There is so complete an absence of any reference to the use of Anglian runes by Bede or any of the Church historians then, though beyond doubt the runes were in use then, that it is probably too far-fetched to suggest that the rune for *w* is scarcely distinguishable from the ordinary letter *p*, and a scribe might possibly transliterate Chilperic or Hilperic as Helwric. In any case it is very interesting to find a king of the effete Merovingian line acting thus apparently in full and royal sovereignty towards a brother king two years after the death of Pepin of Heristal, when the Mayors of the Palace were supreme in actual power. Pepin had been so much assisted by Anglo-Saxon missionaries, and Charles Martel who succeeded him so completely continued the friendly relations with our ancestors, that it is most probable that the king was advised by the Mayor how to act in the matter, as a Prime Minister might advise King George.

Here Bede's history of the Abbats of Wearmouth and Jarrow ends. He had come down to the time of his own abbat, Huetbert, whose life was not as yet a matter for history. In an imperfect list of saints honoured in the North of England, written in the tenth century and to be seen in the library of Corpus Christi College in Cambridge, Benedict, Easterwine, and Ceolfrith all appear as saints, their days being respectively the 12th of January, the 7th of March, and the 25th of September.

We have a very pleasant account of the tone and atmosphere of the Wearmouth monks from Alcuin, written long after he had said his final farewell to Northumbria (Ep. 274, Mon. Alc.). It is specially worthy of record here because of its delightful personal story of Bede. Writing of the time when Alcuin was still in office at the School of York, he says :—

" The place of your dwelling was very dear to me, though the call to foreign travel took me far away from you, in body, not in love. When I was with you, everything that I saw gave me great pleasure, both your buildings and your manner of life. It is your

praise in the sight of men that alike in garb and in all
the discipline of the monastic life you abide firmly
by the institution of your fathers, who were dear to
God and honoured by men. It is certain that the
founders of your community frequently visit the places
of your abode. They rejoice with you when they
find you living rightly and keeping their statutes, and
they cease not to intercede for such with the pious
judge. Nay, there is no doubt that the angels, too,
visit the holy places. It is reported that our master
and your patron the blessed Bede said, ' I know that
the angels visit the canonical hours and the assemblies
of the brethren. What if they do not find me in the
congregation ? Would not they have to say, Where
is Beda ? Why has he not come with his brethren
to the appointed prayers ? ' "

Both in the Commentaries and in the Homilies Bede
speaks of his conviction that the angels are present at
the worship of God on earth.

It may be added that the Abbey of Wearmouth
suffered severely in the Danish wars, and was destroyed
in 867. It was again destroyed by fire in an inroad
made by Malcolm, king of Scotland, in 1070. Jarrow
is said to have been destroyed by the Danes in 793,
and again by the forces of William of Normandy in
1069, when they devastated the country between
Humber and Tyne. Walcher, Bishop of Durham,
restored both monasteries, and in 1083 Bishop William
of Carileph transferred the monks of Wearmouth and
Jarrow to Durham, and made them the chapter of the
cathedral church.

CHAPTER VIII

THE LIFE OF ST. CUTHBERT

Stories of miracle—Many of these stories not miraculous—Melrose and Boisil—Alchfrith and Ripon—Prior of Melrose—Abbat of Lindisfarne—His rule there—Retirement to a small island—Bishop of Lindisfarne—At Carlisle—His death and burial—Relics of St. Cuthbert—Coffin—Pectoral cross—Portable altar—Robes.

BEDE's Life of St. Cuthbert was undertaken at the request of the bishop and monks of Lindisfarne. We have already seen the extreme care which he took to make it accurate. The story is full of miracles from beginning to end, and each miracle comes down to us with the solemn attestation of those who knew Cuthbert well, and had lived under his personal rule. Thus there can be no doubt that in that age the frequent occurrence of miracles was accepted as an incontestable fact. Bede's own feeling in the matter seems to have been that it was, perhaps, as well to give his authority for any miraculous story he related ; but, beyond that, there is no appearance of an expectation on his part that his accounts of miracles would be disbelieved. Even when he describes in a circumstantial manner the steps he took to secure perfect accuracy in his Life of St. Cuthbert, he does not in the most remote way suggest that without such explanations of his method of procedure his account might be doubted because of the miracles it contained. And in his Ecclesiastical History, the latter part of

which contains many miraculous stories, there is no
sign to indicate that a miracle was less likely to be
believed than the fact that two comets appeared in
the year 729. But as we proceed with the life of
St. Cuthbert, we shall see that the great mass of what
is called miracle is susceptible of a simpler explanation, even where it is not to be accounted for by the
natural tendency to exaggerate the influence of one
who showed forth so many of the signs of an apostle as
Cuthbert did.

Cuthbert died in the year 687. Bede was therefore thirteen or fourteen years old at the time, and
Jarrow is no great distance from Lindisfarne. There
is no reason why Bede may not have seen Cuthbert.
Supposing the Life of St. Cuthbert to have been one of
his later works, it must at least have been written
within thirty-five or forty years of Cuthbert's death.
But in the Ecclesiastical History he says that many
years had elapsed since he wrote the Life, and, indeed,
the later part of the Ecclesiastical History contains a
sort of supplement to it. Monks in Lindisfarne who
had reached the age of sixty had spent their boyhood
and early manhood under Cuthbert's influence. Priests
of that age had been ordained by him. In this, as in
some other cases, Bede had talked with men on or for
whom miracles had been wrought, and had heard their
account of the miracles ; indeed, he sometimes gives
the account in the actual words of the narrator. It is
difficult to reject the details of such testimony on the
ground that we know much more than our fathers, and
are sure that they were ignorant and superstitious.
It is unfair to charge superstition, in its accepted sense,
against men who were ignorant of physical explanations
which are familiar to us. Such men were men of pious

faith, and as such deserve our respect. Not only that, they set an example which we might do well to follow in some cases, even in this age of vastly extended natural explanation. If we are to reject all these stories wholesale, so far as their miraculous part is concerned, we must do it on the ground that natural phenomena and remarkable coincidences were interpreted and exaggerated into miracles, in the case of men so remarkable for their piety that the people looked upon them as specially favoured by God, and endued with power over the elements and over diseases. Such exaggeration would, of course, lead sometimes to false claims and pure invention on the part of unscrupulous or overwrought men.

A large proportion of the miraculous stories told by Bede have nothing necessarily miraculous about them. Take, for instance, the first miracle recorded in Cuthbert's life. The future saint was afflicted suddenly with a serious lameness when he was a mere boy. One of his knees became very painful, and an angry tumour formed near it. The muscles of the thigh were contracted, and the leg hung bent and useless. One day, when he had been carried out by his attendants and left to lie a while out of doors in the fresh air, a man, clad in white, rode up on a magnificent horse. Seeing that Cuthbert did not rise, he asked if he had no respect to show for such a visitor. Cuthbert replied that he would most gladly rise and pay him reverence if he were not tied by the leg to his couch. The stranger dismounted and examined the knee. He prescribed what we may call a bread-poultice. " Boil some wheat-flour in milk, lay it on warm, and you will be cured." Cuthbert followed this excellent advice, and in a few days

the leg was healed. Then he perceived that his
visitor was an angel, sent by Him who sent Raphael
to restore the eyesight to Tobit. Curiously enough,
Bede's only doubt in the matter is whether all readers
will believe that an angel rode on horseback. To
satisfy the scruples of such, he refers them to the
passage in the Maccabees where angels came on
horseback to the aid of Judas Maccabeus. The remedy
recommended by the stranger was not quite what the
Saxon leeches would have employed. Their treatment
for the swelling of knees and for shanks was this :—
Take the root symphoniace (Saxon henbelle, or hen-
bane) and pound it, lay it thereto, and it will take away
the swelling. For the racking pain in the joint their
prescription was—Take the netherward part of marche,
and honey, and the smede of wheaten meal, and the
bowels of a wig (ear-wig) ; rub them together, and lay
on. Wheat flour was thus common to two of the
prescriptions.

Or, to take the miracle which comes next in order
in Cuthbert's life. The story is worth extracting, if
it were only for the curious and interesting light it
throws upon the transition from paganism to Christianity, which was by no means complete in Cuthbert's
time. The monks of Tynemouth—they had been
changed into nuns before Bede wrote—had gone to
the Tyne in five vessels to fetch wood for the use
of the monastery. As they floated down the river
again, a violent wind came from the west and blew
them beyond their landing-place, in spite of the
assistance rendered by boats which the remaining
monks launched when they saw that the ships were
unmanageable. Human help being of no avail, and
the five vessels being blown out so far to sea that

they looked like birds riding on the waves, the monks issued forth from the monastery, and grouping themselves on the extreme point of the rocks prayed to God for the safety of their brethren. There seemed to be none to hearken, for the storm continued to rage with unabated fury. Then the common people, who were collected in crowds to see what would happen to the monks, began to revile. The monks, they said, deserved it, for abandoning the ordinary manner of life and conforming to new and unheard-of practices. Cuthbert, a layman and little more than a mere lad, was among the crowd, on the opposite side of the river from that on which the monks were praying. He reproached the people and asked them whether it would not be better to pray for the safety of the monks than to revile them in their misfortune. The people indignantly refused to pray for them. "No one should pray for them! Might God spare none of them! They had taken away from men the ancient worship, and how the new worship was to be carried out no one knew." Then Cuthbert knelt down among them and prayed with his face to the ground. The wind fell at once, and the ships were carried by the waters to the landing-place they had missed. The rustics blushed for their unbelief and became firm Christians. It is evident that this miracle, which Bede had from one of the rustics present, whose truthfulness was unimpeachable, may have been nothing beyond the ordinary course of nature. The monks would start at first with a flowing tide to drift up the estuary to the place where the wood was to be procured. Having spent some time in loading their ships, they would drop down again with the falling tide. The wind and the tide hurried them past their landing-place. The monks prayed in vain till the tide turned, for there was no adequate reason for disturbing the course of nature. It is well known how calm an estuary becomes on a sudden, under certain circumstances of wind, &c., when the " first of flood " is imminent. We have only to suppose that Cuthbert's prayer coincided in time with this calm and with the turn of the tide, and then without any miracle we can imagine the five ships drifting quietly up with the tide to their landing-place. In fact, the whole scene, without the monks and the prayers, has often been enacted in tidal waters.

Another miraculous event in Cuthbert's life may be mentioned, as coming under the same category of coincidence, not miracle. When he was still a young man, and not as yet a member of any brotherhood, he set forth on horseback alone. About nine or ten o'clock in the morning he halted at a village which lay on his road, to rest himself and to give his horse some food. A pious woman begged him to let her prepare dinner for him ; but he refused, on the ground that it was a fast day, being Friday. Bede remarks that on Friday the faithful fasted till three o'clock in the afternoon. It was customary to end fasts other than the severe fasts of Lent at three in the afternoon, on the ground that at that hour, the ninth, the Agony on the Cross ended in the Death. An English Council, held a dozen years after the death of Bede, directed that the Rogation Fasts be kept till three o'clock. The woman assured him that he would find no house on his way, and he must fast all day and all night if he did not take something then ; but he still refused, and after a while he continued his journey. When evening drew on, he halted at some deserted shepherds' huts, the season being the beginning of winter. Here he tied his horse to the wall, and gave it some dried grass which the wind had torn from the roof. Having no food for himself, he turned to prayer and singing. While thus occupied, he saw the horse pull out a bit more of the thatch, and with it a bundle, which fell to the ground. The bundle was wrapped in linen, and contained half a loaf of bread, still warm, and meat enough for a meal. Cuthbert at once gave thanks for this miraculous bounty, on which he proceeded to feast, dividing the bread into two parts, one for himself and one for his horse. From that time Cuthbert was more than ever determined to fast up to three o'clock on Friday, believing that the supply of food when he was hungry from his long fast was a token of divine approbation. An aged monk of Wearmouth, Ingwald the priest, told this story to Bede, and Cuthbert himself told it to Ingwald. History does not repeat what the shepherds said when they found their little store of food gone. A further miracle of feeding is related by Bede as having occurred in Cuthbert's experience. An angel brought him three loaves which surpassed the lily in whiteness, the rose in odour, and honey in taste. From that time forward, Bede states that the saint was frequently supplied with food direct from the Lord.

Cuthbert had become a monk before this last miracle of the loaves happened. He chose the Abbey of Melrose as the place of his profession, knowing, as Bede says in compliment of those for whom he wrote, that the church of Lindisfarne contained many holy men whose precept and example would be of service to him, but attracted to Melrose by the report of the great virtues of Boisil, the prior. The abbat was

Eata, one of the twelve English boys given to Aidan
by King Oswald to be trained for the ministry.
Cuthbert rode up to the abbey gate with his spear in
his hand, the ordinary equipment of a layman in those
days of insecurity.[1] Boisil was standing at the door,
and exclaimed in the hearing of one who told it to
Bede, " Behold a servant of the Lord ! " In a few
days the abbat, who was absent, returned, and on the
favourable report of his prior he admitted Cuthbert
a monk of Melrose. Some years after this event,
King Alchfrith of Deira granted a tract of land at
Ripon to Abbat Eata of Melrose, for the redemption of his soul, and Eata built a monastery there,
and sent Cuthbert and others to occupy it. Melrose,
it must be remembered, being south of the Forth,
was in Northumbria, not in Scotland. Before long,
however, Cuthbert and the monks were expelled from
Ripon, and other monks were established there. Bede
passes over this fact very lightly, for it was delicate
ground. He contents himself with saying that since
everything in this world is frail and changing, like the
ocean when a storm comes on, so the monks of
Melrose found themselves expelled from their new
home at Ripon. In his Ecclesiastical History he
was under no obligation to avoid what might offend
Lindisfarne. He tells us that the Melrose monks
observed the British rule of time for keeping Easter ;
and " being left to their choice " by Alchfrith, either to
give up their Easter, or to give up their lands, chose

---

[1] William Greenwell of Durham, whose praise is in all Archæo-
logical Societies, has shown, in one of his latest papers before the
Society of Antiquaries of London, that the people of these islands
developed, independently of all outside influences, the most perfect
form of spear-head. The paper was written in his ninetieth year.
He died at the age of ninety-six, when this present book was being
written.

the latter alternative and returned to Melrose, Ripon being given to Wilfrith, who had been brought up by the Scotic monks but had now become the eager partisan of the Italian Easter. Thus Cuthbert had an early practical experience of the tender mercies of those who are at variance on ceremonial matters of religion. He himself spoke with unflinching severity of those who differed from him in this matter of Easter, almost with his last breath.

After a time Prior Boisil died. We have a very interesting account of his latest days, which he spent in the company of Cuthbert who owed to him his admission to Melrose. It is clear from Bede's account that Boisil was understood to have prophetic power. In this power he announced that he had only seven days to live and have the use of his tongue ; Cuthbert must therefore learn from him all that there was time to teach him. Cuthbert asked what he had better read, to last through the seven days. " I have here," Boisil replied, " a codex with seven quaternions of St. John's Gospel. We can read one a day, and meditate thereon as best we may." This they accomplished in the time, for they sought simple lessons, and did not enter upon profound questions. Boisil died on the seventh day, having told to Cuthbert all that was to happen to him for the rest of his life. Among other things, he told him he would become a bishop. In course of time, Cuthbert retired to an island and lived as an anchorite. He would not tell any one of this alarming prophecy of a bishopric, but he used to say to the brethren who visited him on his island, " Though I dwell in a very modest little cell, surrounded by the waves of the ocean which cut me off from the sight and knowledge of mortal men, not even so do I think myself safe from the snares of the world, and I fear that somehow or other I shall be carried away by the love of money." We may remember that Bede, too, wrote gravely and comprehensively of men holding bishoprics as a means of making money.

In succession to his prophetic friend, Cuthbert became prior of Melrose, but, in imitation of Prior Boisil, he was very far from confining himself to the domestic business and internal affairs of the monastery which were the special duties of a prior. He performed these duties with pious zeal, but he did much more. He found that the neighbouring people were at best Christians in name only. They led evil lives, and in time of danger and pestilence they neglected the sacrament of their faith and had recourse to idolatrous remedies, as though they could restrain, by means of pagan mysteries and charms, a blow sent from God. Cuthbert made frequent attempts to eradicate these evils. He sallied forth from the monastery, often on horseback, more often on foot, to preach in the neighbouring villages, as Boisil had done. He specially selected such hamlets as were situated in mountainous places, difficult of access, and thus likely to deter teachers of less zeal than himself. In these out-of-the-way places he would often spend a week, sometimes two or three weeks or even a month, finding full exercise for his powers of teaching. He had great gifts, and he met with great success. We gather from his biographer that he possessed three special qualifications for the work. His methods of teaching were skilful ; he was determined to press home to the conviction of his hearers any lesson he had once begun ; and he had a face like an angel. When such a man, impelled by the love of Christ, gave himself for weeks at a time to the ignorant inhabitants of a hamlet buried among the hills, we need no Bede to tell us the result. " No one dared attempt to hide from him the secrets of his heart. All confessed openly   for they felt they could conceal nothing from him, and they hoped to wipe away their offences by the fruits of repentance which he enjoined."

Several of the miracles recorded in Cuthbert's life give significant evidence of the scantness of the population in the north of England, and of the difficulties and dangers of such journeys as Christian teachers had to take.   In addition to the miracles of feeding mentioned above, we read that on one occasion Cuthbert left the monastery of Melrose with two of the brethren on some necessary business which took him to the land of the southern Picts.   This territory Bede calls Niduari, "the land of the Picts which is called Niduari."   If this meant Nithsdale, a land journey of some forty or fifty miles from Melrose would have taken them there.   If the territory of Whithern is meant, forty miles would take them to the Solway, and forty or fifty miles of sea would land them at that promontory.   Northumbrian conquest of the districts west of the Forth had cut these Picts off from the Picts of Fife and Forfar.   They went by sea and arrived at their destination on the day after Christmas Day. As soon as they landed, a severe storm set in, which entirely prevented their return.   Snow fell for days. They found no one to provide food or shelter.   The Epiphany was close at hand, and they were in danger of perishing from cold and hunger.   Cuthbert under these trying circumstances did not lose the cheerful and kindly temper for which he was remarkable, nor did he cease to pray for help throughout each night. One morning he took his companions down to the shore, to the spot where he had spent the night in prayer, and showed them three pieces of flesh of a large fish—a dolphin Bede calls it, probably a porpoise, porpoises were used as food in the Middle Ages, and were considered a delicacy—cut up and prepared for cooking. This he told them was prepared by the Lord, and the number of the pieces, he informed them, signified that in three days' time there would be favourable weather. All fell out as he said. For three days the storm raged violently ; on the fourth day a calm came on, followed by a fair wind, which carried them safely back.

On another occasion he went on foot with one boy as an attendant, to preach at a distant village. Cuthbert became tired with the walk long before reaching the place, and turning to the boy he asked him where they should stop to take refreshment, and whether he knew of any one on their road who would supply them with food. The boy confessed that he was thinking about food when Cuthbert spoke, for they had brought no provision with them, and he knew of no one on their way, and he was hungry. Cuthbert pointed to a bird flying in the air, and told the boy that God could feed them even by that eagle. Soon after this, they came to a river, on the bank of which the eagle had alighted. "There is our handmaid," the saint exclaimed, "run and see what God has provided." The boy ran, and found that the eagle had caught a fish of considerable size. Cuthbert took half for themselves, leaving the other half for the bird, and continued his journey till they reached a village, where the fish was cooked.

King Ecgfrith had a prefect, Hildemer by name, who was devoted to good works with all his house. His wife occupied herself in almsgiving and the exercise of other Christian virtues. Cuthbert often visited them when his business took him in their direction. In the midst of her religious activity, it is said, Hildemer's wife was suddenly afflicted of a devil. She gnashed her teeth, uttered piteous cries, and tossed about her limbs in such a manner as to terrify all who saw her. The prefect saw that she grew worse, and indeed was at the point of death. He rode off in haste to Cuthbert ; begged him to send a priest to visit her and give her the sacrament of the Body and Blood of Christ ; and entreated that she might be buried at Melrose. He was ashamed, Bede says, to tell Cuthbert that she was out of her mind, for Cuthbert had always seen her in the possession of her senses. He feared that this affliction might cause him to think that she had not been a true servant of the Lord. When Cuthbert informed him of his determination to come himself instead of sending a priest he began to weep, for he saw that the saint would detect the concealment of which he had been guilty. Cuthbert divined the cause of his tears, and assured him that so far from thinking such a thing of his wife, he expected to find her well enough to come and meet them and take the reins of his horse. Accordingly, when they drew near to the house, the prefect's wife came out and led Cuthbert's horse by the bridle till they reached the door, declaring that at the first touch of the rein she felt herself entirely restored to her former state of health.

After many years of active life at Melrose, Cuthbert was transferred by Abbat Eata to Lindisfarne to

act as abbat there, apparently as deputy to Eata, who
ruled both Lindisfarne and Melrose. From Aidan's
time Lindisfarne had had a bishop, and, like Aidan,
all its bishops were monks. Bede remarks that it is
surprising that so small an island should have both a
bishop and an abbat. He explains that the bishop
chose some one to rule over the monks as abbat,
with the consent of the brethren, and that the bishop,
priests, deacons, singers, readers, and all the ecclesiastical staff, lived together in observance of the
monastic rule. Cuthbert began to introduce a more
strict discipline, and he soon found that some of the
brethren preferred the old customs to the new rule.
The opposition to him was carried very far. Time
after time, when the monks met in conclave, the acting
abbat was wearied by the bitter hostility displayed by
the party which stood in the way of reform. On such
occasions he would rise suddenly, without a cloud
upon his brow, and adjourn the meeting till the next
day. When they met again, he would repeat his
arguments, as if there had never been any opposition.
By this method he converted them all to his practice
in the end. Bede very significantly says, in recording
the success of Cuthbert's tactics, that he was a man
of endless patience, and that it was impossible to
tire him out in mind or body. Given a chairman
possessed of unlimited patience, and with unlimited
powers of adjournment and unlimited ability to tire
out all opponents, it is scarcely to be wondered at that
in the long run his views prevailed.

One grievance the monks had which they seem to
have persisted in cherishing. They had been accustomed to be free from all chance of being disturbed during their hours of sleep, whether at night

or at noon ; the latter being a general time of repose, as we find from more than one story in Cuthbert's life. Cuthbert rebuked them for their unwillingness to be disturbed when any sudden occasion arose, and for taking it ill when they were roused from sleep. For himself, he assured them that any one who awoke him did him a kindness, by enabling him to turn to something active and useful. Men with less power of existing without sleep might fairly have been excused, one might suppose, for not quite following Cuthbert in his precept and practice. He would spend three or four consecutive nights in watching and praying, neither going to his own bed in the common dormitory nor taking rest elsewhere. On such occasions he kept himself awake by singing or doing some handiwork, sometimes by walking round the island and observing everything on the way. And he had an uncomfortable habit of walking into the sea and standing all night with the water up to his neck. The monks of Lindisfarne not unnaturally drew the line a little below such discipline as this.

In another respect he practised a severity which it would appear that the monks up to his time had not practised, and it is evident from Bede's manner of relating it, that monks in general did not practise it. Cuthbert would not wear garments of rich material or colour. His aim was to find a dress which should not attract attention either by its smartness or by its squalor. The example he set was no doubt enforced by orders issued in his capacity of acting abbat, and this may have been one of the points on which the opposition to his new rule rested. Seventy or eighty years later, the monks of Lindisfarne still continued to dress as Cuthbert had taught them to dress. They avoided all dyed and expensive material, and wore only wool of the natural colour.

The saint was by nature a recluse, though his sympathetic temperament drove him into active works of benevolence. It showed itself also in his dealings with sinners, for we are told that he often wept over those who were confessing to him their sins. And his feelings were so warm, and so ready to respond to any call upon them, that he seldom or never got through the service of the mass without shedding tears and losing command of his voice. When he came to the words " Sursum Corda," " Lift up your hearts," he was so intent upon raising his own heart to God, so anxious that all present should do so, that he could not raise his voice, and he groaned rather than sang the words. After some years, his desire for the life of a recluse mastered all other feelings, and with the permission of Eata, and the blessing of the brethren, he retired to a remote part of the island. He very soon found that even this place was not sufficiently withdrawn from the haunts of men. He determined on a very bold step. There was an island at some distance from Lindisfarne, not, like it, connected with the mainland at low water, but at all times an island surrounded by the sea, lying some eight miles off the coast. This was one of the Farne islands. It was not only not inhabited by man, it was said to be the abode of evil spirits. No one within the memory of tradition had ever lived on this island, till Cuthbert made his home there. On this desert place he made himself an abode in keeping with the surroundings. It was a circular house or hut, of considerable size, with a wall the height of a man or more. Within, the height of the wall seemed much greater, for Cuthbert had excavated the rock and so lowered the floor, his object being to make a house from which he could see nothing of the earth, only the heavens. The wall was built of the excavated materials, and the roof was made of rough timber and straw. The house was divided into two chambers, one an oratory, the other the apartment in which he lived. At the landing-place he built a large house, for the accommodation of such brethren as might visit him. Bede relates that angels assisted him to lift the heavy stones, and that wood and a perennial flow of fresh water were supplied by miracle.

In this hut he passed his days and nights. At first, he had a window open through which he could be seen by visitors and could see them, but he soon closed this, and only opened it to give his blessing or for some purpose of absolute necessity. Among other austerities, it is recorded that he kept on his shoes from one Easter to another, only taking them off then in order to join in the accustomed washing of feet at the Lord's Supper at that season. Even his gaiters, made of skin, he did not take off for months at a time. He sowed wheat, declaring that he must not live on the labours of others ; and when it would not grow, he sowed barley in its place, determining to return to the monastery if it in turn refused to grow. His determination was not put to the test, for an abundant crop appeared. When the barley was ripening, birds came and made great havoc among it, but he delivered a solemn address to them which rid him of their presence :—" If you have received licence from God, do as He allows you ; if not, get you gone." This story he told himself. It was not the only occasion on which he showed his power over birds. There were crows on the island, and he detected them making off with portions of his thatch to build their nests with. He warned them to desist, and when they disregarded the warning, he banished them. Three days after this he was digging in his field. A crow came and alighted at his feet. It spread out its wings, hung down its head, made sounds significant of humiliation, and demeaned itself with so much submission and propriety that the saint gave it leave to return to the island. It then flew off to fetch its mate, and they returned bearing on their beaks a lump of lard as a present to Cuthbert,—a fitting gift Bede calls it. Cuthbert kept the lard for the double purpose of greasing the boots of the brethren and serving as a text for inculcating upon his visitors a lesson of submissive humility.

In the year 684 a great synod was held at Twyford, on the Alne. King Ecgfrith was there, and Archbishop Theodore presided. The business of the synod was the election of a bishop. The vast bishopric once held by Wilfrith, including the whole of Bernicia and Deira, had been divided into two on the expulsion of Wilfrith, when Bosa was made bishop of Deira, with his seat at York, and Eata bishop of Bernicia, with his seat at Hexham or at Lindisfarne. Three years later, Theodore added two more bishops ; he made Trumwine bishop of the Picts north of the Solway, who were at that time included in the kingdom of Northumbria, and Tunbert bishop of Hexham, Eata remaining bishop of Lindisfarne. Tunbert was in course of time deposed, and the synod at Twyford unanimously chose Cuthbert as bishop, to supply the vacancy caused in the episcopate. It was afterwards arranged that Eata should go to Hexham, and Cuthbert should be bishop of Lindisfarne. Even with this concession to Cuthbert they had great difficulty in persuading him to accept the bishopric. Messengers and letters from the synod were of no use ; he would not leave his solitude and present himself before the assembly. Mahomet was obliged to go to the mountain. The king, with Bishop Trumwine and a party of great men and ecclesiastics, crossed over to the island. The brethren of the monastery on Lindisfarne joined them, and they all knelt together before Cuthbert and begged him with tears to come to the synod. He gave way, and consented to be made bishop, chiefly moved by the fact that his old friend Boisil had prophesied that he would be a bishop.

The manner in which Cuthbert fulfilled his episcopal duties completely justified the choice of the synod. He taught with as much vigour as when he had visited the hamlets on the hills in the days of his youth. And, as Bede quaintly puts it, he did that which is the best assistance to a teacher, he practised what he preached. He saved the needy from the hand of the oppressor, and the poor man from him that would destroy him. He comforted the sad and the faint-hearted, and those whom he found unduly elated he brought down to a godly sorrow. In the midst of the bustle and pomp which surrounded him he retained his simple ways and monastic severity. He gave food to the hungry, clothing to the destitute. The miracles which he performed bore witness to his virtues. He is said to have possessed the gift of prophecy, in the form afterwards known as second-sight. Thus, when he visited Ælfleda, abbess of the monastery on Coquet Isle, she adjured him in the most solemn way to tell her how long her brother Ecgfrith would reign. He told her in a somewhat vague and oracular manner that he had scarcely a year to live. She then pressed him to say who would succeed, for Ecgfrith had neither sons nor brothers. " Behold the sea," he said, " how full it is of islands. It is easy for God to provide from the isles some one to reign over England." Then she remembered one Aldfrith, who was supposed to be an illegitimate son of her father, and lived in studious retirement in the Scottish isles. Shortly after his accession to the bishopric, he made a journey to Lugubalia (Carlisle), " which the English incorrectly call Luel," Bede says. His intention was to visit the queen, who was there in her sister's monastery, awaiting the event of the invasion of the Picts by her husband. The people took Cuthbert to show him the walls of their city, and the fountain made in a remarkable manner by the Romans. As he stood by the well, he was suddenly disturbed in spirit. He groaned deeply, and said that the battle was over. He then went to the queen, and urged her to leave Carlisle for the royal city on the following Monday— it was then Saturday evening, and he told her it was unlawful to ride in a chariot on the Lord's Day—lest by chance it should prove that the king had been slain. It was found afterwards that the king was slain exactly at the time when Cuthbert was standing at the Roman well ; and Aldfrith succeeded him, in accordance with the saint's forecast. In the same spirit of prophecy he foretold the time of his own death, and also the fact that one Herebert, who lived a hermit's life on an island " in the great marshy lake from which the Derwent takes its rise," would die at the same time with him. On one occasion we have an incidental notice of that rapt expression of countenance which in later times has accompanied the exercise of second-sight. He was sitting at meat with the above-mentioned Abbess Ælfleda, for whom he was about to consecrate a church. Suddenly the colour of his face changed. His eyes became fixed. The knife dropped from his hand. His attendant priest bent down and whispered to the abbess that he must have seen something they had not seen. Addressing him as " my lord bishop," she asked him for what reason he had dropped his knife. He put off the question at first, but she persisted, and he told her he had seen the soul of a holy man carried up to heaven in the arms of angels. From whence was it carried ? she asked. From her monastery. Whose soul was it ? She would tell him that the next day when he was celebrating mass, he informed her. The next morning the body of a worthy shepherd was found under a tree from which he had fallen, and the abbess, on being informed of it, went to the bishop, who had already begun to consecrate the church, and begged him to remember in the mass her servant Hadwald. Thus all fell out as Cuthbert had foretold.

Cuthbert's miracles were, some of them, wrought in his absence. There is one striking story of a miracle of this kind which will show us how fully the people of his time believed in his wonder-working power. It may show us also, if we accept it as it stands, how powerful over bodily disease is the influence and example of a firm faith. The prefect Hildemer, whose wife Cuthbert had cured, afterwards fell ill himself, and his life was despaired of. His friends were sitting round his bed, consoling him as well as they were able, when one of them remarked that he had with him some blessed bread which Cuthbert had given him "I believe," he added, "that unless the dulness of our faith hinder, the taste of this bread would cure our friend." They were all laymen, but of a reverential turn of mind ; and the English were by nature greatly given to a belief in the efficacy of amulets, and charms, and simples administered with pious words. They turned to one another and made a mutual confession of complete belief that by partaking of that blessed bread their friend could be cured. Then they filled a cup with water, put a little of the bread into it, and gave it to the sick man to drink. He drank, the internal pain ceased, and the wasting of the limbs disappeared. He was perfectly cured.

Cuthbert held ordinations at various places of his diocese. On one occasion we find him ordaining priests at Carlisle. He was diligent in performing the rite of Confirmation. When he cured an earl's wife with holy water he was on a Confirmation tour, as a bishop of these days would say, or, as Bede describes it, he was going through the rural districts, the homesteads, the villages, to lay hands on those who were recently baptized, that they might receive the Holy Spirit. At another time we hear of him visiting the outlying parts of his fold, and reaching a place among the hills where a large number of people were collected from all the villages round about, that he might lay his hands upon them. But there was no church among the hills, nor any place where the bishop and his companions could be housed. The people set up tents for him, and for themselves they cut down branches and made booths. Thus lodged, the bishop preached and confirmed for two days. His short episcopate included the period of a dreadful pestilence ; many villages and estates which had once been well populated were almost or entirely cleared of inhabitants. Cuthbert diligently continued to visit his diocese under these conditions, and exhorted and comforted the scanty remnants of the population.

After two years of an active episcopate, Cuthbert retired once more to his solitary island. He was asked when his people might hope to see him back again, and he answered, when they brought his body. About three months after this he died. Abbat Herefrid was with him at the last, and from him Bede learned all that occurred. When he was first taken ill, he sent away Herefrid and the party of monks who had come to visit him, bidding them bury him in his island of Farne he was to be wrapped in linen which the Abbess Verca had given him, and laid in a coffin which he had received from Abbat Cudda. They were naturally very urgent that he should allow some of them to stay with him, but he was positive in his dismissal, and they obeyed. For five days they were prevented by bad weather from reaching the island, and when at last they did get there, they found him in a miserable state.[1] For five days and

---

[1] A paragraph in the *Newcastle Chronicle* (A.D. 1877), relating to the Farne Islands, may be quoted as an illustration of the difficulties still attending a visit to the islands in tempestuous weather. "An important work—the erection of fog-signals—has been for some months in the course of construction at the Longstone, the scene of the famous deed of Grace Darling. The Messrs. Armstrong, of Alnwick, have the contract for the work, and by some misfortune the men on their return from home got to the island without their provisions, which were to follow them immediately, but continuous storms coming on, it was impossible to reach the rocky island, and the men were reduced to the greatest straits for want of food. The flag signals for flesh, flour, and water were hung out in vain. For a whole week they had to subsist upon three small 'ham shanks,' with hardly any meat upon them. One of the men, when attempting to shoot a Norwegian crow, nearly lost his life, the run of water among the rocks being so sudden and violent. At high water it

five nights he had not stirred from the seat to which
he had gone when they left him, at a distance from
his cell.　He had supported life by gnawing an onion ;
he had a store of five onions, which he kept under his
bed, and they found that he had only eaten about
half of one of them.　His legs, long swollen, were
ulcerated.　He was worn out with pain and want of
food.　From that time to the day of his death, about
a fortnight, he allowed certain monks to stay with
him, especially Herefrid and Bede major, not our
historian who was then a boy of twelve or thirteen.
The monks of Lindisfarne sent a deputation to him,
entreating that he would allow himself to be buried
in their church.　The dying saint's answer was so
curious that it is worth while to transcribe it in full.
" I greatly wish to rest here, where I have fought some
little fight for the Lord, where I desire to finish my
course, whence I hope that the righteous Judge will
take me to receive the crown of righteousness.　And
for you too it would be better that I should rest here,
on account of the influx of fugitives and criminals to
seek sanctuary at my grave.　Humble as I am, they
will seek this asylum, for the fame of me has gone
forth that I am a servant of Christ.　Thus you will
often have to intercede for such with the great men
of the world, and you will have much trouble in the
matter."　When at length their asseverations that labour
of this kind would be pleasing to them induced him to
yield, he gave a curious piece of advice, for which Bede

would have been fatal to attempt to go beyond the rampart that
surrounded the lighthouse, for the boiling surf was continually dash-
ing over it.　The workmen dried their tea-leaves and smoked them
for tobacco.　At last, on Christmas Day, by taking advantage of the
wind, ten of them succeeded in reaching the inner Farne, where they
obtained some refreshments.　On the Sunday they had nothing to eat
but a few crumbs of bread.　They reached Alnwick on Friday last. '

says they thanked him on bended knee. " If you really do wish to take my body to Lindisfarne, I think you should bury it in the inner part of the church ; for then you can visit the sepulchre yourselves whenever you wish, and you will have it in your power to grant or to withhold leave for others to visit it."

About nine o'clock one morning, when the brothers visited him, he asked them to carry him to his cell and oratory. When they reached the door, they asked if one of them might go in with him to wait upon him, for no one as yet had ever entered his cell. He selected from among them one who was himself ill, Walstod by name, and these two spent six hours alone. At the end of that time, Walstod came out to tell Herefrid that Cuthbert wished to see him, and at the same time announced that he had himself been cured of his disease by the saint. Herefrid went to him at three o'clock, and found him reclining in one corner of the oratory, opposite the altar. He sat by his side, and entreated him to leave some last words of counsel for the brethren. Painfully and at intervals, for he was too ill to speak more than a few words at a time, the dying man said these words, as nearly as Herefrid could remember : " Keep peace among yourselves and divine love. When you meet in council, take earnest pains to be of one mind. Have mutual concord, too, with other servants of Christ. Despise none who come to you for hospitality and are of the household of faith, but receive them, keep them, and speed them on their way, with friendly kindness, not esteeming yourselves better than others of the same faith and life. But have no fellowship with those who err from the unity of the Catholic faith, either by keeping Easter at a wrong time or by living perversely. Know this, too, and keep it in memory, that if necessity compels you to choose between two evils, I greatly prefer that you should take my bones from the tomb and abandon this place, carrying them with you, than that you should in any way consent to submit to schismatics. Strive most diligently to learn and to keep the Catholic rules of the Fathers. Practise the rule which God through my ministry has given you ; for I know that, however some have despised me during my life, when I am dead you will see more clearly what manner of man I was, and that what I have taught is not to be despised."

Then he ceased to speak or think of this world. He passed the time till evening, and on into the night, in quiet and prayerful expectation of future bliss. Before the dawn of day he strengthened himself for his departure by the Communion of the Lord's Body and Blood. He raised his eyes and hands to heaven, and breathed out his soul. The brethren carried his body to the ship, and took it to Lindisfarne. There it was met by a great company of monks, with choirs of singers, and it was laid in the Church of St. Peter[1] in a stone coffin, on the right side of the altar. Nine years later, when it was supposed that the flesh would be reduced to dust and the bones might be put into a smaller and more convenient receptacle, the coffin was opened, the monks obtaining the necessary permission from Bishop Eadbert, Cuthbert's successor. To their surprise they found the body unchanged, the joints still flexible. The clothing, too, was neither decayed nor faded. This was

[1] The true dedication was St. Peter and St. Paul.

on the anniversary of his burial, the 20th of April.
A fortnight later Bishop Eadbert himself died, and
was buried below the coffin which contained Cuthbert's remains. The story of the many wanderings of
this coffin with its precious relics belongs to a later
period. Bede's bones were mingled with Cuthbert's,
being found in the same tomb in 1104.

One more miracle we may tell of. After his death
a boy was brought to the monastery in a cart by the
parents, who did not know what to do with him. He
was out of his mind, very noisy and violent ; he
yelled and bit, and would not be quiet. There is a
remedy known to a few persons who are a good deal
about horses, by which the most fractious horse can
be brought to walk quietly past any object which he
has altogether refused to pass. It is a simple remedy.
Throw a little dust or mud off the road into his
mouth, and the horse becomes at once so absorbed
in the endeavour to expel all the dirt that he will
walk quietly past anything. Perhaps this is a remedy
dating from Saxon times ; at any rate the remedy
suggested by one of the priests in the monastery was
very similar both in its composition and in its effects.
He went to the place where the water with which the
dead saint's body was washed had been thrown, and
he brought some of the mud to the sick-room of the
monastery and poured it into the raging boy's open
mouth, from which at the moment dreadful cries
were issuing. The cries ceased instantly, the mouth
was closed, the head fell back in a profound sleep ;
and the next morning the boy got up perfectly cured.

Relics of St. Cuthbert of very great interest and value
exist still. When his tomb was opened in 1104 a
copy of St. John's Gospel was found in it, a sixth-

century manuscript. It is now at Stonyhurst. The famous Lindisfarne Gospels are described on pages 170 and 318. We have other personal relics, shown on Plates 7 and 8.

Plate 7 shows St. Cuthbert's pectoral cross, found on his breast when his grave was opened in 1827. The representation is the full size of the original. It was found deep down among the remains of the robes which were nearest to the breast of the Saint, and its position quite accounts for its not being seen and described by Prior Reginald during the operations of 1104. It is of curiously dulled gold, except the loop at the top, which is of bright pure gold. It weighs fifteen pennyweights and twelve grains. It has a large garnet in the centre and one at each angle, with twelve small ones on each arm. It will be remembered that the Dream of the Holy Rood, which will be mentioned in connection with Caedmon's religious dream-poems, places before the mind's eye a cross of gold, adorned with gems, " four shone at base, on earth, and five on the spreading arms."

Another personal possession of St. Cuthbert which we still have is his portable altar, Plate 8. The anonymous monk of Lindisfarne who describes the last rites for the body of the departed Saint, tells us that they clothed him in sacerdotal vestments and placed upon his breast the sacramental oblations. There can be no doubt that the consecrated elements were placed on this portable altar, which was found on his breast in 1827. When the remains of the Saint were placed in the new Norman Cathedral Church at Durham in 1104 (August 29), the monks clothed the body in an additional robe, " the most costly pall they could find in the church, and they replaced in the coffin all the things they had found there, including 'a silver altar.' " Reginald, writing later on the information of the elders of the church, says, " He has with him in the coffin a silver altar."

The altar consists of plates of embossed silver attached by silver nails to a slip of oak about a third of an inch in thickness, and about six inches by five in area. The fragments of the embossed silver which still remain show very interesting ornamentation, typical of the time, and portions of an inscription which suggest a combination of Greek and Latin letters ; this, too, is typical of the time, for on the breast of Bede's friend Bishop Acca of Hexham there was found in the year 1000 a similar altar, formed of two pieces of wood fastened with silver nails, with the inscription in curiously combined Greek and Latin *" Alme trinitati agie Sophie Sancte Marie "* ("to the Holy Trinity, to holy wisdom or to Saint Sophia, to Saint Mary"). These portable altars are called in the inventories "super altars," the "altar" in Archbishop Ecgbert's time being the solid structure, and the *tabula altaris*, the "altar table," being the specially consecrated plate or insertion on the upper surface on which the elements were placed. The itinerant priests carried with them consecrated plates of metal or stone, to be used where there was no consecrated altar.

Next in order of date come some of the robes found on the body. St. Cuthbert was highly respected by members of the royal family of Wessex, and when King Athelstane proceeded to the north with an army he clothed the body of the Saint with additional robes. It is certain that the robes shown in Plates 9 and 10 are portions of the robes taken to Durham by Athelstane, for they are dated and placed by the inscriptions wrought into them   *Ælflæd fieri precepit pio episcopo Frithestano* " (" Ælflæd caused to be made for the pious bishop Frithestan "). This places the making of the robes in Wessex. Ælflæd was the queen of Edward the Elder, Alfred's son, and Frithestan was the contemporary bishop of Winchester. It also dates the making of the robes. Ælflæd was queen till her death, which took place before 919, Frithestan was bishop of Winchester from 909, and died in 933. Thus they were Queen and Bishop together for at most ten years, during which time these robes were made. So long as Frithestan lived, his robes would remain with him. After his death they might naturally be at the disposal of any one in great position who wished to make a special gift that was to cost him nothing or very little. Possibly they were Palace property, for use at celebrations there. Athelstane, a son, said to be illegitimate, of Ælflæd's husband, succeeded to the throne in 924 and died in 940, seven years after Frithestan. In 933–4 he successfully invaded the territory of the Scots, and on his way he made rich gifts to the body of St. Cuthbert, then lying at Chester le Street, among them a stole and maniple. Both the stole and maniple now at Durham have the inscription given above worked into them in worsted work. The substance of these robes is narrow gold tape, woven with self-edges for the insertion of the lettering, the prophets, the floral ornamentation, and all parts of the subjects, in worsted. It is a marvellous piece of work, just a thousand years old, with an unusually clear and convincing pedigree.

Besides these remarkable portions of the bishop's robes, some portions of a very splendid robe were found.[1] It was of stout silk, ornamented with circular medallions two feet across, containing a vase, symbolical of an island floating on a sea. The floating vessel was laden with fruits, and the whole was enclosed by a circular border of fruits. The sea, covered with ripples, had eider ducks and large fishes, and at the lower margin of the silk, between each two medallions, were pairs of solan geese. The colour of the fruits throughout was gold, the stalks were red. The sea was purple, and the fishes were red. There were portions of another robe, of thin silk.[2] Its medallions were less artistic. They had a very rich border of incurved octagons fifteen inches across, enclosing a man on horseback, with hawk and hound, with a row of rabbits below. These magnificent robes have usually been held to be the work of the Arab weavers of Sicily, and were presumably made between 1085 and 1104, to be ready for the translation of the Saint's body to the new Cathedral Church of Durham. The present writer had blocks made of the full size of each of the two medallions. The former of the two is very handsome, stamped in red on a long piece of thin yellow silk. The blocks were made by Sir Thomas Wardle, of Leek, and are still in the possession of his sons at their silk works at Leek. Each of the Colonial Bishops at the Lambeth Conference of 1908 who attended the gathering of Bishops at Lindisfarne received from Bishop Browne of Bristol two pieces of silk printed from these blocks. The octagonal medallion was found perfect. The island medallion had lost the upper part of the vase, all but a small part at the top which suggested the rude filling in that was purposely made inartistic. The robe with the circular medallion

[1] See Plate 11.   [2] See Plate 12.

must have been made to order; and possibly the other pattern was designed to represent King Ecgfrith. St. Cuthbert and the Farne Islands are connected, in tradition and in fact, with eider ducks, solan geese, porpoises, and rabbits. The suggestion that the man with hawk and hound may represent King Ecgfrith may at first sight seem fanciful. But a good deal can be said in its favour. Hawking was practised in his time, for we have letters not long after this which show that this sport, so fascinating in itself and so very useful as a means for procuring birds for food, had got a firm hold in Anglo-Saxon England. Alchfrith, Ecgfrith's elder brother, is represented on the contemporary memorial cross at Bewcastle with a hawk on his wrist. Further, when Cuthbert persistently refused to accept the bishopric of Hexham, the whole Synod by whom he had been elected, at Twyford on the Alne, with King Ecgfrith at the head, sailed to Lindisfarne and on bended knee entreated him to accede to their request. This visit of the king and synod to the Saint on his island is graphically shown, in very skilful drawing, among the illuminations of the early mediæval Life.

The coffin in which the monks of Lindisfarne enclosed their saint nine years after his death is described in Chapter XV.

The designs on the silk robes of St. Cuthbert are of such exceptional interest that great pains have been taken to produce specially accurate copies of them for this volume. Photographs have been taken from the full-size photographs in the Victoria and Albert Museum, and the missing parts of the designs have been faintly outlined by Mr. Emery Walker's skilful staff. We are greatly indebted to Mr. Kendrick, the Keeper of the Textiles in the Museum, for his courteous help. It has been ascertained that the medallion containing a man with horse and hound is not woven in the silk. It was printed, presumably from a wood block, with some adhesive substance, and gold leaf was then applied to the adhesive substance, some flakes of which still remain. The pattern is now shown on the silk by the remains of the adhesive substance with which it was printed.

The most recent view is that these silks are not the work of Arab weavers in Sicily. Opinion appears to be settling upon Syria and the Mesopotamian region as the centres of this very beautiful art. As we shall see in the next paragraph, " Syrian purple " was the descriptive phrase used in Charlemagne's time.

Plate 13 shows, for purposes of comparison with St. Cuthbert's robes, a circular medallion on silk, found in the tomb of Charlemagne when it was opened in the presence of the Emperor William II. It has been supposed to date from the year 1000, when Otho III opened the tomb, or possibly as late as 1166 under Barbarossa when Charlemagne was canonised ; and to have replaced an earlier robe. Plate 14 shows an elephant robe which is evidently earlier in details of design, and has been attributed to Charlemagne's own time, in the eighth century. These two elephant robes may have been merely Oriental in design. On the other hand, they may have had a direct connection with Charlemagne's interest in his favourite elephant Abulabaz, given to him by Harun al Raschid, which he used to take about with him in some of his progresses. Leo III gave to Charlemagne among other great treasures "two robes of Syrian purple, with borders of cloth of gold wrought with elephants."

The greatest of the treasures connected with St. Cuthbert is the Gospel-book of the Church of Lindisfarne, of the art of which some account is given in chapter XVIII. Some points of interest may be mentioned here.

The Calendar prefixed to the Lindisfarne Gospel-book is evidently not a local Calendar. The list of Saints shows this quite clearly, both by what it does not contain and specially by what it does contain. There are very few entries relating to the festivals of Saints. Two of these very few relate to St. Januarius, and that of course suggests the Church of Naples. Another entry relates to the dedication of the Basilica of St. Stephen, and St. Stephen was the earliest dedication of the Cathedral Church of Naples. Now Abbat Hadrian had dwelt near Naples, and had presumably become possessed of a manuscript with a Neapolitan Calendar, which his friend and colleague Benedict Biscop had taken north with him and placed in the library at Wearmouth or Jarrow. That there was a close connection between the Lindisfarne *scriptorium* and Benedict Biscop's libraries, is shown by the fact that the figure of St. Matthew in the Gospel-book is copied from the figure of Ezra in the Codex Amiatinus, which, as we have seen, had its home in Bede's time at Wearmouth. This gives another special interest to the Lindisfarne Gospels; for the Ezra in the Codex Amiatinus traces back to Galla Placidia and Cassiodorus. Yet another special interest is to be found in the entry in the Calendar of the Lindisfarne Gospels, " *Dedicatio Basilicae sci Stephani* "; for we have seen precisely that phrase employed on the dedication stone of the church of Jarrow, " *Dedicatio Basilicae sci Pauli.*"

CHAPTER IX

CAEDMON AND WILFRITH

Caedmon — His early life — Inspiration — Sacred poems — Death scene—His Memorial Cross at Whitby—The Ruthwell Cross—The Dream of the Holy Rood—The Quinisext Council—Oswald's wooden cross—Bede's Memorial Cross at Rooker Point—Wilfrith's expulsions and restorations—Bede's silence.

BEDE'S account of Caedmon is so exceedingly interesting that it may be well to give it as nearly in his own way as English can give what is stated in Latin. It is a digression from, or a supplement to, his account of Hilda and her teaching work at Whitby, where five bishops had their training under her rule. We could scarcely find a better example of Bede's way of telling interesting facts.

There was in the monastery of this abbess a brother specially marked out by divine grace, in that he was wont to make poems apt for religion and piety, after this fashion, that whatever he learned from the divine Scriptures by interpreters he speedily put into English verse, in poetic words of the greatest sweetness and point. By these sacred poems the minds of many were kindled to contempt of worldly things and desire for the life of heaven. Others of the English race after him made trial of composing religious poems, but none could compare with him, for he did not learn the art of poetry of men or through human agency, but received it as a free gift of God. Hence it was that he could not write poetry of a frivolous kind, or without useful influence ; poems pertinent to religion were the only poems that became his religious tongue.

He lived as a layman up to an advanced age, without any knowledge of poetry. On convivial occasions, when it was arranged that for the sake of merriment each should sing in turn, when he saw the harp coming his way he would rise from supper and walk off to his own abode.

When he had done this on one occasion, and had left the place of feasting and gone to the stable where he was in charge of the draught cattle for the night, in due time he composed his limbs to sleep. As he slept, there stood by him one who addressed him, calling him by his name. " Caedmon," he said, " sing me something." He replied, " I cannot sing, that is why I left the company and came away here, because I could not sing." " Nevertheless," quoth the man who spoke to him, " you have to sing to me." " What," said he, " must I sing ? " " Sing," said he, " the beginning of created things." On hearing that, he at once began to sing verses which he had never heard, in praise of God the Builder of the World. The substance of the verses was this :—" Now must we praise the Author of the Kingdom of Heaven, the power of the Creator, and His design, the deeds of the Father of Glory. How He, eternal God, stood out as the author of all miracles, created as omnipotent guardian of the human race first the heaven as a roof to cover the sons of men and then the earth." That is the sense but not the order of the words which he sang in his sleep. Songs, however well composed, cannot be translated word for word from one language into another without loss of beauty and dignity. When he awoke from sleep he retained the memory of all that he had sung, and presently added further words after the same fashion, a song worthy of God.

In the morning he went to the steward, his master, and told him of the gift he had received. He took him to the abbess. A number of the more learned of the men were called in, and he was told to describe his dream and repeat the verses, that all might judge the nature and the source of what had happened. They were all agreed that a heavenly gift of grace had come to him from the Lord. They expounded to him some passage of sacred history or doctrine, and bade him put that into verse if he could. He undertook the business, and came back in the morning with the passage put into an excellent poem. Thereupon the abbess, understanding that the grace of God was in the man, bade him relinquish lay dress and join the monastic body. Accordingly he entered the monastery, with all his belongings, and was enrolled in the society, and she had him taught the whole course of sacred history. Everything which he could learn by the ear he thought over by himself, like some clean animal ruminating, and turned into the very sweetest verses, and softly repeating them he made his teachers his hearers in turn. He sang the creation of the world, the origin of man, the whole story of Genesis. He made many poems on the departure of Israel out of Egypt and their entry upon the land of promise, on very many other of the Scripture histories, on the Incarnation, Passion, Resurrection, and Ascension of the Lord, on the coming of the Holy Spirit, on the teaching of the Apostles. He wrote many songs on the terror of the day of judgment and the horror of the pains of Gehenna, and on the sweetness of the kingdom of heaven, and many more on the divine blessings and judgments. In all these he was at pains to draw men away from the love of wickedness and rouse them to the love and the pursuit of good deeds. For he was a man of much religion and humbly given to the regular discipline, while against those willed to do otherwise he burned with fervid zeal, and so he made a beautiful ending.

For when the time of his departure was drawing near, he suffered fourteen days from the bodily infirmity which is the herald of death, but in so slight a degree that he could talk and walk all the time. There was a house hard by in which the sick and those who were in a dying condition were placed. On the evening of the night on which he was to die, he asked the attendant to find a place in the infirmary for him to rest in. The attendant wondered at the request, for he did not seem like to die, but did what he asked. When he reached the infirmary, he talked and joked with those who were there before him. After midnight had passed, he asked if they had the Eucharist there.[1] "What need of the Eucharist?" they replied. "You are not going to die yet, you are full of joyous talk, like a man in perfect health." "And yet, bring me the Eucharist." Taking it in his hand,[2] he asked if they all felt kindly towards him, and free from quarrel or rancour. They all replied that their minds were most kindly disposed, completely free from any sort of ill feeling. They asked him in turn, did he feel kindly towards them? "My children," he replied, "my mind is kindly towards all the servants of God." Then strengthening himself[3] with the heavenly viaticum he prepared for entrance into another life.

[1] *Si Eucharistiam intus haberent.* [2] *Qua accepta in manu.*
[3] *Se coelesti muniens viatico.*

He asked how near it was to the hour at which the brethren in the monastery would be called to sing nocturnal lauds. He was told it was not far off. " Well then,[1] let us await that hour." Signing himself with the sign of the holy cross he laid his head on the pillow, and falling into a light slumber he silently passed away. We may well add, Blessed are the dead that die in the Lord.

This present age has seen the erection of two noble crosses in memory of Bede the Historian and Caedmon the Poet. It may be permitted to give here the statement made by this present writer in his work on *The ancient cross-shafts at Bewcastle and Ruthwell* (Cambridge, 1916), pages 52, 53, so far as relates to the Caedmon Cross. On the vigorous initiative of Canon Rawnsley, a number of us determined in 1898 that these two great men must no longer remain without a witness in their own Northumbria. We secured the help of Mr. C. C. Hodges of Hexham, whose unrivalled knowledge and facility of design enabled him to produce monuments not inferior to the design of the Bewcastle and Ruthwell crosses. Caedmon's Cross, which we erected in the churchyard at his own Whitby, is 19 feet 6 inches high, about 2 feet higher than the Ruthwell Cross. The flowing vine, which covers two of the sides at Ruthwell, is replaced by the wild rose on one face and the English apple on the other. The figures we selected are, our Lord in blessing, David playing the harp, the Abbess Hild, Caedmon himself, and four of the Whitby students of his period (A.D. 680), Bosa, Aetla, Oftfor, and John, all of whom, as well as their fellow-student Wilfrid II of York, became bishops. We incised on the face, in modern English, and also in Anglo-Saxon both in

---

[1] *Bene ergo.*

runes and in minuscules, the nine lines of Caedmon's first sacred song on the Creation, beginning :—

> Now must we praise
> The Warder of Heaven's realm,
> The Creator's might
> And His mind's thought,
> The works of the glorious Father.

The Poet Laureate, Alfred Austin, inaugurated the Cross for us.

It is well known that we have in the original Anglo-Saxon the one stanza of Caedmon's song quoted in the preceding paragraph. It is written on the back of a closing page of the Cambridge manuscript of the Ecclesiastical History, a manuscript written in or very near to the lifetime of Bede. It is not written by the hand which produced the invaluable manuscript itself. The early lines of it are given above in modern English.

We possess a long and beautiful early poem in Anglo-Saxon, known as the Dream of the Holy Rood. It runs to a great length in its complete form, indeed the only form in which it is found in Anglo-Saxon manuscript. But it is evident that only the earlier half is the original poem. The later part has lost the simplicity of thought and diction of the early and larger half.

It is of surpassing interest that we have stanzas and lines of this poem, all from the early part, incised in bold Anglo-Saxon runes on one of our two greatest monuments of the early Anglo-Saxon times, the noble cross at Ruthwell in Dumfriesshire, which preserves for us the earliest piece of Anglo-Saxon poetry, as the Bewcastle Cross, already mentioned in connection with King Alchfrith, preserves for us, also in Anglo-Saxon runes, the earliest piece of Anglo-Saxon prose.

There is much reason for assigning the authorship of

portions at least of the early part of the Dream of the Holy Rood to Caedmon, specially including the lines preserved on the Ruthwell Cross. Bede tells us, very frankly, that English people after Caedmon had tried to write English poetry, but none could compare with him. The lines on the Ruthwell Cross are of the highest beauty and power. Clearly they would compete with Caedmon's verse if they were not Caedmon's and if, as seems certain, they were placed on the Ruthwell Cross in Bede's time, that is, before 731, some fifty years after Caedmon's death. Besides, some of us have seen Caedmon's name incised in runes on the top of the Ruthwell Cross. A few words on this question of date and authorship may fitly find room here.

In the first place, the poem is a Dream. That strikes at once the Caedmon note. His poems were dreams, and we do not know of any other Anglo-Saxon poet whose verses were definitely avowed to be dreams.

Next, it is certainly, in its most beautiful parts, simple, and early. Those notes of simplicity and earliness are very clear when we contrast them with the later part, with its dwelling on the legend of the discovery of the true cross, and its tenth-century note.

Then, the insistence on the reality of the suffering of the Lord on the Cross is highly suggestive of Caedmon's date. For in his later days the Christian Church was divided on this very point. So far had some parts of the Church of Christ gone away from this reality, that the reality of the sufferings had become obscured. Shortly after Caedmon's death, a great Council of the Church was held at Constantinople, at which it was decided and ordered that the Saviour should be represented (pictorially and in

sculpture) in His human form, not under the figure of a
lamb. The reason assigned was, that the people might
have their thoughts turned to His Passion and saving
Death, and through His humiliation might learn His
glory. The Dream of the Holy Rood begins with
the preparatory word usual in Anglo-Saxon poems,
as though the reciter had struck a sharp note on his
harp, or uttered a sharp call, to command attention.

> List ! A dream of dreams is now my theme.
> 'Twas midnight when the vision met my gaze.

Then follows a glorious description of the beauty of
the Cross adorned with jewels, a beacon of molten
gold. By a rapid transition, the dreamer passes immediately to the terrible sufferings of the Lord, and, by
poetic imagination of a high order, the sufferings of the
cross itself. The transition is so sharp that we can
imagine an interruption of the dream of beauty and
splendour of a great golden cross bedecked with jewels,
by the divine messenger's insistent voice forecasting
the council's decree, " Sing, that men's minds may
be turned to the Passion and the saving Death, and
through His humiliation may learn His glory." This
is the finest part of the poem, the long-drawn-out
wail of the Cross, compelled to bear its burden. Here
comes in the stanza in the manuscript which is the
main part of the inscription on the Ruthwell Cross.
The Cross is still speaking in the dreamer's ear—it
still speaks thus to the eye in the ancient runes at
Ruthwell :—

> Then the young warrior prepared himself.
> 'Twas God Almighty, resolute and strong,
> brave in the sight of many. He went up upon
> the lofty Cross, to save mankind. I trembled

in his clasp, yet dared not bow nor fall to
earth, I had to stand there firm. A cross
they stood me there, I uplifted the great
King the Lord of Heaven and yet I dared not
stoop. They pierced me with dark nails, you
see the wounds, the open gashes ; I durst harm
no one of them. They scorned us both together. Stained was I with the blood that
streamed

There the runes break off, with fractures of the
stone. In another part they take it up again :—

Christ was on the Cross,
then men came thither, hastening from afar
unto their noble Prince. All this I beheld,
sore pained I bowed me

Again a break in the runes ; then :—

wounded with missiles
Him they laid down limb-weary, stood by
His head, they looked upon the Lord of Heaven.

There are still surviving the breaking of the massive
shafts a few runes which show that a very early part
of the poem was also engraved upon the cross, "a
gallows tree but not of shame."

Certain parts of the early stanzas of the poem
which are now to be found in the runes appear to
refer to the erection of the wooden cross by Oswald on
the day of the great victory of Heaven-field in 635,
some forty-five years before Caedmon's gift of song.
That noble story must have been well known to
Caedmon at the time, and the yearly visit to the field
by the monks of Hexham had naturally kept it fresh
in memory.

On the whole, there is much to be said in favour of

the theory that a dream-poem by Caedmon was the first foundation of the later Anglo-Saxon poem, not later than the tenth century, the Dream of the Holy Rood.

Plate 15 shows across the top and on the right side the two and a half lines " Christ was on the cross I beheld." And on the left side, " with missiles wounded they stood."

The Ruthwell Cross gives exactly those points of the poem, and so far as can be judged from its fractured condition only those parts, which emphasise the reality and the terrible severity of the suffering.

The Caedmon Cross at Whitby was eminently successful, as a memorial of the first of the series of Christian Poets of England, culminating in John Milton, and was a beautiful example of what modern skill and knowledge can do. Under the same auspices, and by the same able designer and workmen, a great cross was erected in memory of Bede himself. The concise account which was quoted for the description of the Caedmon Cross may be completed by adding the part relating to this second cross.

The Bede Cross is higher still, I think too high, 25 feet. It stands in clear air at Roker Point, the fumes of chemical works at Jarrow rendering it unwise to erect it nearer Bede's home. The inscriptions are in Bede's own words, first his death-song, in Anglo-Saxon, in runes and in modern English block letters, and then passages from his writings. I selected these from his prefaces to the Ecclesiastical History of the English and the Life of St. Cuthbert, as an example of minute care for all writers of history. These are in the bold script of Acca's Cross. There are busts of several of Bede's contemporaries, the kings Ecgfrith and Ceolwulf, bishops Acca and Ecgbert (afterwards archbishop), abbats Benedict Biscop, Easterwine, Siegfrith, Ceolfrith of the Codex Amiatinus, and Huaetbercht ; Trumbercht Doctor, and John Arch Chanter. There are five bas-reliefs of scenes from Bede's life. The cross was unveiled on October, 1904, by the Archbishop of York, the Bishop of Durham taking part in the ceremony. The surface ornament is beautiful. It comes nearer to a representation of one of the marvellous pages of the Lindisfarne Gospels than anything else that can be shown.

Before we pass on to speak of Bede's Letter to Ecgbert, which comes near the end of his life, we may note the remarkable silence on Bede's part to which reference is made on page 118. It follows chronologically the point in Anglian history which we have now reached.

Bede's silence on the main facts and details of the long struggle of Wilfrith, his expulsions, his appeals to Rome, is very difficult to explain. It is necessary to take note of this silence here, but to attempt to deal with the whole question of his appeals would be beyond the compass of this work.[1] The story in its entirety is in itself exceedingly interesting, and its relation by Wilfrith's friend and chaplain, Stephen Eddi, many years before Bede's Ecclesiastical History, is the earliest essay in our Church History by an Anglo-Saxon writer, and is a good model for later work. It is to be found in full in the *Historians of the Church of York* (Raine, 1879), vol. i.

Bede begins the story of the expulsions by the bald statement that a discussion arose between King Ecgfrith and the most reverend prelate Wilfrith, who was expelled from his bishopric, two bishops

---

[1] See further, *Theodore and Wilfrith*, G. F. Browne.

being put in his place (iv. 13). This statement suppresses a whole series of most interesting events which must have been before Bede's eyes in Eddi's Life of Wilfrith. Wilfrith, by the way, died in the same year as Aldhelm of Malmesbury and Sherborn, 709, some twenty-five years before Bede's death. The date of the expulsion of Wilfrith from the see in which Bede himself lived was 678, when Bede was about five years of age.

Bede then proceeds to state that on his expulsion Wilfrith travelled long in many parts and went to Rome ; that he returned to Britain ; and that because of the enmity of the king he could not be received in his own country or diocese (iv. 13). This suppresses the whole story of Wilfrith's appeal to the Pope and the decision at Rome in Wilfrith's favour, of which no notice was taken by the authorities of Northumbria so far as Bede is concerned. As a fact, Wilfrith was imprisoned for nine months with great severity when he presented to the king and the Witan the decree of Pope Agatho in his favour. The decree was rejected with contempt, and the Witan declared that it had been obtained by bribery. Bede eventually found it necessary to include in the last book of his Ecclesiastical History a long account (v. 19) of Wilfrith's life, but even here he does not make any mention of the presentment of the decree of Agatho or of the punitive imprisonment. All that he says is that in the second year of Aldfrith, who succeeded Ecgfrith, he was restored to his see on the invitation of the king.

Bede then states (v. 19) that five years after his restoration he was again accused by the king and several bishops and was again expelled from his diocese. He came to Rome, met his accusers, and was by Pope John and the bishops unanimously declared to have been falsely accused, and the Pope undertook to write to the English kings Ethelred and Aldfrith that they should cause him to be admitted to his bishopric. Ethelred was concerned in the matter as king of Mercia ; Wilfrith had done invaluable service in his kingdom on various occasions, and in that kingdom there was nothing against the much-harassed bishop. Ethelred, who was presumably already contemplating the great step he took in the next year, when he resigned the kingdom and became a monk, and abbat, at Bardney, a year before Aldfrith's death, gave a kindly hearing to the Pope. Aldfrith, Ethelred's brother-in-law, refused to overlook Wilfrith's real or supposed offences, whatever they were, and would not admit him to his kingdom. Aldfrith died two years later. His successor was a boy. A synod was held at Nidd, in the West Riding of Yorkshire, of which all that Bede says is that after some conflict of parties they agreed to receive Wilfrith as ruler of his church, and there he remained in peace for the remaining four years of his life. Who they were who came to this conclusion, Bede, who was about thirty-two at the time, gives no hint. It was in fact a dramatic scene. There were assembled the young king of Northumbria, and his three bishops, and the abbats. Elfleda of Whitby was there, Oswy's daughter, the king's aunt, "always the comforter and best adviser of the whole province." Brihtwald, Archbishop of Canterbury 693 to 731, was there ; he and Wilfrith arrived on the same day. The great laymen were there. Brihtwald and Wilfrith received permission to read their letters from the Apostolic See,

the *sedes Apostolorum*. The layman next in rank to
the king, Berechtfrith, rose and said they would like
to know what the words they had heard meant. " The
judgments of the Apostolic See are expressed," the
Archbishop replied, " in a long round of dubious
words ; but there is the same meaning in both letters."
Either they must restore Wilfrith to parts of churches
he formerly ruled, or all must go to the Apostolic See
and have the matter settled there, or king, layman,
priest, all would be cut off from the Body and Blood
of Christ.   The answer was that the whole thing had
been settled by Theodore and Ecgfrith. After that,
at Austerfield almost the whole of the bishops of
Britain in presence of Brihtwald himself had decreed
the like.   How could any one alter it ?   Then some
new evidence of a sacrosanct character was produced.
A special authority attached to the last word and
testament of a man.   Elfleda had been with her
brother Aldfrith when he died.   He had, as we have
seen, refused to pay attention to the papal letters.
But on his death-bed he charged Elfleda to tell his son
in the name of the Lord that for the remedy of his
soul he must fulfil the Apostolic judgment, restoring
Wilfrith.   Berechtfrith gave judgment accordingly,
informing the Synod that when they were closely
besieged at Bamborough, and were sheltering in a
narrow place in the rock, " we vowed that if God gave
to our royal boy the kingdom of his father we would
fulfil the Apostolic mandates.   As soon as our vow was
taken, the hostile forces came over to us ; the gates
were opened ;   we were free ;   the kingdom was
restored."

There must have been some very grave reason which
coerced Bede into omitting the whole of this.

CHAPTER X

THE EPISTLE TO ECGBERT

The Epistle to Ecgbert—Ecgbert's Pontifical—His royal descent—
Master of School of York—Alcuin a pupil—Alcuin's praise of
him—Bede's advice—More bishoprics—York a Metropolitan See
—The Pallium—Cruel treatment of Leo III—Paulinus not a
metropolitan archbishop—Irregular consecration of Archbishop
Honorius of Canterbury—Carefulness in conversation—The
Pastoral Care of Gregory I—The Lord's Prayer and the Creed in
the vulgar tongue—Subdivision of the diocese of York—Number
of Bishops' Sees—Too many monasteries—Monastic endowments for bishoprics—Resident priests in country places—Great
abuses of false monasteries—Evil lives.

ECGBERT, to whom Bede addressed the letter now
under consideration, is an important personage in the
Church of England. He is the first English pontiff
whose Pontifical we possess, the collection, namely,
of forms and services which he used as bishop and
archbishop during his episcopate which lasted from
734 to 766. This book is a possession of inestimable
value. It was published by the Surtees Society in 1853,
from the tenth-century manuscript in the "Imperial
Library, Paris," now the Bibliothèque Nationale.
It is only with a real effort that a writer mentioning it
in this connection deprives himself of the pleasure of
telling something of its fascinating contents. Ecgbert
was a first cousin of Ceolwulf, the reigning king of
Northumbria when he was consecrated, being in the
sixth generation from Ida, the first king of Bernicia.
Three years after his consecration, his cousin Ceolwulf
resigned the sovereignty and became a monk at Lindis-

farne. It was to this sovereign that Bede dedicated his Ecclesiastical History in the interesting preface described in Chapter VI. Ceolwulf was succeeded by his first cousin Eadbert, Ecgbert's older brother. Alcuin, in his long poem on the Pontiffs and Saints of the Church of York, describes the happiness of the time when these two brothers side by side, the one with the pall on his shoulder sent by the Apostolic, the other on his head the diadem of his ancestors, the one wielded the Church's laws, the other ruled the nation's affairs. Eadbert in turn resigned and became a monk after a reign of twenty years and was succeeded by his son Oswulf. As we shall see, Bede's language in the Letter to Ecgbert might be taken as suggesting that he was not sure that he would in all respects be an ideal bishop ; but Alcuin's statements in the poem to which reference has been made not only are favourable but cover apparently the whole of his episcopal work in all branches. He was wealthy, Alcuin says, and he spent his money generously on the poor. This he put in the forefront of his panegyric. We must remember that Alcuin is writing of the head-master of his earliest years at school, as well as of the archbishop ; he was twenty-one years old when his master died. Ecgbert, he continues, was a most illustrious ruler of the Church, an admirable teacher, venerated by all the people, elect in morals, affable to the just, very sharp with the depraved, gentle and severe. He divided nights and days into sacred portions, assiduously active in prayer in the long nights. By day he celebrated the sacred solemnities of Masses. He gave many things for the equipment and adornment of the Houses of God. He beautified them with silver, gems, and gold. He gave hangings of silk, woven with figures, from other lands. He ordained worthy ministers for the altars, of the various orders, to celebrate the Festivals of the Thunderer, and others to sing hymns to the Lord. It is very pleasant to read this testimony to the success of Bede's very frank advice to the bishop in his earliest years of office.

Bede, as we shall see, advised that Ecgbert should put before his cousin King Ceolwulf the advisability of largely increasing the number of bishops in Northumbria; York, and Hexham, and Lindisfarne, and Whithern, being at that time the only sees. Pope Gregory had planned for the province of York, as for the province of Canterbury, twelve bishops and an archbishop. At that number, Ceolwulf, who would certainly do anything in his power for the good of the Church, should be advised to aim ; and then Ecgbert, his most dear relative, would receive the pall from the Apostolic See, and become the metropolitan archbishop. It appears that an application was made to Rome, and the pall was granted, though there was no increase in the number of Northumbrian sees. The short "continuation" of the Ecclesiastical History of Bede has an entry under the year 735, "Ecgbert the Bishop, having received the pallium from the Apostolic See, is confirmed to the archiepiscopate, the first since Paulinus ; and he ordained Fruidbert and Fruidwald bishops ; and Bede the presbyter died." These were bishops of Hexham and Whithern respectively. This and other entries in this "Continuation" raise questions of much interest and importance and considerable difficulty, on which we must not enter here.

The pallium was continued to York. It seems curious that Alcuin made so light of it that he did not mention its having been sought and obtained, he merely mentions it as worn by his old head-master. Some sixty or more years later than the receipt of Ecgbert's pall, Alcuin wrote to Pope Leo III to support an application for the pall for the newly-consecrated Archbishop of York, Eanbald II, whose name, curiously enough, as also the name of his see, he does not mention. The part of his letter which relates to the pall is as follows (Ep. 82) :—

" And now as regards these messengers, who have come from my own fatherland and my own city, to solicit the dignity of the sacred pall, in canonical manner and in accordance with the apostolic precept of the blessed Gregory who brought us to Christ, I humbly pray your pious excellency that you receive benignantly the requests of ecclesiastical necessity. For in these parts the authority of the sacred pall is very necessary, to keep down the perversity of wicked men and to preserve the authority of holy church."

That is a remarkably limited statement of the need for the pall, when we remember the tremendous claims made in later times. Alcuin is evidently writing in his most persuasive way to obtain his end, and all he can say is that to have the pall was *bonum et utile*, good and useful for the two purposes which alone he names. The pall came. Three years later, Leo crowned Charlemagne Emperor.

The letter was written in 797. It is almost impossible to pass by without comment its reference to the authority of the Church as backed by the Pope. We seem to see a great Prince of the Church, serene, benign, and secure, in all the glamour of imperial Rome, and all the glory of the presence of the mortal remains of St. Peter and St. Paul ; crowning kings into emperors of his own mere will. But between the giving of Eanbald's pall and the coronation of Karl, Leo was set upon in the streets of Rome by the followers of the nephews of the late pope, who threw him off his horse and tried to gouge out his eyes and cut out his tongue. They only half did the work, so the nephews themselves dragged him into a church, threw him down before the altar, and set to work to complete the deprivation of eyes and tongue, which, however, they did not fully accomplish. Then, having beaten him cruelly with sticks, they left him weltering in his blood. After partial recovery he fled to Paderborn, where very grave charges were brought against him by messengers from Rome ; these were still under investigation when he returned to Rome and crowned the emperor. He died in 816, two years after Charlemagne.

Ecgbert died in 766.

It is strictly correct to speak of Ecgbert as the first metropolitan archbishop of York. Pope Gregory I had planned two Provinces for England, a Southern Province, with an archbishop and twelve bishops, the metropolitical see to be at Canterbury during Augustine's lifetime, at London after his death, and a Northern Province, with an archbishop and twelve bishops, the metropolitical see to be at York. So far as regards the Northern Province, no part of this excellently desired plan was carried out. Paulinus was sent as a missionary bishop to York to bring about the conversion of the southern part of the proposed province. He is, or was, usually described as Archbishop of York, but he never held that position. He was consecrated at Canterbury, July 21, 625, by Justus of Canterbury, who, unlike his two predecessors, had received the pall from Rome ; but he did not him-

self receive the pall till after he had fled from Northumbria never to return ; thus he was never, in the full
sense of those times, metropolitical Archbishop of
York.   But notwithstanding the absence of the pall,
Honorius, Archbishop-elect of Canterbury, came north
to him, met him in Lindsey, and was consecrated to
Canterbury, thus traversing the whole theory of the
necessity of the pall.   And this irregular consecration
was recognised to the full by the pope of the time,
another Honorius, and confirmed by sending the pall.
Quaintly enough, the pope at the same time sent the
pall to Paulinus, in order that either of the two who
survived might consecrate the successor of the other.
It is a remarkable comment, and from Rome itself, on
the supposed fundamental necessity of the pall.   A still
quainter comment is found in the fact that Paulinus
had fled from York before the pall reached him, and
becoming bishop of Rochester wore his pall there as a
personal ornament.   Ecgbert was thus the first Archbishop of York, Paulinus its first Bishop.

Of Bede's affectionate personal charges to the young
bishop, the most insistent, put in the forefront of the
letter, deal with carefulness in conversation.   Either
Bede had reason to think that Ecgbert in his former
position had been careless in talk, or he knew that
such carelessness was common, almost universal in the
ordinary walks of life, among the clergy as among the
laity ; indeed he specially mentions " certain bishops "
who are credited with being grave offenders in this
respect.   While Bede on his part had to be very careful
to consort only with those who would keep him
straight if he was inclined to let his tongue run wild,
these " certain bishops " were said to have no men of

religion and continence with them, but rather such as were given to revellings and drunkenness and other vices of the careless life. We know a good deal about all the English bishops of the year 734-5, and we wonder.

Then Bede turns with evident relief to the pastoral charge of a bishop. Of course he urges the study of Gregory's Pastoral Care. How little Bede can have thought when he wrote of this invaluable work, and when he turned the pages of the book he used so freely, the " Compendious history of the world by Orosius," that a hundred and fifty years after his death, the greatest of Saxon kings would select these two as two of the few books he would translate and employ others to translate into the vernacular English of the ninth century, and that another of the few books would be Bede's own Church History of the English. Ecgbert was to fill his diocese with priests and teachers who in every village should preach the word and celebrate the holy mysteries, especially the sacred rite of baptism. The people, who did not know Latin, were to be drilled in repeating in English the Apostles' Creed and the Lord's Prayer ; and not they only, but the clergy and monks who were ignorant of Latin. Bede had himself often given English translations of these fundamental documents to uneducated priests. What would not an educated priest or bishop give to-day for one of Bede's little parchment manuscript copies !

The diocese was too large for one man. Bede had heard, and it was common report—we may note the credit Bede not infrequently gives to common report in those days when the accuracy of memory and of repetition was so carefully trained in the absence of literature—that there were country houses and places among the mountains and in the forests where for many years no bishop had been seen, and yet none was free from paying tribute to the bishop though he never came near them for the laying on of hands, and not even any teacher was sent by him to visit them. " My best beloved prelate, I have written this to your holiness, on the calamity under which our race labours, earnestly entreating you to do something to bring things to a wholesome rule of life. You have an excellent opportunity. The king, Ceolwulf, is earnestly religious, you are his near and best-loved relative. Advise him that the number of bishops must be increased."

In connection with Bede's strong complaint of the shortage of bishops, it must be remembered that—as we now know—there was no parochial system in his days. The old idea that Archbishop Theodore of Canterbury (668–690) established the parochial system in England was founded on a misunderstanding. He subdivided bishoprics, and as his name for a bishopric, indeed, the ordinary Anglo-Saxon name in the Latin lists, was *parrochia*, usually so spelled in the lists, he was supposed to have subdivided bishoprics into parishes.

Under our modern parochial conditions, we might have supposed that considering the sparseness of the population in those times, the number of bishops was after all not so very inadequate. There were in 735, the date of the letter, sixteen bishops' sees in England. Till Henry VIII's time there were only seventeen, and of these Ely and Carlisle were of Norman foundation. The sixteen in Bede's time were, Canterbury, London, Winchester, Lichfield, Lindsey, Sherborn, Dunwich, Elmham, Worcester, Hereford, Selsey, Rochester ; and in the north, York, Lindisfarne, Hexham, Whithern.   While Canterbury has more than doubled the number of suffragans suggested by Pope Gregory, York is creeping up to its suggested twelve, having now reached the number of ten.   It is to be hoped that another generation will see the full number of twelve reached and passed.   Six have been added in the lifetime of the present writer, and seven in the southern province.   An Act has been passed which will add one to each province.

Bede had a complete scheme ready.   A great council should be held.   They should aim at completing the number of bishoprics named by Gregory. York should receive the pallium and become metropolitan.   An edict should go forth by pontifical and royal consent, naming a place among the monasteries where a bishop's see should be established, for the foolish donations of preceding kings had so covered the country with monasteries that there was no vacant place where a new see could be formed.   The abbats and monks would naturally oppose the scheme.   To obviate that difficulty, licence should be given to them to choose one of themselves to be consecrated, to rule episcopally the adjoining country belonging to that monastery, and to govern the monastery itself.   Bede thought that Ecgbert would easily carry out this plan, with divine help, and a sufficient number of bishops could thus be obtained.   If a monastery thus selected had less than sufficient property, there were innumerable places, as they all knew, where so-called monasteries existed, the abode of luxury, vanity, intemperance of meat and drink, where by synodical action chastity, temperance, continence, might replace these ill doings, and the property should be added to the endowment of the see.

Further, there were very many and very large monastic establishments of which it was commonly said that they were of no use to God or man. They neither kept the regular monastic rule, nor supplied soldiers or officers for the defence of the realm against the barbarians. If any one were, in accordance with the necessities of the times, to erect such an establishment into an episcopal see, he would do a virtuous deed. We might be reading a letter from Thomas Crumwell to Henry Tudor.

It was not only for additional bishoprics that no lands were left. The kings had no lands to assign to sons of nobles and to warriors who had served their country. Having no means of support, such men either went into foreign parts in search of occupation or lived idle lives at home and fell into all manner of evil ways.

Bad as was the state of many of the monasteries, there was a still worse scandal. Laymen gave money to kings, and under pretext of erecting monasteries acquired possessions by royal writ, where they lived licentious lives. They actually got their edicts confirmed by the signatures of bishops, abbats, and secular authorities, as conferring the rights of inheritance. They got together outcasts and ne'er-do-weels, monks and laymen, and filled with them the cells they had built, and lived riotously. In like manner they procured lands for their wives, who gathered together lay women and ruled them as if they were Christ's handmaids. Well did the common proverb suit them, that wasps could make combs, but they stored them with poison, not honey.

Then Bede goes on to say something which would have cost him his head under a Tudor sovereign. For the last thirty years, ever since King Aldfrith died, their province had been so demented with this mad folly, that there had hardly been one præfect who had not furnished himself during his term of office with a monastery of this type, and his wife with another. This sweeping statement covered four reigns, including the then King Ceolwulf, who had reigned six years, and Ceolwulf's older brother who had reigned two years. The inculpated præfects were no doubt some of them still living in their sham monasteries.

As to the people outside the monasteries, who were the special and anxious care of a bishop, Ecgbert must have much more done for them than had been done. To take one example, they must be taught how salutary it was to receive daily the Body and Blood of the Lord, as was done throughout Italy, Gaul, Africa, Greece, and all the countries of the East. This teaching had been so neglected, that even the more religious of the laity communicated only at Christmas, Epiphany, and Easter, though there were innumerable boys and girls of innocent and chaste life, young men and women, old men and old women, who without any doubt could communicate every Lord's Day and on the natal days of the holy Apostles and Martyrs.

Bede warns Ecgbert that there would be opposition to the proposed reforms, especially from those who felt that they were involved in the offences detailed. Let him remember the apostolic precept, We must obey God rather than man.

Finally, he had dwelled mainly upon the evils of monasteries, and against the vice of avarice which underlay so much of the evil. If he were to dwell at like length on drunkenness, revellings, luxury, and other such evils, his letter must reach an immense length.

CHAPTER XI

POETIC WRITINGS

BEDE'S Latin poems occupy more than a hundred
octavo pages. Four-fifths of them are hexameters, not
very poetic in substance, chiefly metrical prose ; with
some liberties of metre which in his early youth might
have earned penalties if things had been then as they
are now in schools. The bulk of this portion of his
poems consists of (1) the miracles of St. Cuthbert,
(2) the suffering of Justin Martyr, (3) a description of
the seasons of the year. The remaining one-fifth is in
verses of eight syllables each, the favourite metre of
mediæval hymnology. Bede set an example which
was followed in later times, of sometimes disregarding
the shortness of a syllable and relying upon accent to
lengthen it. Literary critics are divided in our own
times on the question of accent against quantity in
English verse. Some at least of Bede's poems in short
lines are intended to be chanted or intoned in church
as hymns. Thus the second part of a long poem on the

Nativity of St. Andrew is noted as to be " said " at the Cross, this second part having sixty-two lines of eight syllables. A study of these hymns informs us or reminds us of the continuity of words and phrases in ecclesiastical hymnology. Time after time we come upon words and usages familiar to students of the charming " sequences " of mediæval Masses which came after his time. It is evident also that Bede used the ornament of rhyme when it came naturally, especially the rhyme of the concluding syllable of a hexameter with a pause syllable in the middle of the line ; but the rhymes in his long lines are only occasional. As we shall see, he wrote a long poem in short rhyming lines.

The short-line hymns are on (1) the universal Works of God, (2) the Natal Day of the Innocents (very pretty), (3) the Ascension of the Lord, (4) the Natal Day of St. Agnes, (5) the Nativity of St. John Baptist, (6) the Apostles Peter and Paul, (7) the Passion of St. John Baptist, (8) the Natal Day of the Holy Mother of God, (9) the Natal Day of St. Andrew, (10) the Second Part of the same.

There is also one short poem of fifty-five hexameters, which gives us what we should like to have more of, a glimpse of the lighter side of our dear lovable Bede. It takes the form, so well known to such a student of Latin and Greek as Bede was, of a set controversy between Spring and Winter. It has to be allowed that the poem may have been wrongly attributed to Bede. It is more like the work of a generation which had been brightened and lightened by the genius of Alcuin.

The controversy related in this poem turns on the cuckoo. We may gather that the cuckoo was a great favourite in Northumbria. Two generations later,

our famous Yorkshireman Alcuin gave the name
Cuculus (cuckoo) as a pet nickname to a dear friend.
Bede sets before us a gathering of shepherds from the
hills, under a tree shadeful with early leaves. They were
come to celebrate the Muses ; the youthful Daphnis
was present, and the elder Palaemon. All were prepared to sing the praises of the cuckoo. Spring enters,
with a fillet of flowers, and winter, bristling with
frosted hair. These two engage in a great contest on the
subject of the cuckoo. Spring begins, with three
hexameters,—Would that my cuckoo would come, the
dearest of birds, most welcome guest to all, modulating
songs with his red beak.—Winter rejoins that he won't
have the cuckoo come ; let him go on sleeping in
dark caves ; he's always a nuisance when he comes.—
Spring repeats his eagerness for the arrival of the
cuckoo, to drive away the colds of winter ; always the
friend of Phœbus ; Phœbus loves the cuckoo.—Winter
won't have him come ; he brings labour in the fields,
he renews war, he breaks up loved repose, he disturbs
everything, he makes labour on land and sea.—O
tardy Winter, Spring replies, why do you sing attacks
on the cuckoo, you, heavy with torpor, covered up in
dark caves, after the feasts of Venus, the cups of
foolish Bacchus.—I have riches, Winter replied,
joyous feastings, sweet rest, warm fires.—But, retorts
Spring, the cuckoo brings flowers, ministers honey,
builds houses, navigates placid waters, begets off-
spring, clothes the happy fields.—I, rejoins Winter,
hate everything you rejoice in. I love counting over
my money in the chest, feeding well, with plenty of
rest.—You slow thing, Spring cries, always ready to
sleep. Who piles up wealth for you, who gathers
together your money, if no Spring or Summer does the

work ?—Quite so, Winter replies, feeling that his turn
has come, quite so, Spring and Summer in all their
work serve me, they are my slaves, I am their lord.—
Nay, Spring asserts, you are not their lord, you are a
mere pauper to those lofty ones. You couldn't even
feed yourself, if the cuckoo, who will surely come,
didn't provide you with food.—Then Daphnis and
Palaemon intervene. Winter's sixth retort is cut off.
Palaemon gives a reasoned judgment. " Say no more,
atrocious Winter. Let cuckoo come, the dear friend of
shepherds. Let sweet herbs spring on the hills,
pastures for cattle, peace in the cornfields, leafy shade
for weary labour, let the she-goats come to the milking-
stool with full udders, and birds of many notes salute
Phœbus. That this may be so, come, cuckoo, come
quick, thou sweet love, thou guest most welcome to
everyone. All things are waiting for thee, sea and
earth and sky. Hail to thee, cuckoo, sweet delight,
for ever hail ! "

Chaucer gives us a charming controversy between
the Cuckoo and the Nightingale, which shows us that
the six and a half centuries from Bede's verse to his
had gone altogether against the Cuckoo. The long
controversy, fifty-eight stanzas of five long lines, turns
upon points of love, not on questions of voice and song.
The Cuckoo has the worst of it because he is a bad
character, so bad that he stirred up the poet in his
dream to dismiss him in a summary manner :—

> Me thoght then that I stert out anon,
> And to the broke I ran and gate a ston,
> And at the Cockow hertely I cast ;
> And he for drede did flie awey full fast,
> And glad was I when that he was gon.

In itself, this specimen of Bede's poetry need not,
perhaps, have been given in full. But it supplies us

with a rather striking example of continuity in Anglo-Saxon—or, more correctly, Anglian—literature. It will be noted elsewhere that Alcuin copied phrases and whole lines of Latin verse from the West Saxon Aldhelm, who died at an advanced age in 709, a whole generation before Bede, three generations at least before Alcuin. Alcuin in turn owed much to Bede, and naturally studied his writings, whether history or homily or verse. He has a long elegiac poem on the Cuckoo. This would not be a very likely coincidence of an accidental character, and there is internal evidence that Alcuin was working on this poetic account of the grave controversy on the cuckoo. Bede introduced a senior character, Palaemon, and a junior, Daphnis. Alcuin introduces a senior, whose name is of the same syllabic construction, Menalcas, and a junior of the same name as Bede's junior, Daphnis. Alcuin gives us the same question, Will the cuckoo come ? But under that name he is writing of a well-loved friend, who is so far as he knows lost to him. Menalcas and Daphnis were real persons, whose names we do not know. Menalcas was a poet, in charge of the royal table ; Daphnis was a pupil of Alcuin, to whom he addressed part of his exposition of the *Canticum Canticorum*, Solomon's Song. It would appear that this friend, Cuculus or Cuckoo, had been a very favourite companion, of a jovial and tuneful character, with a will too weak to resist the temptations to which such a character is liable. But it seems impossible to make Alcuin's lamentations on the absence of the cuckoo suit the case of the disciple whom Migne's editor supposes to be referred to here. That disciple is the subject of two long and very sad letters, the one urging a change from gross moral evils by the example of a fellow-student now a bishop, the other urging change for fear of Gehenna. It can hardly be that the much-loved cuckoo was the man to whom Alcuin wrote thus :—" Why have you broken with the father who from infancy trained you in liberal discipline and in morals, and furnished you with the precepts of perpetual life ? Why have you joined yourself to troops of harlots, gatherings of drinkers, the vain things of pride ? Are not you he who in budding manhood wert laudable in the mouth of all, lovable in the eyes of all, desirable in the ears of all ? Alas ! Alas ! You are now reprehensible in the mouth of all, execrable in the eyes of all, detestable in the ears of all. Drunkenness and wantonness have done it all." Probably Alcuin's reference to Bacchus in his poem has given the idea to the editor, but it will be remembered that the poem which is credited to Bede and must have been in Alcuin's mind, makes Spring name the goblets of Bacchus, foolish Bacchus, as a usual occupation of Winter.

A few of Alcuin's elegiac lines on the cuckoo run thus :—

> Let us mourn for our cuckoo, Menalcas and Daphnis,
> Ah me ! how the cuckoo sang sweetly to us.
> Never perish the cuckoo ! he will come back in spring,
> And coming will sing us the songs of his joy.
> Ah me ! what if Bacchus has drowned our dear cuckoo !
> That impious Bacchus who seeks to destroy.
> Let us mourn for our cuckoo, mourn all for our cuckoo.
> Send verses to cuckoo, send verses of sorrow,
> It may be our verse will bring cuckoo again.
> May he alway be happy wherever he be
> May he think of us ever, and ever fare well.

It can scarcely be a mere chance that Bede's last word is *Salve !* and Alcuin's is *Vale !*

Bede does not hint at any knowledge of the careless

conduct of the cuckoo mother, or the selfish conduct of the cuckoo poult. Alcuin's poem has three expressions which are or may be in point. He attributes the loss of his friend Cuckoo to the action of a savage stepmother. He begs Cuckoo to return to warm nests ("a warm nest " would have fitted the Latin verse equally well), and hopes the crow will not tear him with fierce claw. And he asks—Who tore thee from the paternal nest ?—a curiously *mal à propos* manner of saying that the mother didn't sit the egg. All through, the cuckoo is the victim, as though in those days the mother-errant chose large nests of fierce birds, instead of small nests from which the young could be squeezed out by the growing poult.

In Chaucer's dream the Cuckoo was a powerful bird. When the poet had driven him off with a stone :—

> Than spake o bird for all, by one assent,
> " This matter asketh good avisement,
> For we ben birdes here in fere,
> And sooth it is the cuckow is not here,
> And therefore we woll have a parliment.
> And thereat shall the egle be our lord,
> And other peres that been of record,
> And the cuckow shall be after sent,
> There shall be yeve the judgement,
> Or els we shall finally make accord."

It was not to Alcuin and his immediate companions alone that the friend called by them Cuculus or Cuckoo was dear. The Archbishop of Salzburg, Arno, the most important of Alcuin's non-royal correspondents, wrote thus (Ep. 287) " To the very dear bird the Cuckoo, the Eagle [Arn is an eagle in Northumbria] sends greeting. I have dipped my pen in love to write this letter. Rise, rise, most pleasing bird. Go higher, never lower. Let your friends, the angelic dignities, hear your voice. Your voice is sweet to them."

Alcuin employed Cuculus as his messenger to Archbishop Eanbald of York. Dümmler, the joint editor of the *Monumenta Alcuiniana*, feels sure that the Cuckoo's real name was Dodo, there being two or three men with that bird-name in those times. But we have a letter of Alcuin to Dodo his pupil, and there is nothing in it which seems to fit the case of the Cuckoo. Alcuin definitely says that he " took him as a pupil late and speedily dismissed him. That savage stepmother the flesh had snatched him by the whirlpool of lust from the paternal breast." At the same time it is curious that he uses here two of the expressions which he applied to the case of his lost Cuckoo. Also it is a fact that this letter is three years later than the letters in which he writes of his friend as his messenger, so there had been time for a man given to wine to fall very low.

It seems probable that the Cuckoo's actual name was like that of some bird, for he is spoken of as a bird in the letters, apart from the mention of the Cuckoo. We must hope that the learned Dümmler, when he tells us he is sure that Dodo—to whom Alcuin wrote—was the student in question, did not imagine that Dodo was the name of a bird in Anglo-Saxon times. The now extinct Dodo of Mauritius was only discovered in 1507 by the Portuguese, who named it Dóudo (simpleton) from its silliness. Linnæus named it *Didus ineptus*. The German equivalent would be *dumm*.

To return to the short-line poems of Bede, we naturally find one dealing with the Apostles Peter and Paul. The Abbey of Monkwearmouth, in which Bede's earliest days of boyhood were spent, was dedicated to St. Peter Jarrow, in which all of his days from budding youth were spent, was dedicated to St. Paul.

He combines these two chief princes of the Church of Christ in one poem of ninety-two eight-syllable lines, " Of the Apostles Peter and Paul." He strikes the note of equality at the very beginning :—

> The glory of the Apostles
> Let us sing in due verse,
> Barjona Simon Peter
> And the dear teacher of the Gentiles.

It is needless to say of Bede, or of his predecessor in date Aldhelm, that we shall not find the Petrine claim in their writings. Rome was in their eyes the Apostolic See because it was the death-city and the sleeping-place of the two great martyrs. Bede makes this very clear in the closing lines of the poem under consideration, as we shall see. He also makes it very clear in the opening lines of his long poem on the Miracles of St. Cuthbert, when he speaks of the several parts of the earth made illustrious by the presence of apostles and other great teachers. He speaks first of Rome, and all he says of it is :—

> Rome, delighting in the splendour of Peter and Paul,
> Will ever live rejoicing in the trophies of the Apostles.

In his poem on the two Apostles, he skilfully states the parallel claims of the two chiefs, parallel rather than equal, with no note of superiority or inferiority ; he gives the palm to each in his own sphere. Both, he says, drew by their teaching the various errors of the nations to the grace of truth. The sacred Prince of the Church saw Jesus in the Mount and heard the voice of the Father from the fiery sky ; Paul ascended to the third heaven of the bright pole and heard hidden things which it is not lawful to utter to any other. The steps of Cephas on the waves are aided by the right hand of Christ, who raises his own that they be not drowned in the sea of the world ; Paul showed that the dangers of the world can be overcome by the faith of them that believe, when he saved from the waves his shipwrecked companions.   Simon draws the faithful from the lowest depths of the world, to set the good fishes free ; Paul teaches the just inhabiting the earth to dwell in safe camps, by his making of tents like camps.   The shadow of Simon passing by raises the sick, cleanses the leper, makes the lame to walk ; the dear Master of the Gentiles, full of power, puts to flight the evil spirits and every disease by his hand- kerchiefs.   Peter, desiring to follow the footsteps of Christ, fears not to come to Him by the cruel ladder of the Cross ; Paul enters the palace of the everlasting realm by the sword, for who fears God gladly gives his head to the block.   Thus the Princes of the Church, thus the true lights of the world, by noble triumph over death received the palm of glory ; whose illustrious trophies happy Rome now contains, whose crowns the circuit of the whole world celebrates.

Reference was made above to the West-Saxon Ald- helm,—St. Aldhelm, as his canonisation by Arch- bishop Lanfranc made him.   He was older than Bede by a full generation, and was a marked man at Malmes- bury before Bede was born.   Bede knew his writings, for he used one of Aldhelm's lines on Judas Iscariot,

Culmen Apostolici celsum perdebat honoris,

and half a line from his verses on St. Thomas Didymus,

Coeli qui sceptra gubernat.

Aldhelm wrote a short poem, in twenty-one hexa- meters, on the new and larger church which he had built in the sacred enclosure of Malmesbury in honour of the Saviour and the chief Apostles Peter and Paul.

In the collected works of Aldhelm (J. A. Giles, Oxford, 1844) the poem is said to have been written on entering the Church of St. Peter and St. Paul at Rome; what church that may have been we cannot say. But William of Malmesbury, who knew if any one did know all about the Malmesbury churches, gives the account as above; he describes the Apostles Peter and Paul as *Primi Apostoli* or *Primi Apostolorum*, the chief apostles. This is what Aldhelm himself says of them :—

" Here in this fair place Peter and Paul, the lights of a dark world, the chief Fathers who guide the reins of the people, are venerated in frequent song.

Key-bearer of heaven, who openest the portal of the upper air, and unclosest the white realms of the Thunderer of the skies, mercifully hear the vows of the people who pray, moistening the dry ground with showers of tears. Accept the sobs of those who groan for their offences, who burn up with fragrant prayer the sins of their lives.

Lo ! thou greatest Doctor, Paul, called from the heavens Saul, now with changed name Paul, when thou didst aim at setting the Old Law above Christ, and after darkness didst begin to see the clear light ; open now benignant ears to the voice of them that pray, and as their guardian stretch forth with Peter thy right hand to the trembling ones, who flock to the sacred thresholds of the church ; that here may be granted continuous indulgence of offences, flowing from abundant piety and the fount on high which never through the ages grows sluggish for men of worth."

Another of Aldhelm's poems might be expected to throw even further light upon this question of the relative importance of the two avowed and recognised

Chiefs of the Apostles, the two in whose joint names a
Papal Bull must to this day run if it is to be valid. The
poem referred to is described as " On the Altars dedicated to the blessed Mary and the Twelve Apostles,"
presumably in the Basilica on which he has a poem
with a delightful description of the church and services,
and with the first mention of an organ in an English
church. But this poem has no distinguishing reference of the kind ; it describes the labours and the
sufferings of each of those to whom altars were dedicated. Thirty-six hexameter lines are given to
St. Peter, and thirty-six to St. Paul, as also to St.
James the Lord's cousin. Next in order of number
comes the Virgin Mary. Aldhelm names St. Paul
second in the list and St. Matthias last, omitting Judas
Iscariot, and having thus dealt with thirteen apostles
he concludes by saying, " I have now gone through the
twelve names of the Fathers."

William of Malmesbury has preserved for us yet
another poem comparing and contrasting the merits
of the two Princes of the Apostles. Writing at
Malmesbury in the twelfth century, about 1130, he
tells us that King Ina built a church at Glastonbury
and dedicated it to the Saviour and the Apostles Peter
and Paul. We know from another source that this
work was undertaken on the advice of Ina's relative,
Aldhelm. William adds that Ina set up an inscription
in Latin elegiacs which still existed in his time. We
know of no one in those parts who could write them
then, other than Aldhelm. It may be well to give an
English rendering of this inscription, for to some not
inconsiderable extent Bede was a student of Aldhelm's writings, of which he speaks in high praise.
He mentions particularly " a notable book of his on

the errors of the Britons in not celebrating Easter at
the right time and in doing several other things not
consonant to the purity and the peace of the Church.
Also an illustrious book on Virginity, which after the
manner of Sedulius he duplicated, writing it in hexameters and in prose. He wrote other books also, being
a man most learned in all branches, writing in a clear
style, wonderful for both liberal and ecclesiastical
erudition." It is of importance to press this connection of Bede with Aldhelm's writings, for we have then
the connection of Alcuin with Bede's writings, and
thus we can point to Alcuin as the final power of the
great English trinity of learning, Aldhelm, Bede, Alcuin,
covering by their lives the period from 635 to 804.

The substance of ten lines of the remarkable inscription referred to is as follows, Paul being named first :—

Two gates of the heavens, two lights of the wide world,
   Paul thunders with voice, Peter lightens from the sky.

The one loftier in degree, the other more learned in teaching.
The hearts of men are opened by the one, the stars by the
   other ;
   Whom the one teaches with the pen, the other receives in
   the pole.
The one opens the way to heaven with doctrine, the other with
   keys ;
   To whom Paul is the way, to him Peter is the trusty gate.
The one remains the firm stone, the other is the architect.

Against the hostile torch two bulwarks rise,
   The city the head of the world has these as its towers of
   strength.

The view of the equality of the two Princes of the
Apostles which Aldhelm and Bede held was supported
by—probably was based upon—the earliest Masses for
the Day of St. Peter and St. Paul. We may fairly take
it that in writing their hymns on the relative merits of
the two Apostles, they were expanding the details of

the Mass for their day. As an example, we may take
parts of the very early Mass which was probably
current in England at their time. The Collect is as
follows   O God, whose right hand raised the blessed
Peter, walking on the waves, so that he should not
sink, and saved from the depth of the sea his co-
Apostle Paul when shipwrecked for the third time,
mercifully hear us, and grant that by the merits of
both we may attain to the glory of eternity : who with
God the Father, etc. The Secreta is as follows :—
We offer unto Thee, Lord, prayers and gifts ; and
that they may be worthy of Thy sight, we beseech the
help of the prayers of Thine Apostles Peter and Paul,
through, etc. The Post-communio :—Protect, O Lord,
Thy people, and preserve with perpetual defence
them who trust in the patronage of Thine Apostles
Peter and Paul, through, etc.

Or we may turn to the very early French Mass in
the so-called *Missale Gothicum*, where the *Oratio* is that
the holy Church throughout the world may ever be
governed by the mastership of these two, through
whom it received the beginning of the Christian
religion. The Collect invokes the patronage of the two
Apostles. In the *Immolatio Missae* we have just the
kind of comparison that Aldhelm and Bede make.
Paul was made blind that he might see, Peter denied
that he might believe. To the one the keys of the
heavenly kingdom were given, to the other the skill of
bringing the Gentiles ; the one brought them in, the
other opened ; both therefore received eternal rewards.
The one was raised by the right hand of the Lord when
sinking in the water, the other was saved when shipwrecked a third time. The one overcame the gates of
hell, the other the sting of death. Paul's head was

smitten off because he was the head of faith to the Gentiles, Peter followed on the cross in the footsteps of Him who is Head of all.

It is said to be impossible to prove a negative ; and there are many cases in which that is true, literally. In the present case, it does not appear that these great ancestors of ours recognised in St. Peter a Bishop of Rome, or recognised in him a supremacy over St. Paul. The continual balancing of the one with the other is a strong evidence against the existence in their minds of any such views. They had nothing in Scripture or in earliest history to balance against St. Paul's long and close personal connection with the imperial city ; nor have we.

It is a mere commonplace to say that Bede describes the frequent visits to Rome of the English of his time and of earlier times as visits to " the thresholds of the Apostles," not " of the Apostle," *ad limina Apostolorum.* The *Sedes Apostolica* was the *Sedes Apostolorum* to Bede's trained mind, not the *Sedes Petri* alone or supremely.

Of one class of versification in which Alcuin and especially Aldhelm rejoiced, Bede has not left any example, the *Ænigmata*, Enigmas. We have ninety of Aldhelm's Enigmas, more than 750 lines in all.

The absence of Enigmas from Bede's writings is no great loss, if we may judge from the specimens of Aldhelm's and Alcuin's efforts in this kind of work. Here is one of Aldhelm's :—

> Once was I water, full of scaly fish.
> My nature changed, by changed decree of fate.
> I suffered torments torrid by the flames,
> My face now shine like whitest ash or snow.

The answer is *salt*, produced by boiling sea water.

Alcuin preferred tricks with the letters of words :—

As evil you treat me yet gladly you eat me
And changing my vowels you mount me and beat me.

The answers are, *malum*, evil ; *malum*, an apple ;
mulam, a mule.

Or again :—

I'm a power and a charm of the highest degree,
And every man born is but one-half of me ;
The other half burns when in worship you fall ;
Let me part with one letter, I can poison you all.[1]

The answers are, *virtus*, virtue, power ; *vir*, a man ;
tus, frankincense ; *virus*, poison.

As an example of the playfulness and the typical
affectionateness of an early Anglo-Saxon scholar, we
may take one of Alcuin's Latin riddles, transferred into
modern English :—

A beast has sudden crept into my house,
A beast of wonder, who two heads has got,
And yet the beast has only one jawbone.
Twice three times ten of horrid teeth it has.
Its food grows always on this body of mine
Not flesh, not fruit. It eats not with its teeth,
It drinks not. Its open mouth shows no decay.
Tell me, Damoeta dear, what beast is this ?

We have the letter to Damoeta, that is, Riculf
Archbishop of Mainz, in which Alcuin acknowledges
the gift of this formidable creature :—

" I am much delighted with your loving present,
and I send you as many thanks as it has teeth. It is
a wonderful animal, with two heads and sixty teeth,
not of elephantine size but of the beauty of ivory. I
am not terrified by the horror of this beast, but

---

[1] " Sex mihi litterulae sunt et praeclara potestas
Disrumpis nomen medio de tramite totum
Pars colet una Deum, hominem pars altera signa
Littera tollatur faciet mox quarta venenum."

delighted by its appearance ; I have no fear of its biting me with gnashing teeth. I am pleased with its fawning caresses, which smooth the hair of my head. I see not ferocity in its teeth, I see only the love of the sender."

We can imagine the beauty of this ivory comb with one row of sixty teeth, the solid piece at the top being ornamented at each end with a lion's head looking outwards. A hundred years later, the comb, if made in Northumbria, might have had two bears' heads, the muzzles looking inwards along the ridge.

This no doubt was the comb which wrought so many miracles in cases of acute pain after the death of Alcuin, as described by the biographer who wrote from personal knowledge soon after his death. " Father Sigulf, while performing the last offices for the body of the deceased abbat, had a great pain in his head. Raising his eyes above the couch of the master, he saw the comb with which he was wont to comb his head. Taking it in his hands he said, ' I believe, Lord Jesus, that if I combed my head with this my master's comb, my head would be cured at once by his merits.' The moment he drew the comb across his head, that part of the head which it touched was immediately cured, and thus by combing his head all round he lost the pain completely." He might have echoed his master's words, " I love its fawning caresses."

We may fairly claim Bede as the source from which Alcuin derived his exalted idea of the practical value of the Psalms in prayer. Indeed, we can go further than that, for Alcuin wrote to Arno, the Archbishop of Salzburg, after the year 798, to the following effect. "He was sending to him a little handbook, manual, containing much on divers matters, short expositions of the seven penitential psalms, of the 118th Psalm (our 119th), and of the fifteen psalms of degrees. In this little manual," he says, "there is also contained a small psalter, called the Psalter of the blessed Presbyter Beda, which Beda put together, with sweet verses in praise of God and prayers from the several psalms and very beautiful hymns, one especially noble hymn in elegiac metre on Queen Etheldreda. Also Beda's hymn on the six days of creation, and the hymn on the six ages of the world. Also an old hymn on the fifteen psalms of degrees, and prayers." This actual "little book," with a full description of its contents and the assignment to Bede of all the parts which follow the mention of his name, has been found in the Cathedral Church of Cologne, where its class-mark is cod. 106.

We have Bede's Psalter, and the hymns named, and the prayers, in Dr. Giles's edition of Bede in twelve volumes already referred to. They are given in the first volume, pages 221–245. The Psalter occupies nineteen octavo pages. It is a gathering of verses of the Psalms of a comforting and prayerful character, beginning with the first verse of the first psalm, *Beatus vir,* our "Blessed is the man that hath not walked in the counsel of the ungodly," and ending with the last verse of the last psalm, *Omne quod spirat,* our "Let everything that hath breath praise the Lord." In all, about three hundred verses of the Psalms are selected for this interesting purpose.

We have also Bede's *Canticum graduum,* Song of degrees. It is placed by Dr. Giles among the "Moral Works," volume i., pages 239–241, not among the poems, and so is liable to be overlooked by anyone who desires to read this pretty example of his poetry.

This Canticle he forms on the fifteen psalms of degrees. It consists of fifteen stanzas of four eight-syllable lines, rhyming in couplets. Each is taken from the first verse of one of the fifteen psalms of degrees, extended to form a stanza, and altered to make rhymes. Thus, taking the first verse of Psalm 126, " When the Lord turned again the captivity of Sion, then were we like unto them that dream," in the Latin, *In convertendo Dominus captivitatem Sion, facti sumus sicut consolati* (Jerome, *somniantes*), Bede's stanza runs :—

> In convertendo Dominus
> Captivitatem protinus
> Sion, satis in omnibus
> Consolati nos fuimus.

That is, 'when the Lord turned again the captivity of Sion forthwith we were in all things consoled.' Tate and Brady were forestalled by Bede. Bede's sixteenth stanza prays the Father of power and the Prince of knowledge that by these thrice five steps he may be able to mount to the heavens.

We have also the prayers which are part of the contents of the hand-book. It should be added that with the Cologne MS. there is a copy of the letter of Alcuin to Arno from which we have quoted. This is fair evidence that the Cologne Codex is the actual hand-book, as indeed its contents make clear.

It is well to note how Alcuin acted in the use of the Psalms, having this direct lead from Bede in his hands and in his mind. A contemporary biographer informs us that Alcuin taught Karl, whether Charlemagne or his son Karl who died three years before him we do not know, which of the Psalms he should sing throughout his whole life for various occasions ; for times of penitence, with litany and entreaties and prayers ;

for times of praising God ; of any tribulation ; and for
his being moved to exercise himself in divine praise.
The biographer adds that any one who wishes to know
all this, may read it in the little book which he wrote
to Karl on the principles of prayer.

This little book is Epistle No. 244 in Wattenbach
and Dümmler's *Monumenta Alcuiniana*. Its first
words state that King David gave us a rule " for
singing psalms," and Alcuin's instructions show that
he meant the Psalms to be chanted, in private as well
as in public use. He himself on his death-bed sang the
evangelical hymn to the Virgin Mary, with the Antiphon, *O clavis David et sceptrum domus Israel*, and
then chanted the Psalms " Like as the hart," " O how
amiable," " Blessed are they," " Unto Thee lift I up,"
" One thing have I desired," " Unto Thee, O Lord,"
and others of like kind.

In the little book under consideration, Alcuin
arranged three courses of Psalms for the night and
seven for the day, and then passed on to explain, in
accordance with a special request from Karl, the order
in which a layman in active life should pray to God
at the stated hours :—

" When you have risen from your bed, say first ' O
Lord Jesus Christ, son of the living God, in Thy name
will I lift up my hands, make haste to deliver me.'
Say this thrice, with the psalm ' Ponder my words, O
Lord, consider my meditation. O hearken Thou unto
the voice of my calling, my King and my God, for unto
Thee will I make my prayer. My voice shalt Thou
hear betimes, O Lord, early in the morning will I
direct my prayer unto Thee.' Then, ' Our Father,'
and the prayers ' Vouchsafe, O Lord, to keep us this
day,' ' Perfect my steps,' ' Praised be the Lord daily,'

' Direct and sanctify,' ' O Lord, let Thy mercy lighten upon us.' Then, rising, begin the verse ' Thou shalt open my lips, O Lord.' When that is ended, with the Gloria, begin the psalm ' Lord, how are they increased.' Then follows ' God be merciful unto me.' Then, ' O come let us sing unto the Lord.' Then psalms, as many as you will."

Thus, through our own Alcuin, our own Bede taught and sang to Austrasians and Neustrians alike, the Franks on both sides of the Rhine, and England profoundly influenced not private life only but also the choral parts of the services of the Mass. And who can say how much of the fundamental position of the Psalms in the religious phraseology and the religious thought of our own race is due to the constant work of Bede and of Alcuin, twelve and eleven and a half centuries ago.

CHAPTER XII

THE SCIENTIFIC WORKS OF BEDE

On the Reckoning of Times—Interest of the subject—Indication of
numbers with the fingers—Anno Domini—Dionysius—Telligraffs—On the Nature of Things—Bede's indebtedness, to
Isidore—Bede and Isidore in Paradise—Isidore's indebtedness
to others—Why the sea is salt—On the rainbow—On Mount
Ætna—Agostoli—Have stars a soul?—On thunder and thunderings.

ONE volume of the twelve of Dr. Giles's edition of
Bede's works is devoted to his scientific treatises.
These are treatises on Orthography, on the Art of
Metre, on the Schemes and Tropes of Holy Scripture,
on the Nature of Things, on Times, on the Counting
of Times.

The treatise on the Counting or Reckoning of Times
is by far the bulkiest of the treatises. It occupies more
than two hundred octavo pages. The history of its
production is interesting in itself, and it speaks well
for our early Northumbrian ancestors. Bede was
supported and encouraged in his many labours by the
interest and keenness of his companions in the
monastery. We learn this from the treatise on the
Reckoning of Times. He tells us in the preface that he
had written in concise language two small books, one
on the Nature of Things and the other on the Reckoning of Times. These he had put into the hands of some
of the brethren, and they had told him that they were
too brief, especially the one on Times. He believed

that the desire for a longer treatise on Times was due to their special interest in the calculation of Easter. This longer treatise, he says, he had now written, and he submits it to them. One general remark he makes in the preface,—he has taken the chronology of the Hebrew Scriptures, not that of the Septuagint. That this was right he says in a delightfully firm manner,— " It stands my fixed opinion, and I assert that no prudent person will gainsay it." In these modern times of ours, the reviewers would speculate upon the particular colleague at whom he was aiming. We may perhaps acquit Bede and each and all of his colleagues of that suggestion.

The first chapter is devoted to an explanation of the method of showing numerals, numbers, with the fingers. One example may be given, selected because of the pretty way in which it is put by Bede and the still prettier way in which Jerome put one detail of it in writing of the hundredfold, sixtyfold, and thirtyfold fruits of the sower's seed. You join, Bede says, to show " thirty," the nails of the index finger and the thumb in a caressing embrace. Jerome says that the " thirtyfold " refers to marriage, because the conjunction of the digits, clasping and binding in a soft kiss, indicates the husband and wife. To show " sixty," the thumb is bent and the index finger is bent over it. This, Jerome says, the " sixtyfold," refers to widows, oppressed with want and sorrow, the thumb pressed under the index finger. To show "a hundred " ("I beg you attend diligently, Reader," says Bede), you use the right hand instead of the left—he has not said that thirty and sixty are shown on the left hand— and make the circle with the same digits ; that shows the highest and best state, virginity. We naturally find in Bede's writings various applications of these numbers, so suggestive of culminating merits.

Bede commences the treatise itself with the obvious explanation that the Latin word for " times " (*tempora*) is derived from a verb which means " to divide into portions " (*tempero*). It may be of some interest to add that our words " time " and " tide " come from a Teutonic base meaning " to divide," " apportion."

It is in this treatise that Bede introduces into use in England the method of counting time to and from the Incarnation of Christ. He tells his readers that a certain venerable abbat of the city of Rome, Dionysius by name, a man with no mean skill in Greek and Latin,[1] found that chronologers were calculating years from the date of Diocletian. Dionysius was writing on the calculation of Easter, and was unwilling to count his cycles of years, in a calculation dealing so closely with the Incarnation of the Lord, from the date of an impious and persecuting tyrant. He therefore chose the Incarnation itself as the event from which his calculations should count. Dionysius published his cycle in the year 527, beginning with March 25, the Annunciation to the Blessed Virgin. It is from this epoch that the dates of bulls and briefs of the Popes are supposed to run.

In this connection, we may quote the latest authoritative statement on the subject of the gradual introduction of this method of dating. Dr. Reginald L. Poole writes thus, in a paper on " Imperial Influences on the Forms of Papal Documents" (*Proceedings of the British Academy*, vol. viii). " Though the system of reckoning from the *Annus Domini* was devised as

---

[1] It may perhaps be inferred from this that Bede was aware of the fact that Dionysius Exiguus (the lowly) was a Scythian.

early as 525, it was not till just two hundred years had
elapsed that it was brought into currency by the
publication of the Venerable Bede's treatise de Tem-
porum Ratione. From that time it became an
established element in the dating of charters in
England, but in England only. It passed to the
Continent by the means of Anglo-Saxon missionaries
and scholars. St. Boniface took it with him into the
Frankish kingdom, see Carloman's capitulary of
21 April, 742. But it does not appear to have been
regularly employed in the Royal Chancery until the
last quarter of the ninth century, from which time it
became a fixed element in diplomas. The Popes never
adopted it till after the Imperial coronation of Otto
the Great in 962."

The English synod of Chelsea in 816 ordained, it is
said, that all bishops should in future date their acts
from the Incarnation. This detail is taken from its
context and so appears to be of more direct importance than in fact it is. The 9th decree of the Synod of
Celchyth ordered that acts of synods should be put
down in writing in due order, stating in what year of
the Lord they were passed, under what archbishop,
and so on. The general force appears to be that the
Anno Domini date was a matter of course, if a date
was given at all, being in common use, not that the
decree ordered the use of this method of dating. It
may be mentioned in passing that the 7th decree of
this synod ordains that monasteries shall have in
possession their telligraffs. That very modern-sound-
ing word is a hybrid formation to represent the Anglo-
Saxon Land boc, in other words, their title deeds.

The treatise on the Nature of Things is the most
interesting of the Scientific Works of Bede. It cannot

fail to be interesting to see what our ancestors twelve hundred years ago thought of the phenomena of nature. Those phenomena were very carefully observed and noted in those far-off days, and deductions were made from them by long experience, and were handed down by tradition and improved upon. They had a larger share of attention then than now, nature being then a much more uncontrolled power than now. The original commission given to man by the Almighty Creator, to replenish the earth and subdue it, has been acted on with results which are vastly beyond the utmost imaginings of the most imaginative genius of that distant age with which we are dealing ; as also has the commission which gave dominion over the fish of the sea and the fowl of the air, and over every living thing that moveth upon the earth.

A great deal of Bede's learning in subjects other than historical and theological did not come from research, for which indeed there was in his time but little scope. It came mostly, in many cases in bodily bulk, from Isidore of Seville, a man of astonishingly general knowledge, who was not as good a Latin scholar as Bede was. This very remarkable man became Bishop of Seville in 601. His merits, Professor William Ramsay said, are but imperfectly acknowledged when he is pronounced to have been the most eloquent speaker, the most profound scholar, and the most able prelate, of the barbarous age and country to which he belonged. His numerous works display a marvellous amount of knowledge, of necessity in that age superficial and of necessity inaccurate considering the subjects which he treated, covering almost every branch of learning known even by name in those times. If we compare Isidore's forty-seven short chapters on the Nature of Things with Bede's fifty-two short chapters under the same name, we find them both equally incapable of giving any approach to a correct explanation of thunder, earthquakes, the rise and fall of the Nile, and other physical phenomena. But we must remember that when twelve centuries had passed from the time when Isidore became bishop, the whole world was in ignorance of the true explanation of many of the phenomena with which he dealt.

We owe to Dr. Plummer's delightful volumes on Bede the reference which shows us Bede and Isidore next each other in Paradise :—

> Vedi oltre flammegiar l'ardente spiro
> D'Isidoro, di Beda (Parad., x. 130, 131),

and the remark that Dante wrote of Bede to the Italian Cardinals as one of his subjects of study.[1]

While we refer much of Bede's scientific work to his direct use of Isidore's writings, it is necessary to state that Isidore in turn used directly the writings of Ambrose, and he in turn the real or supposed work of Dionysius,[2] a man of very large range of knowledge in the time of the earliest Cæsars. Hyginus, too, is quoted by name, another writer of the time of Cæsar, of whom Suetonius in his lives of illustrious grammarians tells us that he was a freedman of Augustus, and had charge of the Palatine Library. It has been remarked, and it is a pregnant remark, that in spite of all the overthrow of the vast empire of Rome by the barbarians, with devastations which are being repeated in our own time by barbarians of even worse character,

---

[1] Plummer, I, xli., note 4.
[2] Dante mentions Dionysius and St. Gregory in connection with the *De Coelesti Hierarchia*, Parad, xxviii. 126.

the learning of the Augustan age not only was not blotted out, but was eagerly retained and handed down by the races who had counted among the barbarians themselves. Isidore was a Goth by descent, Dionysius the humble a Scythian. It was a repetition of the *Graecia capta.*

Sharon Turner goes further than that. He says of Bede's book on the Nature of Things that it " has two great merits ; it assembles into one focus the wisest opinions of the ancients on the subjects he discusses, and it continually refers the phenomena of nature to natural causes. The work of Bede is evidence that the establishment of the Teutonic nations in the Roman Empire did not barbarise knowledge. He collected and taught more natural truths, with fewer errors, than any Roman book on the same subjects had accomplished. Thus his work displays an advance, not a retrogradation of human knowledge ; and from its judicious selection and concentration of the best natural philosophy of the Roman Empire, it does high credit to the Anglo-Saxon good sense.''

Isidore was quite frank on the subject of his indebtedness. He quotes directly from Origen, Victorinus, Ambrose, Jerome, Cassian, Augustine, Hyginus, and " especially in our own times," he says, " from the eloquent Gregory." *Quod ego loquor, illi dicunt   vox mea ipsorum est lingua* (" I speak what they say   my voice is their tongue ").

One or two examples of the scientific argument which Isidore takes from previous writers and Bede takes from Isidore, and of the manner in which Bede uses the work of Isidore, will be of interest to the reader.

Isidore, Chapter 42, *Why the sea has salt water.* The learned doctor Ambrosius says, The old philo-

sophers say that the sea has salt and bitter water
because a large quantity of water from many rivers
daily flows into it and is caught up by the heat of the
sun and the blasts of the winds, as much being thus
taken up each day as each day flows in. They hold
that the sun has a power of selection, and takes up to
itself what is pure and light, leaving behind what is
heavy and earthy and what is bitter and undrinkable.

Bede, Chapter 41, *Why is the sea bitter.* They
say that the sea remains salt though so many rivers
and so much rain pour into it, because the sweet and
light liquid, which is very easily attracted by the
force of fire, is drawn out by the sun, while the harsher
and thicker fluid is left behind ; and thus the upper
part of the sea water is sweeter than that below. But
the aliment of the moon is of sweet waters, as is that
of the sun.

Here Bede appears to have been caught by Isidore-
Ambrose's idea that the sun selects drinkable water,
and so unluckily adds a remark of his own about the
food of the moon.

Isidore, Chapter 31, *On the Bow*, and Bede, Chapter
31, *On the Bow of Heaven.* They agree that the rays
of the sun are impressed on a cloud and give the form
of a bow, as a ring is impressed on wax. Isidore says
that the roundness of the sun causes the circular form
of the bow. Isidore says that the bow never appears
without sun and cloud ; Bede says that it appears
more seldom in summer than in winter, and seldom at
night, when it is only seen at full moon ; that is a
very interesting addition, considering the great rarity
of a lunar rainbow. They agree that the rainbow is of
four colours, and they agree as to the causes of this.
The colour of fire, red, is taken from the heaven ;

purple from the waters ; white (Isidore) hyacinthine (Bede) from the air ; black (Isidore) grass-colour (Bede) from the earth. Bede, who does not follow Isidore in quoting Clement of Rome, and omits most of his physical argument, does not give a word of his allegorical notes. The bow, Isidore says, shining from the sun in the clouds, represents the glory of Christ shining in the prophets and doctors ; others say that two of its colours, the purple from the waters and the fiery from the heaven, set forth, the one the destruction of the impious long ago by the deluge, the other the future burning of sinners in the infernal regions.

Isidore, Chapter 46, *On Mount Ætna*, and Bede, Chapter 50, *The burning of Ætna*. Here Bede uses the actual phrases of Isidore. They agree that the interior is composed of sulphur and bitumen, and that internal blasts of wind fight against the internal fire and so force out from the mountain smoke and vapour and fire. They agree that the Æolian Islands —that is, the Lipari Isles, near Sicily, understood by the ancients to be the abode of Æolus the god of the winds—have much to do with the eruptions of Ætna. The clashing of the waves drives the winds down to the bottom, and there they are kept captive till they make their way through the breathing-holes of the land, and in this way they fan the flames in the interior of Ætna, and now and then are so powerful that masses of sand (Isidore), sand and stones (Bede), are cast up. It is these showers of sand and stones that keep up the bulk of Ætna ; but for them it would have been burned away long ago. To them and to the Æolian Islands it is due that the burning lasts like the fires of hell ; that is all that Bede says of the similitude of hell ; it is characteristic of him that he does not follow Isidore in his remarks, which are much more drastic. The fire of Ætna, Isidore says, lasts as the fire of hell lasts perpetually to punish sinners, who shall be tortured to all ages, world without end. The mountain goes on blazing and can never be put out, and so the eternal flame for torturing the bodies of the damned can never be extinguished. There are little touches in Bede's treatment which indicate literary taste. Thus Isidore says that the internal blasts of wind drive out of the mountain flame and vapours and smoke. Bede gives the more natural and correct form, an ascending series of vigour, the smallest and most frequent being mentioned first, smoke, vapours, flame ; and he adds an accurate piece of information, that these indications break out at many places on Ætna.

In connection with this strange theory of air being forced down to the bottom of the Mediterranean Sea by storms of wind, and then blowing as it were the bellows of volcanoes, it may be well to mention a remarkable fact. At Agostoli, in Cephalonia, the Mediterranean sea is always pouring down into a chasm, working mills on its way down, and going no one knows where. Modern science has suggested, curiously enough, that it finds its way to fissures where the rock is at a great heat, and being converted into steam helps to produce eruptions.

Bede had a sound instinct which led him to avoid some of the speculations of those who had gone before, whom in so very many parts of their work he was thankful to follow. Besides words and ideas in the course of their attempts at explanation of physical phenomena which do not appear in Bede's quotations, he sometimes goes further than that. Thus Isidore has one curious chapter, No. 27, which Bede omits entirely, on the question, Have stars a soul ? Isidore tells that it is wont to be asked, as the holy Augustine says, whether Sun and Moon and Stars are nothing but material bodies, or have spirits of their own, which rule their course as animals are animated—the phrase is Isidore's—by an *anima* or soul. Some such cause there must be of their observed conduct, he thinks, for they move in such wonderful order and proportion that they never go wrong.

Bede's treatise on Thunderings, if it be Bede's, is very remarkable, both for what it contains and for what the author fears he may have to suffer for acceding to a friend's request to write it. Of Thunder itself he and Isidore had of course written. Bede declares (ch. 28) that Thunderings are generated by the clashings of clouds, driven by the winds which are conceived among them, this violent clashing producing a noise like that of chariots rattling over the stones as they rush forth from the stables. The treatise on the Presages of Thunder is a very different affair. It is full of the erroneous views of the time, which an age of more knowledge calls superstitious, a fate the future may have in store for a good many of the views of the present time, to specify or indicate which, in this volume, might raise the " howls " which Bede felt that his treatise would be sure to raise. In order to shelter himself so far as he could against hostile " howls," he keeps himself personally clear, in a very marked and curious manner, of responsibility for any one of the statements of presage which appear in his book. His anxiety is evidently real and great. He is clear that the work is open to the " howls " and blasphemics of hostile critics, who may assert that he had thought out and uttered new presages of events in a diabolic spirit ; or puffed up with dwelling on the art of magic and not illuminated by the grace of the Holy Spirit ; or in a mere rhetorical spirit, as though his friend Herefrid, at whose request the treatise was written, had bid him foretell the future with prophetic mouth. Three points should be noticed. He tells Herefrid that he has translated the work into Latin, which suggested that he is putting into his book the common sayings of the people of the time. He does not name any one of the persons whom he describes in extravagantly complimentary terms ; in our flippant times they might well be pungently ironical. And he does not say by whom he is so sure to be abused for writing the treatise. Herefrid was probably his friend at Lindisfarne, not a member of Jarrow, for he begs in his defence the shield of the prayers and the anchor of the holy speech of Herefrid and his faithful followers. There is evidently something serious in the background, at which it is more or less idle to guess.

The actual request addressed to him by Herefrid was, that he would collect the opinions of learned writers on the events which thunder foretold according to the day of the week, the month, etc., of its occurrence. He gives the received presages for the four winds, the twelve months, and the seven days of the week ; and in every case, without exception, he expressly states that he only gives an account of what others have discovered. The shifts to which he is put to vary his phrases are amusing. Twice, and twice only, he contents himself with the remark, "as they say." For thunder with an east wind, which signifies " the copious effusion of human blood," he quotes " the traditions of subtle philosophers." For thunder with a west wind, signifying "a very bad pestilence," he quotes "wise men in their exceeding subtlety actively investigating the presages of events." For thunder with a south wind, signifying "a great destruction of the inhabitants of the seas," he quotes "philosophers of sagacious disposition, who, by intellectual study and great prudence, have noted the presages of events." For thunder with a north wind, signifying "the death of the worst sinners, viz. pagans and perverts," he relies upon "the subtlety of those who have taken in hand to investigate the causes of events." Through the twelve months of the year he rings the changes on the activity, subtlety, and sagacity of the philosophers. By the time he comes to the end of the seven days of the week he is in extreme straits for something fresh to say. For thunder on Friday, signifying "the slaughter of the king," or "a mighty war with much slaughter," he quotes, "the noble teachers who almost from the cradle have been fed and nourished on the breast of maternal Philosophy, their intellects adorned by most careful and acute contemplation, and the varied flowers of philosophic subtlety." And for thunder on Saturday, signifying either "a mighty pestilence," or "a very great war," he quotes the "philosophers, who with practised knowledge, according to the excessive ardour of their most sagacious disposition, have attempted to discern by subtle intellectual speculation, the causes and presages of events." The whole treatise might be a satire upon the folly of those who believed that natural phenomena were prophetic of remarkable events in such a manner that their presages could be tabulated. The fact that some of the coincident presages are of the most contradictory character, would seem to point in the same direction. Thus, if thunder

came on one of the Tuesdays in January or November,
it signified, by coming on a Tuesday, most copious
abundance of fruits of the earth, and by coming in
January, that fruits of the earth would fail, or in
November, that there would be barrenness of everything. And the presages are so arranged that there
are only twenty-nine days in the whole year on which
thunder can mean anything really good, and on those
twenty-nine days it is subject to the presages of the
wind, which, as will be seen from the wind portents
given above, might considerably discount the amount
of good. It seems difficult to suppose that the writer,
whether Bede or not, believed the presages which he
describes. He must have known that observation
failed to support the tradition. It is very unlike the
simple direct character which Bede's known works
enable us to realise in him, that the writer should give
no hint of his sense that the presages practically failed
to come true. The treatise is not mentioned in Bede's
own list of his works, and those who love him cannot
bring themselves to believe that he wrote it.

CHAPTER XIII

THE COMMENTARIES AND HOMILIES OF BEDE

His method as a preacher—His method as a commentator—An
example from Acts ii.—The Song of Solomon—Ambiguities of
the Latin language—Bede's dedications of his commentaries—
Bishop Acca—Celibacy—Answers to Nothelm—The wood-
worm—The lion in the pit—The Virgin Mary—The Two Sacraments—Ælfric's homily—Bede outside his monastery—Anointing with oil—Confession—Purgatory—The vision of Drythelm—
Figurative interpretations—Bede sung as a heretic—The parable
of the Good Samaritan.

THE Homilies of Bede which have been preserved
are in one sense disappointing ; they throw little or
no light upon the state of society in his time. There
is no approach to anything at all resembling the
personal interest of which the sermons of Chrysostom
are so full. There is no rebuking of notorious sinners,
no sarcastic scourging of fashionable follies and
vices. The reason of this is obvious, even if we
overlook the difference between the two men. Chrysostom preached in a great metropolis, full of luxury
and dissipation. Bede read theological lectures in a
quiet monastery, where he seems to have had no
vices to rebuke, or where, if vices there were, he
rebuked them tenderly in private. His Homilies
reflect the quietness and confidence of the faithful
Christian student, addressing a body of his brethren in
good works and in a God-fearing life.

Like others of the early preachers, he supports his

statements with texts of Scripture more often than is usual in the present time. The Bible was of course very much less familiar to ordinary people then than it is now ; indeed it was not familiar at all. There was instruction in Christianity to be found in the quotation of texts possibly novel to some hearers even in a monastery which was a famous seat of learning. Many points of doctrine were much less assured then ; they needed support from every quarter where it could be found, and no support was so good as that which was derived from apposite texts of Scripture.

There is a singular absence of rhetorical attempts in these Homilies. It would seem never to have been Bede's intention to work upon the feelings of his hearers by impassioned words. He said what he meant to say clearly and simply, and he left it to its own inherent force to make its way. It would be difficult to find, in the sermons of Bede, passages dwelling in vehement terms upon the horrors of hell and the happiness of heaven. Threats and profuse promises are no more parts of his teaching than are invective and sarcasm parts of his style.

As a rule, Bede took a passage of some considerable length, one of the lessons for the day, for example, and went through it verse by verse, expounding rather than preaching. He frequently insisted upon the special doctrines which centre round the Incarnation, such as the two natures of Christ, and upon the relation of the Persons in the Blessed Trinity. Such themes suited him better than the more practical subjects which are fitted for those preachers who are conversant with the world and have a mixed and secular congregation to address. It is to be feared that many of Bede's sermons would be stigmatized in these days as "doctrinal," or, by those who say more distinctly what they mean, as "dull."

There is very little indeed of criticism of the text in Bede's sermons. He takes it as he finds it, and he expounds it. This is only what might be expected in those early days ; but from a theological student and scholar like Bede we might, perhaps, have expected more reference to the Greek text and to the manner in which the Latin text in use represented it. In some cases where the Greek has a special emphasis which the Latin has not, Bede's remarks take no account of the emphasis in the original. As an example of his textual criticism—there are very few examples indeed in his sermons—the passage in St. Mark "He came into the parts of Dalmanutha" may be cited. On this Bede remarks that St. Matthew has "Magdala." He thinks that the same place is intended by the evangelists, for "many codices" have "Magedan" in St. Mark instead of "Dalmanutha." It may be noticed as typical of Bede's method of preaching that he makes no point of the emphatic *ye* in John iii. 7, "Marvel not that I said unto thee, *ye* must be born again," though the emphasis of the word is brought out in the Latin text as well as in the Greek original.

Bede's method as a commentator was very different from his method as a preacher. His commentaries are voluminous. Those on the Old Testament fill 1338 octavo pages, and those on the New Testament 1250. In these days of critical study of the Holy Scriptures in the original languages, it is interesting to observe the manner in which he used the Greek of the New Testament in writing his commentaries. The Bible which was in the hands of his readers and hearers was

of course the Latin Bible. Bede did not treat this as
later writers treated it, as being sufficient in itself. He
was careful to point out omissions, and to warn his
readers against mistranslations into which the Latin
might lead them if they were not warned. Thus, to
take half a chapter as an example, on Acts ii. 20,
" the sun shall be turned into darkness," he tells
them that though the Latin might suggest " dark-
nesses," it was only because the Latin word had no
proper singular ; the Greek word, which he gives in
his commentary, shows that the correct translation
is " darkness." On Acts ii. 23, " Him, being delivered
by the determinate counsel and foreknowledge of
God, ye have taken," where the Latin omits " ye
have taken," he informs his readers that a very important word is omitted in their Latin version, very
important because the Jews had the choice between
the robber and Jesus, and they *took* Him. Again,
in the 30th verse of the same chapter, " that of the
fruit of his loins, according to the flesh, He would
raise up Christ to sit on his throne," where the Latin
omits " according to the flesh, He would raise up
Christ," he points out that there is more in the Greek
than in the Latin, and tells them what should be
added. Similarly in verses 33 and 34 he notes differences between the Latin and the Greek. On verse 41
he remarks that while the Latin text on which he was
commenting seemed to say that all who gladly received
the word were baptized, another manuscript gave more
correctly the true force of the Greek, limiting the statement to the particular individuals who heard the word
on that occasion.

The uncial MS. of the Acts known as E is believed
to have been the actual manuscript used by Bede. It

has a Latin rendering (not the Vulgate) in addition to the Greek text. It was given to the University of Oxford by Archbishop Laud, whence its name *Laudiensis*.

Alcuin's quotations from Solomon's Song, the Song of Songs, *Canticum Canticorum*, are numerous. Its impassioned beauty of language and joyousness of thought appealed powerfully to the secular side of his complex temperament. How much of his attachment to the book is due to Bede we cannot know. It is sufficient to say that Bede's Commentary on its eight chapters fills 218 octavo pages, a bulk exceeding the amount of commentary on much longer books of Scripture.

The preface to this Commentary is specially interesting to us because it warns the reader to be very cautious how he read a work on the same subject by Julian of Campania, Bishop of Celanum (?). This Julian was a very able and learned man, with a pleasing and powerful style, who began his manhood in affectionate intimacy with Augustine of Hippo and Paulinus of Nola, the latter of whom wrote an epithalamium on his marriage when he held the office of Reader. He afterwards became very earnestly in favour of Pelagianism, on which account Bede describes him as the sharpest impugner of the Grace of God next to Pelagius. He played the largest part in the controversy under more than one Pope and through a long series of years, apparently retaining his charm of manner and his deep earnestness; but evidently writing many things he had better not have written, especially in his treatise *De Amore*, On Love, in which he made so much use of the love-song of Solomon.

On one point Bede was very careful to warn the

readers of his commentaries. He constantly pointed out the ambiguities caused by the want of an article in the Latin. Thus on Acts i. 6, " Wilt thou at this time restore again the kingdom to Israel ? "(*restitues regnum Israel ?*) the Latin gives no hint to enable a reader to determine whether he shall translate it " restore the kingdom of Israel," or " restore the kingdom to Israel." Bede tells his readers that the Greek article decides the question in favour of the latter. Another source of ambiguity in the Latin is found in the fact that some words are the same in all genders. Thus in the words *cum Maria matre Jesu et fratribus eius*, in the 14th verse of the same chapter, "with Mary, mother of Jesus, and His brethren," the Latin leaves it open to any one to translate " and her brethren," against which translation Bede gives a warning. And so, too, to take one more example from the same part of the Scripture, in Acts ii. 3, " there appeared unto them cloven tongues, as of fire " (*linguae tanquam ignis*), the Latin may be rendered " cloven tongues, as it were fire," where Bede informs them that in the Greek there is no ambiguity, the form of the genitive being different from that of the nominative, whereas in the Latin they are the same. An instance of another kind is found in the next verse, " began to speak in other tongues " here the Latin has " in various tongues," but Bede corrects the translation, and says that it should be " other." From these numerous examples, taken from so small a portion of Scripture, it may be imagined how careful and close was Bede's study of such manuscripts as he possessed. We feel that we are in the hands of a man who, at least so far as the desire to be accurate is concerned, may be trusted either as commentator or as historian.

We find some interesting evidences of the working of Bede's mind in his prefaces to the Commentaries on the several books of Scripture. We may take as an example his dedication of the Commentary on the first book of Samuel, which he heads with the title " An allegorical Exposition." It is addressed to Acca, the Bishop of Hexham, one of the two noble cross-shafts at either end of whose grave we have in our time rescued from the various places where its fragments used to rest and have set up in the Dorter at Durham. He addresses Acca as the best-loved and most desirable of all the bishops then living. It is evident from this and other like sayings of Bede, that he had a very warm affection for him as a man, and a very high respect for him as a bishop. This makes still more unintelligible the fact that Acca was driven from his bishopric in 732, and as we have seen, Ecgbert consecrated Frithubert as his successor in 734. It cannot have been any grave misdoing on his part which caused the loss of his diocese, for when he died in 740 he was buried at the east end of the church at Hexham and two stone crosses of very large size and of wonderfully skilful carving were set up at the ends of the grave.

To Acca Bede wrote on a very personal line in this particular dedication. In explanation of his reason for giving an allegorical turn to his commentary, he points out that the man Elkanah had two wives, Hannah and Phenenna, the Septuagint form of Peninnah. " Now," he puts it to Acca, " we two are by the custom of ecclesiastic life far from the embrace of a wife and remain celibate. We therefore are specially bound to extract some allegorical meaning from this fact of the two wives, which shall chasten, instruct, and console

us." This accounted for Bede's determination to make
his commentary allegorical. Elkanah, one man with
the two wives, was the Redeemer and the Ruler of
Synagogue and Church alike. Peninnah, with the ten
children, was the Synagogue with the ten commandments and the numerous progeny, Hannah was the
Church, desolate and in long waiting. Elkanah's
comforting appeal to her, Am I not dearer to thee
than ten children ? was the appeal of the Church,
more loving and more loved than the Synagogue.

In his dedication of the Commentaries on the book
of Genesis to Acca, he first states his authorities, from
whom he has obtained the materials for his two books.
They were Basil of Cæsarea, Ambrose of Milan, and
Augustine of Hippo. Their works were so copious and
high (*alta*) that only the rich could acquire them, and
so deep (*profunda*) that only the learned could understand them. Therefore it was that his holiness had
bid him pluck from the loveliest plains of this wide-
flowering Paradise (park) that which might seem to
suffice for weaker brethren.

We have a quaint dedication of answers to thirty
questions sent to Bede by Nothelm the Arch-priest of
London, that is, of St. Paul's. Nothelm has been
mentioned already as a main source of Bede's knowledge of the affairs of the earliest period of the Southern
Province. These thirty questions Bede describes as
the graver questions among many sent to him, the
others having been answered briefly in a schedule
already sent to Nothelm. It must be allowed that a
good many of the thirty are not in themselves of a
grave character. Bede clearly saw that this was so,
and he takes great pains to explain away any hint of it.
He tells Nothelm that there were very many passages

more obscure, but he knows that a man who has read and understood the explanations of great writers often finds himself doubtful about less obscure passages which the great writers had not thought it necessary to explain.

An example of a laboriously patient explanation may be found in the greatly disputed passage 2 Samuel xxiii. 8, where in place of the words "Adino the Eznite" the Vulgate has the statement that the Tachmonite was like a very tender wood-worm. Bede begins his answer by mentioning that in the parallel passage 1 Chronicles xi. 11, the name of the hero is given. He was not concerned with the passage beyond the question of Nothelm. This was fortunate for him. If any one wishes to feel really puzzled, he can obtain his wish by reading these two passages in the Authorised and Revised English Versions, in the Latin Versions, and in the Septuagint, to say nothing of the several Hebrew readings. The passage in 2 Samuel has been correctly called one of the most disputed passages in the Bible. Of this Bede knew nothing. He called attention to the parallel passage, and then simply answered Nothelm's question. He explains this curious description of a mighty man of valour by pointing out that the most tender wood-worms can in the course of time so eat away the substance of the very strongest beam of wood that it becomes rotten. Jerome arrived at the "very tender wood-worm" from the words rendered "Adino the Eznite" in the Authorised Version, "Eznite" being near the Hebrew word for "wood."

In 2 Samuel xxiii. 20, he has to explain for Nothelm the statement that Benaiah went down and slew a lion in a pit in time of snow, where the Vulgate has *cisterna* in the place of " a pit. How this was done, Bede says, Josephus tells more clearly. The hole was not very deep, and in time of much snow it was filled up and the surface was level with the whole area of snow-covered ground. The lion was passing over it, unconscious of the danger, and fell in. Finding himself caught he set up a mighty roar, which brought people to see what was the matter. Benaiah came among others, and seeing what it was he jumped down into the hole, attacked the lion with his sword, and slew him.

He speaks in terms of the highest respect of the Virgin Mary, as blessed above all women. But he goes no further than that. His manner of speaking of her may be gathered from a remark which he makes in preaching on one of the festivals in her honour. A most excellent and salutary practice, he says, has long been established in the Church, that her hymn (he is speaking of the *Magnificat*) is sung by all every day at vespers. The object and use of this practice he believes to be that the continual commemoration of our Lord's Incarnation may incite us to deeper devotion, and the recollection of the example set by His mother may strengthen us in virtue. He is careful to explain that the expression " first-born son "—" she brought forth her first-born son "—in no way implies that there were other children born later ; and he maintains the theory of the perpetual virginity of the Virgin Mary so strenuously that he prays God to avert from his hearers the blasphemy of holding otherwise. Of " Mariolatry " there is no sign in Bede's Homilies. In the Ecclesiastical History, Bede relates that Bishop Wilfrith was told by the Archangel Michael, in a vision, that the prayers of his disciples and the intercession of the Virgin Mary had moved the Lord to grant Wilfrith a recovery from a dangerous illness.

There are frequent references to the two great Sacraments of Christ, Baptism and the Supper of the Lord. But there is a rather marked absence of any homily on one or other of these subjects specially. It would have been very interesting, and it might have been instructive, to read what Bede thought and taught in detail on these cardinal points of Christian faith and practice. His method of homiletic exposition was such that his views were stated rather incidentally and in passing, than in any very full and formal manner we find nothing like an elaborate treatise on these and similar points. His mention of the validity of Baptism in the name of the Holy Trinity, by whomsoever administered, is a good example of this. He is preaching on the visit of Nicodemus to Christ, and in commenting on the words of the master in Israel, " How can a man be born when he is old ? " he remarks that the same is true of spiritual birth, a man cannot be born again. " No one who has been baptized in the name of the Holy Trinity, even though by a heretic, a schismatic, or an evil person, may be rebaptized by good Catholics, lest the invocation of so great a name be annulled." In the case of a notoriously ignorant baptizing priest, Bishop John of Hexham had had to order him to desist from baptisms, and repeated the rite. Passing allusions to the necessity of Baptism will be mentioned when we come to speak of Bede's figurative interpretation of the parable of the Good Samaritan, and of the miracle of the Four Thousand. In another place, speaking on the words of St. Mark vii. 33, " He spit, and touched his tongue," Bede says that from this passage a custom prevalent in his time grew up, the priests touching in like manner the nostrils and ears of those whom they were about to present for Baptism, saying at the same time the word Ephphatha. The touching of the nostrils he understood to be a sign that thenceforward they should be a "sweet savour of Christ" (2 Cor. ii. 15) ; and he urges all who had received the rite of consecration by Baptism, and all who were about to receive it at the forthcoming season of Easter, to avoid all occasion of falling back into that from which Baptism washed them. In this passage he speaks at some length on the subject of Baptism, and its cleansing power ; and it is perhaps rather remarkable that he makes no reference to the question of original sin. In another homily he repeats his reference to the practice of baptizing at Easter ; "rightly do we on this night"—the commencement of the festival of Easter—"hallow to the one true God in the font of regeneration the new people of His adoption brought out of the spiritual Egypt."

To the Sacrament of the Supper of the Lord the references in the Homilies are frequent and most reverential. English readers not familiar with the usual names of things in early times must not be surprised to find that Bede uses the ordinary name *Missa*, the Latin word represented by "Mass," to describe the celebration of this Sacrament. In King Alfred's time, "mass-priest" was the accepted designation of officiating clergy in Priest's Orders. In speaking of this Sacrament, Bede uses stronger expressions than he might have done had he known what controversies would rage round almost every word that could be used in connection with it. He uses words well known in Eucharistic controversy, to a greater extent than he uses controversial words in speaking of Baptism. And the reason for this is clear. Our Lord Himself used words as strong as any that can be used, when He said, " This is My Body," " This is My Blood "; and any language framed on these two statements must seem strong, however free it may be in fact and in intention from any element of materialism. This is not true of the language used in baptismal controversy. But while it is true that Bede uses words which a cautious writer of the present day might avoid using in public utterances, because of the misconceptions to which his use of them might possibly give rise, it is at least as true that we search in vain for any sign of a belief on Bede's part in the doctrine of transubstantiation. It is so well known that transubstantiation did not appear as a doctrine till long after Bede's time, that it may seem unnecessary to remark that no sign of it is found in Bede. Since, however, some of his expressions have a recognised force in modern controversy, it is not out of place to preface a mention of them by some such caution.

In the passage quoted above from Bede's Homily on the Eve of the Resurrection, after mentioning the Easter rite of baptism, he proceeds as follows :— " and rightly we celebrate the solemn Mass, we offer to God for the advance of our salvation the holy Body and precious Blood of our Lamb, by whom we have been redeemed from our sins." And in another place, speaking of the " manger " of Bethlehem, he says, " He chose the manger, to which animals came to feed, as His resting-place, foreshadowing the refreshing of all the faithful, by the mysteries of His

Incarnation, on the table[1] of the holy altar." These are the words of a man who had not been taught by sad experience what mischief may be supposed to lurk under harmless expressions when once they have been appropriated by one side or another in a controversy. Against them we may set such words of his as the following, words which no one who held the views afterwards known as the doctrine of transubstantiation could have used " The time of our Passover is at hand. Let us come holy to the Altar of the Lord, not to eat the flesh of a lamb, but to receive the sacred mysteries of our Redeemer. Let no one who abides still in death presume to receive the mysteries of life. Let us pray that He may deign to come to our feast, to illumine us with His presence, to hallow His own gifts to us." And in another passage he tells his hearers that the sacrifices under the new covenant are spiritual :—" The two altars in the Temple signify the two covenants. The first was the altar of burnt-offerings, covered with brass, for offering victims and sacrifices. This was the Old Covenant. The second was at the entrance of the Holy of Holies, covered with gold, for burning incense. This was the inward and more perfect grace of the New Covenant." Something to the same effect is a passage on the priesthood after the order of Melchisedech :—" Melchisedech, a priest of the most high God, offered to God bread and wine long before the times of the priesthood of the Law. And our Redeemer is called a Priest after the order of Melchisedech, because after the priesthood of the Law had come to an end, He established a similar

---

[1] The " table of the altar," *tabula altaris*, was the specially consecrated part of the surface of the altar on which the consecrated elements were placed at the celebration.

sacrifice by offering the mystery of His Body and Blood." Again, in preaching on the words, " *Behold the Lamb of God that taketh away the sins of the world,*" in conjunction with the verse from the Apocalypse, " *Who hath loved us and washed us from our sins in His blood,*" Bede speaks in words which set his views before us in a clear and satisfactory manner. " He washed us from our sins in His blood, not only when He gave His blood on the cross for us, or when each one of us by the mystery of His holy Passion was washed clean by baptism of water, but He also daily takes away the sins of the world. He washes us from our sins daily in His Blood, when the memory of the same blessed Passion is renewed at the altar, when the creature of bread and wine is transferred into the sacrament of His flesh and blood by the ineffable sanctification of the Spirit ; and thus His Flesh and Blood is not poured and slain by the hands of unbelievers to their own destruction, but is taken by the mouth of believers to their own salvation. The paschal lamb in the Law rightly shows forth the figure of this, the lamb which once freed the people from their Egyptian slavery, and in memory of that freeing was wont year by year to sanctify by its offering the same people, until He should come to whom such a victim bare witness ; and being offered to the Father for us as a victim and a sweet-smelling savour, after He had offered the lamb, He transferred to the creature of bread and wine the mystery of His Passion, being made a priest for ever after the order of Melchisedech."

It may be worth while to quote on this point the words of a learned divine who is supposed to have presided over the Anglo-Saxon Church two centuries and a half after Bede's death, Ælfric,[1] Archbishop of Canterbury. " When the Lord said, *He that eateth My flesh and drinketh My blood hath everlasting life*, He bade not His disciples to eat the Body wherewith He was enclosed nor to drink that Blood which He shed for us ; but He meant that holy morsel which is in a ghostly way His Body and Blood ; and he that tasteth it with believing heart hath everlasting life." Thus it would appear that neither early nor late in the history of the Church of England in Saxon times were erroneous views held by the chief divines on this cardinal point of Christian doctrine.

It has already been remarked that there is very little indeed of personal allusion in Bede's sermons. There is not, however, an entire absence of such allusion. In a remarkable sermon on the text, " Every one that hath forsaken houses,   shall receive an hundredfold," Bede refers to the high esteem in which those who professed the religious life were held by those who remained in the world, so that they actually did receive much more than they surrendered when they gave up their property and worldly prospects. The "hundred" he takes to be not a mere numeral but the symbol of perfection. He who gives up human possessions and affections will find an abundance of the faithful eager to receive him, to put their houses and goods at his disposal, to love him with a more perfect affection than wife or mother or child. He reminded those whom he addressed that they had practical proof of this. When

---

[1] There was an Ælfric Archbishop of Canterbury 995–1005, and an Ælfric Archbishop of York 1023–1051. If the homilist was one of these two, he was probably of Canterbury. The homilies were dedicated to Siric, the Archbishop of Canterbury who preceded him. It is, however, not certain that the homilist was of higher rank than Abbat when he wrote the homily.

they passed on rare occasions beyond the bounds of the monastery, they found welcome and support wherever they went. In another homily he speaks of the use of the intellect in a manner which shows how highly he estimated intellectual gifts, and how seriously he felt that he himself devoted to God the hours of study. The text was, " Wist ye not that I must be about My Father's business," or, as Bede completed the expression left indefinite in the Greek, " in My Father's house." This, Bede says, refers not only to the material temple in which Christ was, but also to that temple of the intellect in which He was exercising Himself when He heard the doctors and asked them questions, a temple constructed for the eternal praise of God.

We find Bede's views on the anointing with oil which was afterwards changed into the doctrine of Extreme Unction, in his remarks on the Epistle of James, v. 14-20. The Gospels, he says, show us that the Apostles acted as Christians are there bidden to act. In his own time the custom prevailed that sick men were anointed with oil by the priests, with prayer accompanying, that they might be healed. This is exactly not the purpose of Extreme Unction. As Pope Innocent had written, not priests only but any Christians might *use* the oil for this purpose, in their own or their relations' need. But only bishops might *make* the oil, for the words " anointing him with oil in the name of the Lord " implied two things, the one that the name of the Lord was to be invoked when the oil was used, the other that the oil was to be " oil in the name of the Lord," *i.e.* made and consecrated in the name of the Lord. Of Confession he proceeds to say that many are in sickness and near death because of their sins. If such confess to the priests of the Church, and earnestly set about to amend, their sins shall be dismissed.

The views of Bede's time, and of Bede himself, on Purgatory, are clearly given in the account of a vision in the Fifth Book of the Ecclesiastical History. We have already seen in the life of Benedict Biscop some parts of this vision,[1] but we have not seen all. In addition to the valley one side whereof was burning heat and the other was piercing cold, and to the flaming pit, the place of torment, the man to whom the vision or trance was vouchsafed saw also the abodes of blessedness of two degrees. After passing the place of utmost torment, his guide and he came to a wall whose height and length were infinite. Presently, by what means he knew not, they were on the top of the wall. At their feet lay a vast and joyous plain, full of so sweet a fragrance of vernal flowers as drove away the vile odours of the pit with which his senses had been impregnated. The light was clearer than the day, more splendid than the sun. On the plain were innumerable congregations of white-robed men, and crowds seated by companies rejoicing. Not unnaturally he thought within himself that these were the plains of Heaven. But his companion, knowing his thoughts, answered him, " Not this is the Kingdom of Heaven."

And then, as he moved on, there dawned upon him a yet fairer and more splendid effulgence, from out of which proceeded the sweetest strains of singers and a fragrancy so marvellous as far to transcend the exquisite fragrance of the former abode. His guide allowed him but to perceive these heavenly delights and then led him back to the lesser degree of bliss. Standing

[1] See page 120.

there, he expounded to him what he had seen. The valley of overpowering heat and cold was the place where the souls of those were tried and punished who had delayed to confess their sins and amend their lives, but who, having at the last moment confessed and repented, should enter into the kingdom of heaven at the day of judgment. Many of these, the guide declared, were so aided by the prayers and alms and fastings of living men, and especially by masses, that they would be released even before the day of judgment. The flowery plain on which he had seen the happy bands of youth bright and fair, this was the place to which the souls of those were sent who, dying in good works, were yet not sufficiently perfect to pass at once to the plains of Heaven. At the day of judgment, they would pass to the higher glory.

It will be seen that while the latter class of souls represented men whose lives had been almost perfect, even those who were tormented in the valley had repented before death. It appears that for those who died without repentance, there was no hope from prayers or alms or fasting, not even from masses. A similar lesson is taught by another striking vision of which Bede tells. When Bede was about thirty years of age, there was in Mercia a man high in the military service of King Coenred, but he was a man of evil life. When he was very ill, indeed on his death-bed, the king came to exhort him to repent. The unhappy man said that he would amend his life if he recovered, but his companions should never have it to say that he repented under the fear of death. The king came to him again when he was much worse, and again exhorted him. It was too late, the dying man cried ; he had seen a vision, and it was too late. There had come into his room two youths very fair to look upon ; the one sat down at his head the other at his feet. They produced a little book, very beautiful, but exceedingly small, and gave it him to read. He found written therein all the good deeds he had done ; and behold they were very few and inconsiderable. They took back the book, and spake never a word. Then on a sudden there rushed in an army of malignant spirits, horrid to see, and they filled the whole house where he was. One among them, who seemed to be chief in horror and in place, brought out a book of terrible appearance and intolerable heaviness, and bade a satellite give it to the dying man to read. Therein was written, alas, all that ever he had done ill, in word or deed or thought. Then the prince of the demons said to the white-robed youths who sat at the head and the foot of the victim, " Why do ye sit here, whereas ye know of a surety that the man is ours ? " And they said, " It is true ; take him and cast him on to the heap of your damnation " ; and having so said, they departed. Then there arose two of the worst spirits, having forks in their hands, and they struck him, the one in the head and the other in the feet. Such was the vision, but the wounds, the desperate man said, were real ; they were spreading to meet one another in the midst of his body ; and so soon as they should meet he would die, and the demons were at hand to drag him to hell. On which Bede, writing five-and-twenty years after, remarks, that the sinner was now suffering without avail in eternal torments that penance which he had refused to suffer for a brief period with its fruit unto forgiveness of sins.

The feature in Bede's Homilies which would probably seem the most prominent to a reader not very familiar with early compositions of the kind, is the somewhat far-fetched figurative interpretation in which he constantly indulges his imagination. To take first an instance of such interpretation which bears on a singular charge of heresy brought against him. The six water-pots at the marriage in Cana of Galilee were the six ages of the world down to the first showing forth of our Lord's divinity. The first was the age of Abel ; the second commenced with the Flood ; the third with the call of Abraham ; the fourth with David ; the fifth was the captivity ; the sixth was the birth of our Lord, His circumcision, presentation, and subjection to His parents. In connection with this subject Bede wrote a treatise, " On the Ages of the World." In an epistle to Plegwin, a monk of Hexham, he refers to the charge of heresy of which mention has been made. Plegwin's messenger had come to him with pleasant greetings, but he had reported one dreadful thing, namely, that Plegwin had heard that Bede was sung among heretics by wanton rustics in their cups. Bede confesses that he was horrorstruck on hearing this. He turned pale. He asked, of what heresy was he thus accused. The messenger replied, " that Christ had not come in the flesh in the sixth age of the world." He breathed again. That Christ had come in the flesh no priest of Christ's Church could be supposed to have denied. That He came in the sixth age was another matter, and Bede traced the report to one of Plegwin's monks to whom he had shown his book " On the Ages of the World." In this book he made it clear that the fifth age ended with the Incarnation, with which also the sixth began. Thus the question to which of the two ages the Incarnation was to be assigned might be resolved in either way. He had himself assigned it to the sixth age, both in the book and in a homily, so that the report was a calumny. What a curious picture of the age is this singing of heretics by rustics in their cups. It may remind us of the use made of popular songs by Arius in spreading his views and discrediting his orthodox opponents.

That conjugal chastity is good, widowed continence better, virgin perfection best of all, Bede proves as follows, apparently on the assumption that those things which are symbolized by the earliest parts of our Lord's life on earth are more holy than those symbolized by parts more remote from His birth. " Jesus was born of a virgin ; therefore virgin perfection is best of all. He was soon afterwards blessed by a widow ; therefore widowed continence is next after virgin perfection. Later in His life He was present at a marriage feast ; therefore conjugal chastity comes third only in order of merit."

In his Homily on the Feeding the Four Thousand, he remarks that the seven baskets signified the sevenfold gifts of the Spirit. And he proceeds to say that baskets made of rushes and palm-leaves were employed, to signify that as the rush has its roots in water, so the Christian is rooted in the fountain of life ; and as the palm-leaf is the symbol of a conqueror, so the Christian is a conqueror, and more than a conqueror. The two fishes were added to show by means of these creatures of the water that without the water of Baptism man cannot live.

The parable of the good Samaritan affords as good an example as any of Bede's figurative interpretations. The " certain man " is the human race in Adam.

Jerusalem is the heavenly city of peace, from which Adam went down to " Jericho," that word (meaning " the moon," according to some early commentators) signifying the world with its changes and its wanderings. The " thieves " were the devil and his angels, who stripped him by taking from him the glory of immortality and the garb of innocence. His wounds were the blows of sin. He was left only " half dead," because while man was deprived of the gift of eternal life, there yet was left him sense to discern God. The Priest and Levite were the priesthood and ministry of the Old Covenant. The Samaritan, or "guardian "—Samaria is supposed to have taken its name from its admirable position as a place of observation, or watch-tower—was the Lord Jesus. Binding up the wounds was restraining the sins of men. Pouring in oil was saying, " The kingdom of heaven is at hand " ; pouring in wine was saying, " Every tree that bringeth not forth good fruit is hewn down." The beast of burden was the flesh in which He deigned to come to us. The inn was the Church on earth, where pilgrims are refreshed on their way to heaven ; the bringing to the inn is Baptism. The " next day " is after the resurrection of the Lord. The two pence are the two Testaments, said to be given to the innkeeper then, because there it was that He opened their eyes that they understood the Scriptures. The innkeeper had something over—" whatsoever thou spendest more "—which he did not receive in the two pence, something beyond the requirements of the two Testaments. This Bede illustrates by such passages as " Now concerning virgins I have no commandment of the Lord, yet I give my judgment " and again, " The Lord hath ordained that they which preach the Gospel should live of the Gospel ; but I have used none of these things." To those who obeyed these " counsels of perfection," who did more in such matters than the Scriptures actually required them to do, the debtor would come again, and would pay them, when the Lord came and said, " Because thou hast been faithful over a few things, I will make thee ruler over many things ; enter thou into the joy of thy Lord."

The Homilies contain incidental allusions which throw light upon some of the ceremonies of the time. In this way, for example, we learn that for the anniversary of the dedication day of the church of Jarrow, they adorned the walls of the church, increased the number of lights and of lections and the amount of singing, and passed the previous night in joyful vigils.

The best means of giving the English reader an idea of a sermon to an educated audience in England in Bede's time, will be to reproduce one of his Homilies entire in an English dress.

CHAPTER XIV

A SERMON BY BEDE

Collections of Homilies—Two books of Bede's Homilies—Manuscript evidence—The Text—" Whom do men say that I, the Son of Man, am ? "

A LARGE number of sermons, written by Bede or at least attributed to him, have been preserved. Some of these are certainly not Bede's, but there are fifty which may definitely be taken as his. They were not intended for a mixed congregation, being addressed to his brethren in the monastery. They consist for the most part of a running exposition of passages of Scripture, seldom elaborated and almost invariably brief. On one occasion he apologises for having preached a long sermon ; but the sermon in which the apology occurs could be read without any haste in twenty-eight minutes. The sermon of which a translation is now given, as a specimen of the more practical of Bede's sermons, would take about eighteen minutes to deliver in the Latin, reading slowly.

There is a fine manuscript, in large quarto, which Dr. Giles found in the Library of Boulogne and assigned to the eighth or ninth century, that is, possibly to Bede's own century, containing fifty of his Homilies. It appears from Bede's own list of his works that he issued two books of Homilies on the Gospel. It would appear that each contained twenty-five, and that the fifty at Boulogne, the manuscript having belonged to the monastery of St. Bertin at St. Omer, are the two books in one, and are to be taken as indubitably his. The usual collections of Homilies by other preachers contain fifty-two, as though one for each Sunday in the year, but of Bede's fifty, only ten were written for Sundays. In the collected works of Bede in the editions of Basle and Cologne there are nearly two hundred Homilies attributed to him, very many of them, as has been said, evidently not his.

The occasion of the sermon selected to illustrate Bede's homiletic style was the Nativity of St. Peter and St. Paul. The passages of Scripture chosen for comment were the parallel passages, St. Matthew xvi. 13–19 ; St. Mark viii. 27–29 ; St. Luke ix. 18–21 ; being the passages containing the Confession of Peter "Thou art the Christ," the passage of St. Matthew including the promise "Thou art Peter," etc. The whole sermon is devoted to the particular occasion in the Gospel history which provides the text, and as St. Peter is the actor on that occasion the whole sermon is about him. Naturally there are no gospel occasions or texts dealing with St. Paul. The sermon which precedes this in the printed list is on the Vigil of St. Peter and St. Paul, and in that sermon St. Paul is dealt with, the text (St. John xxi. 15–19) containing words capable of a more general application, "This He spake, signifying by what death He should die." On those words Bede founded his remarks on "the Apostle" *par excellence*, St. Paul.

The sermon on the Nativity of the Apostles Peter and Paul is as follows :—

The holy Gospel which has been read to you, my brethren, is worthy of your utmost attention, and should be kept in constant remembrance. For it commends to us perfect faith, and shows the strength of such perfect faith against all temptations. If you would know how one ought to believe in Christ, what can be more clear than this which Peter says to Him, " Thou art the Christ, the Son of the living God " ? If you would hear of what avail is this belief, what can be more plain than this which the Lord says of the Church to be builded upon Him, " The gates of hell shall not prevail against it " ? These points will be more fully considered hereafter, each in its own place. I will now proceed to the explanation of the whole passage, taking the sentences in their natural order.

And first, of the place in which the Lord's words were spoken. " *Jesus came into the coasts of Cæsarea Philippi.*" Philip, as Luke informs us, was tetrarch of Iturea and of the region of Trachonitis. He built a city in the district where the Jordan rises, at the foot of Mount Lebanon, a district which bounds Judea towards the north, and he named it Cæsarea Philippi, after his own name, and at the same time in honour of Tiberius Cæsar, under whom he governed the country.

" *Jesus asked His disciples, saying, Whom do men say that I, the Son of Man, am ?* " He does not ask as though He knew not what His disciples and others thought of Him. He questions the disciples as to their opinion, in order that He may worthily reward their confession of a true faith. For as, when all were questioned, Peter alone answered for all, so what the Lord answered to Peter, in Peter He answered to all. And He asks what others think of Him, in order that the erroneous opinions of others might be exposed, and so it would be shown that the disciples received the truth of their confession not from the common belief, but from the very secrets of revelation from the Lord. " Whom do men say that I, the Son of Man, am ? " He asks. Right well does He call them " men " who spoke of Him only as Son of Man, because they knew not the secrets of His Divinity. For they who can receive the mysteries of His Divinity are deservedly said to be more than men. The Apostle [meaning of course St. Paul, known in the mediæval times as " The Apostle "] himself beareth witness, " Eye hath not seen, nor ear heard, nor have entered into the heart of man, the things which God hath prepared for them that love Him." And having premised this of men, that is, of those whose knowledge is from the human heart, the human ear, the human eye, the Apostle presently adds, of himself and of those like him who surpassed the ordinary knowledge of the human race, " but God hath revealed them unto us by His Spirit." In the same way here, when the Lord had questioned the disciples as to whom men held Him to be, and they had stated the different views of different persons, He says to them :—

" *But whom do ye say that I am ?* " as though setting them apart from ordinary men, and implying that they were made gods and sons of God by adoption, according to that saying of the Psalmist, " I have said, Ye are gods, and ye are all the children of the Most Highest."

" *Simon Peter answered and said, Thou art the Christ, the Son of the living God.*" He calls Him the " living " God by way of distinction from the false gods which heathendom in its various delusions made to itself to worship, either of dead men, or—greater folly still—of insensate matter. Of which false gods it is sung in the Psalm, " their idols are silver and gold, the work of men's hands." And mark well, my beloved, for it is worthy of all admiration, how, when the true view of both the natures of the same Lord our Saviour is to be expressed, it is the Lord who sets forth the humility of the manhood He had taken upon Him, the disciple who shows the excellency of the divine eternity. The Lord says of Himself that which is the less, the disciple says of the Lord that which is the greater. So, too, in the Gospel, the Lord was accustomed to speak of Himself much more often as Son of Man than as Son of God, that He might admonish us of the dispensation which He undertook for us. And we ought the more humbly to reverence the high things of His divinity, the more we remember that for our exaltation He descended to the low estate of manhood. For if among the mysteries of the Incarnation, by which we have been redeemed, we cherish always in pious memory the power of the divinity by which we have been created, we too with Peter are rewarded with blessing from on high. For when Peter confesses Him to be the Christ, the Son of the living God, see what follows :—" *Jesus answered and said, Blessed art thou, Simon Bar-Jona.*" It is certain, then, that after true confession of Christ there remain the true rewards of blessedness.

Let us now consider attentively what and how great is that name with which He glorifies the perfect confessor of His name, that by a true confession we may deserve to be partakers of this also. " Blessed art thou, Simon Bar-Jona." Bar-Jona in Syriac signifies " son of a dove." And rightly is the Apostle

Peter called son of a dove, for the dove is without guile, and Peter followed his Lord in prudent and pious guilelessness, mindful of that precept of guilelessness and truth which he and his fellow-disciples received from the same Master—" Be ye wise as serpents, and harmless as doves." And surely, since the Holy Spirit descended upon the Lord in the form of a dove, he is rightly called " Son of a Dove " who is shown to have been filled with the grace of the Spirit. And justly does the Lord reward him who loved Him and confessed Him, by declaring that he, who asserted Him to be Son of the living God, is son of the Holy Spirit. Of course no faithful man doubts that these two sonships are very different. For the Lord Christ is Son of God by nature Peter, as also the other elect, son of the Holy Spirit by grace. Christ is Son of the living God, because He is born of Him Peter is son of the Holy Spirit, because he is born again of Him. Christ is Son of God before all time, for He is that virtue of God and wisdom of God which saith, " The Lord possessed Me in the beginning of His way, before His works of old." Peter is son of the Holy Spirit from the time when, illumined by Him, he received the grace of divine knowledge. And because the will of the Holy Trinity is one, and the operation one, when the Lord had said, " Blessed art thou, Simon Bar-Jona," that is, son of the grace of the Spirit, He rightly proceeded to say—

" *For flesh and blood hath not revealed it unto thee ; but my Father which is in Heaven.*" It was indeed the Father who revealed it for the grace of the Father and of the Holy Spirit is one, as also that of the Son, which may be proved very easily from sacred Scripture. For the Apostle says of the Father,

" God hath sent forth the Spirit of His Son into your hearts." The Son Himself says of the Holy Spirit, " But when the Comforter is come, whom I will send unto you from the Father." The Apostle says of the Holy Spirit, " But all these worketh that one and the selfsame Spirit, dividing to every man severally as He will." The Father therefore sends the Spirit, the Son sends the Spirit the Spirit Himself breatheth where He listeth, because, as we have said, the will and the operation of the Father, the Son, and the Holy Spirit, is one. And hence it is fittingly said, that the Father which is in heaven revealed to the son of the dove that mystery of faith which flesh and blood could not reveal. Now flesh and blood we rightly understand to mean men puffed up with the wisdom of the flesh, ignorant of the guilelessness of the dove, and thus as far as possible removed from the wisdom of the Spirit. Of whom it has been said above, that in their ignorance of Christ some said that He was John the Baptist ; some Elias ; and others Jeremias, or one of the prophets. Of such men the Apostle saith " But the natural man receiveth not the things of the Spirit of God."

To proceed. *" And I say unto thee, That thou art Peter, and upon this rock I will build my Church."* Peter, who was before named Simon, received from the Lord the name of Peter on account of the strength of his faith and the constancy of his confession ; for his mind clung firmly to That of which it is written, " that rock was Christ." " And upon this rock," that is, upon the Lord and Saviour who gave to him that knew Him, loved Him, confessed Him, a share in His own name, so that from the Rock he should be called Peter ; on which Rock the Church is builded, because only by believing and loving Christ, by receiving the Sacraments of Christ, by observing the commandments of Christ, can man arrive at the lot of the elect, at eternal life. To this the Apostle [again of course St. Paul] beareth witness when he saith, " For other foundation can no man lay than that is laid, which is Jesus Christ."

" *And the gates of Hell shall not prevail against it.*" The gates of Hell are wicked doctrines, which seduce men and bring them to Hell. The gates of Hell, further, are the tortures and the blandishments of persecutors, who by terrifying and enticing unstable souls, open unto them an entrance into eternal death. Further, the gates of Hell are the evil deeds and the unseemly words of believers, inasmuch as they show the way of perdition to those who allow them or follow their example. For even faith, if it have not works, is dead in itself, and evil communications corrupt good manners. Many, then, are the gates of Hell ; but not one of them prevails against the Church which is builded on the Rock for one who has received the faith of Christ with the inmost love of his heart, easily puts down every temptation from without. But a believer who has depraved and betrayed his belief, either by wrongdoing or by denial, is to be taken as having built the house of his confession, not on a rock with the Lord as his helper, but on sand with no foundation that is, he must be held to have made pretence of being a Christian, with no simple and true determination to follow Christ, but with some frail earthly purpose.

" *And I will give unto thee the keys of the kingdom of Heaven.* He who confessed the King of Heaven with a devotion beyond that of others, had worthily conferred upon him beyond others the keys of the kingdom of Heaven ; that all might know, how that without such confession and faith none may enter into the kingdom of Heaven. And He describes, as "the keys of the kingdom of Heaven," that knowledge and power of discerning by which the worthy would be received into the kingdom, the unworthy rejected. It is evidently on this account that He added :—

"*And whatsoever thou shalt bind on earth shall be bound in Heaven: and whatsoever thou shalt loose on earth shall be loosed in Heaven.*" This power of binding and of loosing seems to be given by the Lord to Peter alone ; but without the slightest doubt it is given to the other Apostles also. Christ Himself bears witness to this, for after the triumph of His Passion and Resurrection He appeared to them, and breathing on them said, "Receive ye the Holy Ghost : whosesoever sins ye remit, they are remitted unto them ; and whosesoever sins ye retain, they are retained."[1] Nay, the same function is committed now, in the person of the bishops and priests, to the whole Church, so that after knowledge of the case of sinners it may take pity on those whom it sees to be humble and truly penitent, and absolve them from the fear of eternal death ; while it marks as bound under ever-

---

[1] In another passage Bede discusses the relative position of Peter and the chief Apostles. He remarks, that though Peter is named first in the catalogues of the Apostles, Paul says, "James, Cephas, and John," and that the order of the Catholic Epistles is the same. The reason for this order he understands to be that James ruled in Jerusalem, the fountain-head of the Church ; also, James wrote to the tribes from whom the first believers came, Peter to the Gentile proselytes the next believers, and John to the Gentiles who were not proselytes, the third class of believers in order of time. Bede could scarcely have said more than he does had he foreseen the claims which later ages would make in St. Peter's name.

lasting punishments those whom it finds to be persistent in their sins. Whence in another place the Lord says of one who is once and again taken in a fault and yet repenteth not,—" But if he neglect to hear the Church, let him be unto thee as an heathen man and a publican." And lest any should deem it a light thing to be condemned by the judgment of the Church, He adds presently these terrible words, " Verily I say unto you, whatsoever ye shall bind on earth shall be bound in Heaven ; and whatsoever ye shall loose on earth shall be loosed in Heaven." To the whole Church, then, of the elect is there given authority to bind and loose according to the measure of sins and of repentance. But the blessed Peter, who confessed Christ with a true faith, and followed Him with a true love, received in a special manner the keys of the kingdom of Heaven and the first place of the power of judgment ; in order that all believers throughout the world may understand that no man who in any way separates himself from the unity of faith and fellowship can be absolved from the chains of sin or enter the gate of the kingdom of Heaven.[1] So that, my dearest brethren, we must of necessity learn with the utmost care the sacraments of the faith which he taught, and show forth works meet for faith. We must with all vigilance beware of the manifold and subtle snares of the gates of Hell, that so we may be worthy to enter into the gates of the daughter of Sion, that is, into the joys of the city

---

[1] In another sermon Bede expounds our Lord's words as follows : Thou art Peter, and on this rock from which thou hast received thy name, that is, on Myself, I will build My Church ; on this perfection of faith which thou hast confessed I will build My Church, and whosoever departeth from the fellowship of this confession belongeth not to My Church.

which is on high. And let us not suppose that it suffices for salvation that we be like unto the crowds of careless and ignorant persons in faith or in deeds, for there is in the sacred writings one only rule laid down for faith and life. But as often as the examples of those who err are brought before us, let us turn away the eyes of our mind lest they behold vanity, and carefully investigate what truth itself teaches. Let us follow the example of the blessed Peter, who rejected the errors of others, and made with the mouth an unwavering profession of the hidden things of the true faith which he had learned, and kept them in his heart with invincible care. For in this place we learn of the faithfulness of confession ; while of the virtue of single love for Christ He beareth witness Himself in another place, when some of His disciples went back, and He said unto the twelve, " Will ye also go away ? " " Peter answered Him, Lord, to whom shall we go ? Thou hast the words of eternal life. And we believe and are sure that Thou art that Christ, the son of the living God." If we set ourselves to follow his example, my brethren, according to our ability, we too shall be able with him to be called blessed and to be blessed ; to us, too, the name of Simon will be meet, that is, of one that obeys Christ ; we too, on account of the guilelessness of our faith that is not feigned, and the grace we receive from the Lord, shall be called sons of the virtue of the dove ; and He Himself, rejoicing with us in the spiritual progress of our soul, shall say, " Behold, thou art fair, my love ; behold, thou art fair ; thou hast dove's eyes." And so it cometh to pass that if we build on the rock of faith, gold, silver, precious stones, that is, the perfect works of virtues, the fires of tribulation shall bring no harm, the storms of temptation shall not prevail. Nay, rather, proved by adversity, we shall receive the crown of life, promised before the ages by Him who liveth and reigneth God, with the Father, in the unity of the Holy Spirit, for ever and ever. Amen.

CHAPTER XV

FURTHER MIRACLES

The power of faith—Miracles wrought on Bede and by his relics—
General belief—Further miracles by Cuthbert—Preservation of
his body—His coffin—Its ornamentation—Later miracles—
Bishop John of Hexham—General conclusion on miracles.

BEDE's Life of St. Cuthbert is full of miracles, as we
have seen in Chapter VIII. And the later portions of
his Ecclesiastical History abound in miracles, carefully attested by many witnesses, and told in honour
of the saints by whose power or prayers they were
wrought. And there can be no doubt at all that Bede
himself entirely believed in the existence and frequent
display of miraculous power in Northumbria and other
parts of England, while it is evident that in many of
his examples the result might have been due to
natural causes.

In fairness to that age it is right to point out that
our own generation has learned to recognise the power
of faith to help the physician in his efforts to expel
disease or ward off death. We have to remember
how active faith is among early converts from
paganism. Missionary experience has taught us to
understand Bede's view and Bede's stories of
miracle. An unseen power produced or helped on
the effect. That unseen power was not in any real
sense miraculous, it worked from within the patient
not from without. But Bede, if he were here, might

plead that the spirit which operated in the faith was specially vouchsafed for the occasion by Divine operation ; and I do not know what spiritually minded person would be bold to assert that Bede would be wrong in so pleading.

Besides a statement that Bede's relics had in one case a miraculous effect, we have it from himself that by interposition from St. Cuthbert, after the Bishop's death, a miracle was performed upon him. It appears that he had some difficulty with his tongue. "I," he wrote to Bishop John of Hexham, "was, as I have told you, the receiver of miraculous help through him. For, as I was singing his miracles, my affection of the tongue was cured." It may remind us of the many cases of recovery of speech by wounded soldiers in a moment of emotion of one kind and another.

It is evident, too, that the stories of miracles were generally believed in his time. The manner in which he relates miraculous stories without any comment is sufficient to show this. There is direct evidence of it, also, in his account of the compilation of the Life of St. Cuthbert—a history full of miracle. When he had finished the life, he submitted it, as we have seen already, before publication— or rather, as the equivalent of publication in those times, before allowing it to be transcribed—to the monastery in which Cuthbert had lived. The monks read it, and considered it carefully, and gave their testimony to its accuracy as a faithful account of their saint's life. Thus the story of Cuthbert's many miracles was held to be true by those among whom his life had been spent.

After his Life of Cuthbert was written, Bede received a number of fresh stories of miracles con-

nected with that saint. These he gave in the fourth
book of the History, prefacing them with an account
of the discovery by the brethren of Lindisfarne that
the body of Cuthbert remained fresh and lifelike,
and its joints pliable, eleven years after death. In
the course of this account, by the way, we find
that Cuthbert's successor, Eadbert, made a practice
of spending the forty days of Lent in perfect solitude,
on a remote bit of land surrounded by the sea. The
contrast between the life of a bishop of Durham,
with the demands upon his time, in those days and
these, could scarcely be brought out more strongly.

There was in the monastery at Lindisfarne a
brother whose name was Bethwegen, whose office it
was to attend to the wants of visitors to the monastery. He was a great favourite with every one, and
was a man of much piety. He had been washing the
linen in the sea on one occasion, and when returning
to the monastery he was seized with palsy, one side
of his body being completely paralyzed. He managed
to drag himself to the church, and prostrated himself
before Cuthbert's tomb. Falling into a stupor, he
felt a large and broad hand touch his head on the
injured side, and he was immediately made whole
from head to foot.

Another story is made vivid by Bede's introductory
remark that the miracle occurred " three years ago,"
and was related to him by the brother on whom it
was wrought. The monastery was in Cumberland.
It took its name from the river Dacore, near which it
was built. The place is now Dacre, near Penrith.
The abbat was the religious Suidbert. The brother
had a swelling on his eyelid, which grew so much as to
threaten the loss of his eyesight. The doctors

fomented it in vain,[1] and then they disagreed. Some said it must be cut off ; others said that would be worse than the disease. It happened that one of the priests of the monastery, Thridred, who was abbat when Bede wrote, had kept in a box some of the hair of the sainted Cuthbert, taken from his body when it was exhumed eleven years after his death. This box he entrusted one day to the brother with the swelling on his eyelid. The brother, by a salutary instinct, took some of the hair from the box and applied it to the eyelid. This was—" as he is wont to say "—about the second hour of the day. He went about his business, and four hours later he chanced to touch his eyelid, when he found it as sound as the other.

We have seen in Chapter VIII that eleven years after the death of St. Cuthbert his body was found to be quite fresh and undecayed, and its limbs supple. It seems clear from Bede's phrase that the brethren regarded this as of something like a miraculous character. The purpose of their investigation was, to place the remains of the saint in a more suitable coffin. This coffin is one of the most remarkable of all the many remarkable relics of the saint. It is the innermost of the three coffins in which the body was enclosed, the coffin made in Lindisfarne eleven years after the saint's death, namely, in A.D. 698.

The great translation of the body, in its coffin, to the new Cathedral Church of Durham on the 29th of August, 1104, is described by an anonymous author. It is evident that remarkably clear notes were made of the ornamentation of the coffin at that

---

[1] The remedy for swollen eyes in the Saxon leech-book was less simple than this :—take a live crab, put his eyes out, and put him alive again into water ; and put the eyes upon the neck of the man who hath need   he will soon be well.

time, for Reginald, who wrote fully of it sixty years
later, describes it as accurately as if it had been seen
again in his time. The very careful examiners of the
sacred relics in 1827 were astonished with the accuracy
of Reginald's description. He tells of the unusual
shape of the coffin, and of its flat lid, which was not
fastened to the great rectangular chest and had rings
" in its middle breadth in the direction of his feet and
his head," whereby the lid could be raised. One of
these two rings was found in 1827.

Reginald stated that the inner coffin was found in
1104 to be externally carved with very admirable
engravings, of minute and most delicate workmanship, and that in small and circumscribed tracts or
compartments, there were beasts, flowers, and figures
(*imagines*) engrafted, engraved, or furrowed in the
wood. Many of these were found in 1827, and
portions of the wood were kept. In 1898 a further
effort was made to find completing portions, not
without some success. In 1827 the figures and names,
or parts of the figures and names, of Apostles and
Evangelists were found, St. John, St. Mark, St.
Thomas, St. Peter, St. Andrew, St. Matthew, St. Paul.
The drapery and the lettering are of the highest value
as illustrations of early art and of palæography.[1]
There were also the Virgin and Child, the fore feet of
a Lion, and the head and neck of an Eagle in a
nimbus.

A few additional examples, taken from the later
parts of Bede's " Ecclesiastical History," will illustrate the claims to miraculous powers made on
behalf of saints and relics in those ages. They will

[1] See *The ancient cross-shafts of Bewcastle and Ruthwell*, G. F.
Browne, pages 28 and 45.

at the same time give incidentally some further idea of the manner of life of important ecclesiastics. By going to the later parts of the history for our examples, we obtain accounts of miracles which have the actual attestation of those who took part in them, some of whom related the details to Bede with their own mouth.

Guthfrid, afterwards Abbat of Lindisfarne, told Bede of a miracle which had happened to him and two other brethren. They had gone in a boat to the island of Farne to speak with a hermit who had taken up his abode there. When they were half-way back again, a violent storm came on, and death appeared to be imminent. In their distress they saw the hermit, Ethelwald, come out of his cave and call upon God. The storm at once assuaged ; they got safe to shore ; and as soon as they had dragged their boat to a safe distance from the sea, the storm came on again and raged for a whole day.

Berthun, Abbat of Inderawuda (Beverley, in the wood of Deira), who was alive when Bede wrote his History, used to tell the following story of Bishop John of Hexham, who ordained Bede. There was a certain retired dwelling near the church of Hagulstad (Hexham), but on the other side of the Tyne. It was surrounded by a narrow wood and an earthen mound and was a cemetery dedicated to St. Michael the Archangel. Here Bishop John used to come whenever he had an opportunity, and especially in Lent, to pray and read quietly with a few companions. In the village near there was a dumb man, who, in addition to that affliction, had some disease of the scalp, which prevented the hair from growing on the top of his head. It grew lower down, but that was no improvement, for it stood out bristling in a ring round his head. Bishop John sent for this man, and had a little hut made for him within the inclosure of the cemetery. On the second Sunday in Lent he called the dumb man into his presence and told him to put out his tongue. The bishop made the sign of the Cross on the tongue and told him to draw it back into his mouth and say " Yes." " Gae," said the man, which in the then English language meant " yes." " Say A," said the bishop. " A," said the man. " Say B," said the Bishop. " B," said the man. They went through the alphabet, and then got into syllables and words and sentences. The first effect must have been rather trying, for we are told that he talked nearly the whole of that day and all the next night as long as he could keep awake. Not satisfied with this success, the bishop put the man's head into the hands of a doctor,[1] aiding his skill by blessings and prayers, and the scalp became sound and a good head of hair grew. Thus, as Bede sums up, the poor man became possessed of good looks, a ready tongue, and very beautifully crisp and curly hair. The bishop offered to take the fortunate fellow into his own household, but life was brighter to him now and he preferred to go home.

Two of this bishop's miracles were wrought when he was visiting great men for the purpose of consecrating their churches. About two miles from the monastery a certain Earl Puch had a country house, where his wife had long lain ill ; for three weeks she had not

---

[1] The Saxon leech-book had remedy for this as for everything :— If a man's hair fall off, work him a salve ; take the mickle wolf's bane, and viper's bugloss, and the netherward part of burdock, and ferdwort ; work the salve out of these worts and butter on which no water hath come.

been moved from her bed. After the consecration of the church, the earl asked the bishop to dine with him. The bishop refused, saying he must get back to dinner. Probably he was afraid to face a Saxon noble's feasting. The earl pressed him to stay, and vowed that if he would break fast in his house he would give alms to the poor. Bede's informant, who accompanied the bishop, joined his entreaties to those of the earl, being not indisposed to partake of secular hospitality. At length the bishop yielded. He had already sent to the earl's wife some of the holy water he had blessed for the consecration of the church, with instructions to apply it both outwardly and inwardly.[1] The lady had done as she was bidden, and had been healed. On the bishop's arrival she presented the cup to him and his companions, and she continued to serve them with drink as long as the meal lasted, ministering to them after the example of Peter's mother-in-law. The other occasion was at the consecration of Earl Addi's church. The earl begged the bishop to pay a visit to one of his servants, who had lost the use of his limbs : he was supposed to be at the point of death ; indeed, the coffin had been prepared. The earl was sure that if only the bishop would lay his hand upon him and bless him, he would even yet be healed. Addi was moved to tears in the earnestness of his request, and the bishop consented to see the man. He found him lying all but dead, with a coffin ready at his side. He said a

---

[1] Holy water was an ingredient in the Saxon leech's somewhat complicated cure for " Lent addle " (typhus fever) :—Work to a drink wormwood, everthront, lupin, waybrond, ribwort, chervil, attorlothe, feverfue, alessandus, bishopwort, lovage, sage, cassock, in foreign ale ; add holywater and springwort. Holy water was employed in making a somewhat similar drink for a fiend-sick person ; in this case the potion was to be drunk out of a church bell.

prayer, gave him the blessing, and left him with what
Bede calls the usual speech of comforters, " I hope
you will soon be better." They then sat down to
dinner, and before long a message came that the
servant was thirsty and would like some wine. The
earl sent him some at once, and it had such an effect
upon him that he got up and dressed himself and
joined the bishop and the other guests, saying that he
would be glad to dine with them. They invited him
to sit down, he greatly enjoyed his dinner, and lived
happy for many years.

Herebald, Abbat of Tynemouth, told Bede of a
miracle which Bishop John had wrought in his favour.
When he was a young man living with the saint, and
studying reading and singing, but not altogether
weaned as yet from youthful pleasures, he and a
number of other youths accompanied John in one of
his expeditions on horseback. In the course of their
journey, they came to a large level piece of ground,
well suited for a race. They begged their master to
let them try their horses,—the lay youths especially,
as Herebald used to tell. He at first refused, saying it
was an idle request ; but after a time he gave his consent, with the proviso that Herebald did not race with
the rest. Herebald begged hard to be allowed to race,
for he was on an excellent horse which the bishop
had given him ; but he could not get leave. The
sight of his companions racing was too much for him,
and he set off without leave, the bishop calling out
after him reproachfully. In a very short time the
horse made an unexpected leap over a hole in the
ground, and Herebald was thrown. On all the
plain there was only one stone, and exactly on that
one stone was Herebald landed head first. He put

one hand to his head to break the fall, but his thumb was broken and his skull was fractured. As he lived to tell the tale in his old age, it is unnecessary to say that he was saved from death by a miracle, wrought in his favour by his forgiving master.

If Herebald had been left to the secular leech, he might have been treated in accordance with the Saxon prescription from Apuleius :—If a man's head be broken, take the herb betony, scrape it and rub it very small to dust, then take by two drachms weight and swallow it in hot beer ; the head healeth very quickly after the drink. Or the Saxon leech-book might have been followed Take betony, bruise it, and lay it on the head above, then it unites the wound and healeth it. And take garden cress, such as waxeth of itself ; put it in the nose, that the smell and juice may get to the head. And if the brain be exposed, take the yolk of an egg and mix with honey, and fill the wound and swathe up with tow ; and so let it alone.

It is worthy of notice that although Bede had in a few cases actually conversed with persons on whom these " miracles " had been wrought, the events had in almost all cases occurred some considerable time before Bede wrote, as much as a generation before. They were almost without exception things of the past, stories told of the early heroes of Christianity in the land. Bede could not or did not name any one living in his time who had any claim to miraculous power. He does, however, state that miracles were still wrought in his time by relics ; we may note that his own relics in their turn performed a miraculous cure. We have seen the efficacy of the wood of Oswald's cross. We have also an account of frequent

miracles wrought at the tomb of St. Chad. A man out
of his mind had lodged on the spot for a night, un-
observed by the guardians of the tomb, and in the
morning he went forth in his right mind. The place of
the sepulchre was a wooden monument, like a small
house ; there was a hole in the wall, through which
men put their hands and brought out some of the
dust, which they gave in water to sick men and cattle
as a general specific. Bede asserts that this remedy
continued to be efficacious in his time, Chad having
died about the year of Bede's birth. Similarly Bishop
Earconwald of London, who died a year or two later,
left behind him a miraculous influence. His horse-
litter, in which he had travelled when he was out of
health, was kept by his disciples as a cure for agues
and other distempers. The litter would probably not
exist long, for Bede relates that chips of it were
carried to sick persons, and they healed them.

On a review of Bede's writings as a whole, we may
fairly say that the miraculous influence claimed for
illustrious missionaries was confined to the first and
second generation of Christian teachers in the land.
To say that even in the first and second generation
there was no such influence at work would be to say
more than we are entitled to say. In the earliest
years of a mission, as the experience of times later
than those of Bede has shown, there are occasions
on which it is very difficult to say whether the Divine
power which the Christian believes to be really
working has wrought openly, whether the Lord has, in
fact, in the sight of men, confirmed the words of His
Apostles with signs following.

CHAPTER XVI

THE STATE OF MORALS IN BEDE'S TIME

Ecclesiastics—Monasteries—Lay people—Nuns—Kings—Remains of paganism.

IT has been remarked that Bede's sermons throw no light upon the state of society in his time. They were not addressed to a mixed audience, and they did not profess to deal with subjects relating to practical life or with ordinary moral questions. We have, however, the long letter described in Chapter X which he wrote to Archbishop Ecgbert of York, and in this we find many references to the prevailing state of morals. The picture he draws is a dark one ; and he remarks, towards the end of his letter, as we have seen, that if he were to write in detail about drunkenness, gluttony, and debauchery, the letter would extend to an immense length. If the ordinary date of Bede's death be correct, we have in this letter some of his last words. For our present purpose we must repeat some parts of what is said in Chapter X.

Ecgbert, to whom this interesting letter was addressed, was the cousin of King Ceolwulf, who reigned in Northumbria from 729 A.D. to 737. He became Archbishop of York, and head of the great cathedral school of that city. Bede, having spent some days with him in study and interchange of ideas, was invited to repeat his visit in the following year. His state of health prevented his accepting this invitation, and, in consequence, he wrote at considerable length some of the things he had intended to say to the bishop, had he been able to pay him another visit The main subject of the letter is the covetousness of bishops, and the disorderliness of many establishments which called themselves religious houses. Incidentally we learn a good deal on points which would not naturally be included under those heads.

The conduct of the bishops in general seems to have been unsatisfactory. Bede urges the archbishop himself, who was as yet bishop of York, not archbishop, to abstain with episcopal dignity from unseemly conversation, and from the evils of an unrestrained tongue. He advises him to read carefully and often the Epistles to Timothy and Titus, as specially suited to his position, and also the *Pastoral Care* of Pope Gregory. Above all things, he should surround himself with devout persons—the best check upon impurity of speech or action. Of some bishops it was commonly reported that they had no pious or continent men near them ; their companions were men given to rioting and drunkenness, thinking more of feeding the body than of nourishing the mind with heavenly sacrifices.

As to the priests, Bede tells us that he has often given an English translation of the Creed and the Lord's Prayer to priests who were ignorant of Latin. What a picture this offers of the state of things for which he thus provided some sort of remedy,—the priest repeating words of which he did not know the meaning, the congregation listening or not listening in ignorance as complete.

We find an illustration of the ignorance of priests

in a story told by Bede of a miracle wrought by
Bishop John of Hexham on Herebald afterwards
Abbat of Tynemouth. Herebald told Bede that
after he had had a fall from his horse,[1] which must
have proved fatal but for the intercession of John, the
bishop asked him whether he knew for certain that
he had been baptized. Herebald said there could
be no question about it ; and he named the priest
who had performed the ceremony. " Then," the
bishop rejoined, " you are not rightly baptized. For
I know the man, and though he was ordained priest,
he was too slow to learn the offices of catechising
and baptizing ; and I had to order him to desist
from the attempt to perform them." The bishop at
once proceeded to catechise Herebald ; and, after
some time, he baptized him. What interesting controversial questions this case would raise if it occurred in
these modern times, as it quite possibly might. The
Canons of the Church of England in Anglo-Norman
times show that this ignorance of priests was by no
means confined to Anglo-Saxon times. And it will be
remembered that the " hocus pocus " of the conjurer
is said to be the layman's imitation of the ignorant
priest's pronunciation of the *hoc est Corpus* at the
consecration of the elements in the Eucharist, by which
the priest was supposed to bring about a miracle.

Other dioceses were as large in proportion as
Ecgbert's, and were still more neglected. There were
many outlying places on the hills and among the woods
where no bishop had been seen for many years ; nay,
where there was no one to teach the people the difference between good and evil. The source of this
mischief was the covetousness of bishops. Every such

[1] See page 275.

hamlet paid tribute to the bishop, and for filthy lucre's
sake bishops undertook a much larger number of
villages than they could possibly attend to. In this
way the rite of Confirmation, on the importance of
which Bede insists, was very generally neglected. The
remedy was, the appointment of more bishops ; but
the kings had been so careless and profuse in assigning
one district after another to existing bishops, that it
was hard to find any place for a new see. Still, since
the reigning king was Ecgbert's first cousin—the next
as we have seen was Ecgbert's brother—Bede argued
that the opportunity was a favourable one for extend-
ing and completing the ecclesiastical establishment of
the kingdom. Pope Gregory had intended in Augustine's time that the metropolitan see of York should
have twelve suffragan bishops, and a great effort ought
to be made to carry out this idea. Ceolwulf, it may
be remarked, was himself much interested in Church
matters, and it was to him that Bede dedicated his
Ecclesiastical History ; indeed, two years after this,
the king was tonsured and became a monk.

The question of the subdivision of bishoprics was
no new one in Northumbria, and it had before this
time led to very serious results. Ecgfrith, the king of
Northumbria, and Theodore, the famous archbishop
of Canterbury, had agreed that the vast Northumbrian
diocese over which Wilfrith ruled—that Wilfrith who
had played so important a part at the Council of
Whitby—must be subdivided. Wilfrith offered an
unflinching resistance to the plan, and he was in consequence deposed by the authority of the king and
parliament, as we should say. We have seen in
Chapter IX something of the events which followed.

With a view to providing funds for the new bishop-

rics, Bede had a practical suggestion to make, which
throws great light on the evils attendant upon the
monastic system in such times, and leads him to make
remarks which help us in our search for evidence as to
the state of morals at that time. He proposed, first of
all, that some of the large monasteries should be appropriated for the foundation of episcopal sees, the
opposition of the monks being got over by putting into
their hands the election of the bishop, who should also
be abbat. In cases where the funds of the monastery
would not bear the additional charge entailed by the
necessary expenses of an active bishop, there were only
too many so-called monasteries which might well
be suppressed by synodical authority and annexed to
the new sees. Bede describes these monasteries as
very numerous and very large. The common saying
about them was that they were of no use to God or
man ; for the life of the inmates was not godly, and
the property, being free from secular claims, provided
no assistance against the barbarians. Hence, any one
who did what he could to meet the pressing requirements of the times, by annexing such monasteries to
episcopal sees, would do an act of virtue, not of con-
fiscation. If Ecgbert and the king did not take some
prompt steps in the way of cancelling the grants of
former kings, on the one hand religion would cease
altogether, on the other there would be no one to
defend the country against the barbarians. Already
so much land was absorbed by these foundations, that
there was none left to give to the sons of nobles and
of retired soldiers, so that a large number of young
men were at a loose end, some deserting their country
and going across the seas, others living a life of the
grossest licence at home.

This introduces the mention of what Bede describes as a greater scandal still. Men who had no knowledge or love of the monastic life, purchased grants of land from the king under pretence of desiring to found monasteries, and had the grants made to them and their heirs for ever. They then erected buildings, collected a number of worthless persons, outcast monks or dependents of their own, whom they tonsured, and over this medley they ruled, living most disgraceful lives, some married, some worse. Many of them got lands for their wives in the same way, and established disorderly convents, over which the wives ruled. To such an extent was this wicked folly carried, that for the thirty years preceding the time of Bede's writing, that is, for the whole time since king Aldfrith's death, there had never once been a prefect who did not furnish himself with an establishment of the kind, and his wife also, if he had one. Bede plaintively remarks that this evil might have been put down by synodical and episcopal authority, but unfortunately the bishops themselves fostered it for the sake of the money they earned by confirming the grants of the kings.

Ecgbert had informed Bede that he claimed the right to visit all monasteries in his diocese, a right which he denied to the king and nobles, except in cases where the inmates had committed some offence against the king himself. Bede replied that the bishop was in consequence responsible for the state of things which prevailed in many monasteries, and urged him to proceed against unworthy abbats and abbesses and also against disobedient monks.

Finally, Bede remarks, as has been said above, that if he dealt in a similar manner with the prevailing drunkenness, gluttony, and debauchery, his letter would be of unmeasurable length.

Bede drew, as we have seen, so dark a picture of some of the clergy and many of the monks, that we might naturally expect to find in other parts of Bede's writings remarks of a similar character about lay people. But we do not find such remarks, or we find them very seldom. In the Ecclesiastical History there is a general absence of contemporaneous accounts of men or women of wicked lives, and in the Homilies there is an all but total absence of allusion to any prevalent vices. It may well be that Bede opened his heart to his friend in a private letter, but did not feel called upon either to make his History a homily against vice, or to make his Homilies, preached to the brethren of Jarrow, a history of the vices in the world outside.

There are, however, various indications that if Bede had cared to do so, he might have given darker details than he has done. We have seen[1] that a certain priest, a certain layman, and a certain woman were specially mentioned by Drythelm as among the shrieking crew of those whom demons were dragging into the pit of destruction. We have seen, too, how evil a life had been led by the military officer of King Coenred.[2] On one occasion, and only one, Bede departs from his usual practice, and enters into a detailed account of the evil life of a brother in a monastery. We cannot but understand that he is writing of a monk of Jarrow. He shall tell the tale in his own words.

" I knew a brother myself—would God I had not known him—a brother whom I could name if it would profit anything. He lived in a noble monas-

------

[1] See page 121.   [2] See page 249.

tery, but he lived ignobly. He was diligently rebuked by the brethren and by the superiors, and was exhorted to turn to a better-disciplined life. He would not hearken, but yet he was borne with by them patiently, because they needed his help in temporal matters, for he was singularly skilful as a carpenter. He was much addicted to drunkenness and other vices. He would rather stay in his workshop night and day, than go to church to sing and pray and hear the word of God with his brethren. And so it happened to him, according to the saying, ' He that wills not into the gates of the church of his own will in humbleness to enter, shall needs into the gate of hell against his will in damnation be driven.' He fell sick, and being at the point to die, he called unto him the brethren, and with much groaning, like unto one damned, he told them that he had seen hell opened and Satan plunged in the depths of Tartarus, and Caiaphas and the rest who slew the Lord being tormented in the flames of vengeance. ' Nigh unto whom,' he said, ' I see a place of eternal perdition prepared for me.' The brethren urged him to do penance while yet he lived ; but ' No,' he said, ' I have no time now to change my life, now that I myself have seen mine own judgment.' Since he held this language, he died without the viaticum of salvation, and his body was buried in the remotest part of the monastery, and none presumed to say masses for him, or to chant psalms, or even to pray."[1]

We may safely conclude that this was the usual manner of dealing with those who died impenitent in Bede's time. And that the case of the carpenter was not singular, we may gather from Bede's statement that the account of his terrible death had

[1] See also page 250.

brought many to do penance for their sins without delay, and from the fervent wish he expresses that the publication of the account in his History might produce a like effect on others.

Though this is the only case in which Bede speaks from his own personal experience of an evil life in a monastery, he gives a startling account of the state of things which prevailed among the nuns of Coldingham. He relates the story as it was told to him by his most reverend fellow-presbyter Edgils, who was living in the monastery of Coldingham at the time when the events occurred, and afterwards lived long at Jarrow, and died there.

There was among the inmates of Coldingham a monk, by name Adamnan, a Scot. He had committed some crime in early youth and had confessed to a priest, offering to fast for a whole week and stand all the night through praying. To fast for the whole week was too much for his strength, the priest replied ; let him fast two or three days at a time for the present ; he would return soon and tell him what to do as a permanency. The priest went over to Ireland and died there, leaving Adamnan under the promise to fast always two or three days at a time, and this promise he kept by eating only on Thursdays and Sundays.

One day Adamnan and a companion had gone out for some distance from the monastery, and as they returned they marked its lofty buildings. Adamnan wept over it, saying, " All these buildings which thou beholdest, whether public or private, shall in no long time be consumed with fire." The companion told this to Abbess Ebba on their return, probably on the principle that the inmate of a monastery is usually accompanied by one of his colleagues when he walks abroad, not as a check only upon his actions, but also as a reporter if need be. Ebba not unnaturally made further inquiries. How did he come to know that her monastery was to be burned down ? Then he told her. He had been busy one night in watchings and psalms, when one stood by his side at whose presence he was terrified. The visitant told him he did well to spend his night thus ; few in that establishment did so ; he had been round to all the cells and the beds, and had found no one but Adamnan occupied in heavenly things. Men and women, they were all either sleeping idly, or awake to sin ; it may be noted that many famous monasteries had both monks and nuns in the early times. The very cells which had been specially made for prayer and reading were converted into dens for eating and drinking and story-telling, and other such things. The virgins who were vowed to God had laid aside the reverence which was a part of their profession, and, whenever they had any time to spare, devoted themselves to making dresses, to deck themselves out like brides or to obtain the friendship of men outside. The consequence would be, that fire would come down and devour the place. The abbess asked why Adamnan had not spoken sooner. Adamnan told her it was out of respect to her ; the thing was not to happen in her time, and he did not wish to worry her. Either she or Adamnan's companion told the tale, and the inmates of the monastery were dreadfully alarmed. For a few days they gave up their sinful life, and subjected themselves to penance. But when the abbess died they returned to their old ways, and just when they were saying peace and safety, the blow fell. This was some few years after Bede's birth.

There was one order in the social scale to which Bede made but slight personal reference, namely, the kings. It is quite clear from the story of King Ceolwulf, to whom we have referred as being much interested in Church matters, that the times were terribly troublous, especially for kings in Northumbria. The continuator of Bede's History gives us a brief record of events down to 766, the death of Archbishop Ecgbert. He has entries for each of the four years 731–734 which elapsed between the completion of the History and the year of Bede's death. His first entry, for the year 731, is very startling, Ceolwulf the King was taken and tonsured, and restored to the kingdom ; Acca the bishop—Bede's greatest friend—was driven from his see. If we turn to Bede's History for his remarks on Ceolwulf (v. 23) we find that the king, to whom he dedicated his History after its completion, had succeeded to a very difficult position. " The beginning and progress of his reign were so overfilled with disturbances of opponents that it was impossible to know what ought to be written about them, or what the result of each of the many troubles would be." William of Malmesbury describes Ceolwulf as ascending the shaking throne of his predecessor Osric, which Osric had bequeathed to him, and suggests that his two predecessors, namely Coenred his brother and Osric, had murdered the disgraceful young man Osred, who as a boy had succeeded his father Aldfrith on the throne of Northumbria.

Osred was specially wicked. His wickedness was remembered thirty years after his death, when six German bishops, two of them English by birth, wrote to entreat Ethelbald of Mercia to live a decent life and enter upon a lawful marriage ; they named Osred as the first to set a terribly bad example, the *stupratio et adulterium nonnarum*. But they had worse things to say of Europe than of England, bad as Ethelbald was and Osred had been till his early and violent death. " If the race of the Anglo-Saxons follow the example set them in various parts of Europe, and enter upon unlawful unions, and live impure lives, the race will degenerate and the faith will be lost, as has already happened—and from that cause—in Spain and Provence and parts of Burgundy, at the hands of the Saracens." They write of *meretrices, sive monasteriales sive seculares ;* and the chief of the six bishops, our own Boniface of Crediton and Mainz, writing to Archbishop Cuthbert of Canterbury, begs that the English Council will forbid the pilgrimages to Rome so often made by women and nuns. They are mostly ruined on the way, few remaining chaste. There are very few cities in Lombardy, or in France, or in Gaul, where there is not some English woman leading a life of open sin.

Well might Bede say that it was impossible to see what would be the result of the evil times on which the nation had fallen. It was not till the year 793 that the Danes came and ravaged Northumbria and destroyed the monasteries on the coast, Lindisfarne and Wearmouth and Jarrow, but that catastrophe, all unexpected as it was, demonstrated the correctness of Bede's calculation in his letter to Ecgbert, that unless some great change for the better came, the country would find its men unable to defend it against the barbarians. So great was the wickedness in high places, that the change was very much for the worse. Ceolwulf was succeeded by the excellent king Eadbert, Ecgbert's brother, who retired to a monastery in 758.

After him came chaos, as the following summary of the succession will show only too clearly.

Eadbert was the 21st king, beginning with Ida who created the kingdom in 547, giving an average of ten years as the duration of a reign. That average in itself is indicative of rough times for royal people. His successors, down to the end of the kingdom of Northumbria, fared even worse, averaging not much more than eight years. The reigns of English kings from William of Normandy to Edward VII, both included, averaged twenty-three years each. Eadbert was succeeded by (22) Oswulf his son, who was within a year slain by his household officers, and was succeeded by (23) Ethelwald, of whose parentage we do not know anything. In 765 he was deposed by a national assembly, and (24) Alchred was placed on the throne, a fifth cousin of the murdered Oswulf. In 774 he was banished and went in exile to the king of the Picts, being succeeded by (25) Ethelred, the son of his deprived predecessor Ethelwald. Ethelred reigned from 774 to 779, when in consequence of cruel murders ordered by him he was driven out, and (26) Alfwold, son of (22) Oswulf, and therefore of the old royal line, succeeded. Alfwold was murdered in 788, and was succeeded by (27) Osred, the son of (24) Alchred, sixth cousin of his predecessor, and therefore of the royal line. After a year he was deposed and tonsured, and was eventually put to death in 792 by (25) Ethelred, who had recovered the throne lost by his expulsion in 779. He was killed in 796 in a faction fight, after he had put to death the last two males, so far as we know, of the royal line of Eadbert, Ælf and Ælfwine, sons of (26) Alfwold. Simeon of Durham tells us (A.D. 791) that they were persuaded by false promises to leave sanctuary in the Cathedral Church of York ; were taken by violence out of the city ; and miserably put to death by Ethelred in Wonwaldrenute. He was succeeded by (28) Osbald, of unknown parentage, but a patrician of Northumbria ; he only reigned twenty-seven days, fled to the king of the Picts, and died an abbat three years later, in 799. He was succeeded by (29) Eardulf, a patrician of the blood royal,[1] who had been left for dead by (25) Ethelred, but had recovered when laid out for burial by the monks of Ripon. In 806 he was driven out by (30) Elfwald, of unknown parentage, but by the help of the Emperor Charlemagne he was restored in 808. He died in 810, and was succeeded by his son (31) Eanred, who was the last king but one of the royal house, and the last independent king of Northumbria, dying in 840, and being succeeded by his son (32) Ethelred II, expelled in 844, restored in the same year, and killed *sine prole* in 848. That was the inglorious end of a kingdom which had lasted 300 years and had at more than one juncture seemed likely to become the dominant kingdom, as Wessex eventually did. Alcuin's letters to the kings and chief people of Northumbria show that immoralities were terribly rife in that order of the social scale.

Bede's opportunities for observation of the life of people in general were very small, and we cannot expect to learn much from him on this point. It is sufficient to say that a hundred years before he was made priest the people were wholly given up to paganism. We have seen how on one or two occasions the innate paganism still showed itself. There had not been that complete breaking off from pagan

[1] We cannot trace his pedigree.

rites which we might at first have expected that the Roman missionaries would enforce. Augustine had specially referred the matter to Gregory, who had replied in a spirit which has generally been called sensible and wise, but is at least open to less favourable judgment. If the temples of idols were well built, the idols only were to be destroyed ; the temples were to be purified with holy-water and kept as churches, so that the people might continue to frequent the accustomed places, and might hear the truth. Men had been used to slaughter oxen to devils at certain times. Let them still slaughter oxen, but for festive purposes, so that on dedication days, and nativities, and so on, they might build huts and booths about the churches and enjoy themselves as they had been wont ; only they must thank God for their sustenance, and so by degrees they would come to look upon these festivals of the Church with Christian eyes.

To this source we must attribute such of the festivities which accompany Christmas-tide as are independent of the joyousness of religious feeling. We find these festivities mentioned in the Life of St. Cuthbert, when the saint was entreated to come out of his retirement and keep the feast with his brethren. He refused for some time, but at length he came forth and sat down with them, indulging in a good dinner, much merriment, and story-telling. Their enjoyment was spoiled by his mysterious hints of something terrible, which proved to be a pestilence that swept off almost all the brethren ; but that does not affect the fact that Christmas Day, which coincided with one of the great pagan festivals, was kept then much as it is now. The use of holly and other evergreens is, of course, a survival of the huts made of boughs, in which our Saxon ancestors kept their pagan feast.

There was one part of Gregory's advice which led to a good deal of trouble. He spoke of the people being allowed to slaughter, for the purpose of feasting, the animals they had been accustomed to slay in sacrifice to their gods. We find from various canons of the Anglo-Saxon Church, that the love for horse-flesh could not be eradicated. The most idolatrous sacrifice the Teutonic races could offer was a horse, and at their most idolatrous feasts they fed on the flesh of the horse. In times rather later than those of Bede, when the Anglo-Saxon Church was being put into order and was framing its laws, it is clear that the propensity to eat horse-flesh was looked upon as much the same thing as a propensity to relapse into paganism, or to keep the heart of a pagan with the name of a Christian, and it was accordingly strongly condemned in one council after another.

CHAPTER XVII

STUDY AND MISSIONS

Enthusiasm for study—Education—The School of York—Its masters—Alcuin—Missions, Irish influence—Egbert—Willibrord —Boniface—Englishmen's influence on the rulers of the Franks from Pepin to Charlemagne.

It is natural to ask how far the example set by Bede so early in the Christian life of the Anglo-Saxons was followed by those who came after ; how far he can be said to have founded, or been the precursor of, or been an important link in, a great school of learning.

The answer to this question is easy, and is satisfactory. It is not too much to say that the Anglo-Saxon Church in the north was in the van of learning and study down to the sad times of the Danish invasions.

Beginning with the enthusiasm of Benedict Biscop as early as 653, an enthusiasm which set the fire burning in his young companion of travel Wilfrith, we see that the early Northumbrian Christians were naturally inclined to learning. Benedict's repeated visits to Rome and Gaul furnished them with plenty of material. He taught, as we have seen, the archiepiscopal school at Canterbury for some two years about 668–70, until such time as the African Hadrian and the Greek Theodore were ready to take up the work. With that exception, Northumbria was the recipient of his stores of mind and material. To him

Bede and all the much that he did in and for study are directly due. The twelve volumes of Bede's Works tell us something of what that "much" was. Among the West Saxons, Aldhelm was a bright early example of study and learning. He was a generation earlier than Bede.

Educationally, we must assign a high place to Benedict's companion Wilfrith. When he became Bishop of York, we find that he opened a school for the sons of—we must suppose—the people in important position. We gather that from his invitation to parents. Secular princes and noblemen were to entrust their sons to his care. He would so educate them that when the time of choice came they would be found fitted for the work they chose, whether it was to serve God in the ministry or to serve the king in arms. Those of us who were educated in the School of York regard this admirable plan of bringing all up in one school, as an evidence that the school was in its beginnings exactly what is meant by a "public school" as contrasted with a seminary or a secular school.

Bede was responsible for a change in the character of this chief school of the north. Ecgbert had told him that he found difficulty in obtaining an adequate supply of priests and other ministers. Bede advised that he should take boys quite young into his cathedral school, in earliest boyhood, and train them from the first for the ministry. It was in this way that a little boy by name Alcuin was taken into the school, almost in infancy, and in this way that he was trained in learning of all kinds, so that he became the leading scholar of Europe, the teacher, adviser, and friend, of Charlemagne.

Ecgbert secured for his school the services of Albert as master. If we may trust Alcuin's report, and everything seems to confirm it, the school and the diocese were equally fortunate in this selection of a master. Albert was good, just, pious, and liberal ; he taught the faith in the spirit of love ; he could be stern to those who would not yield to his persuasion ; he was a friend to the poor, the fatherless, the oppressed. The youths who frequented his school had the opportunity of studying everything that was then known. Languages, then called " grammar," mathematics, natural history, rhetoric, law, poetry, astronomy,—these and other branches of study formed the liberal curriculum ; and with and beyond all, the exposition of the Holy Scriptures. Albert had a keen eye for youthful promise, and when he found among his pupils one of whom he thought that he might make a scholar or an eminent Christian, he took all possible pains with him. He travelled on the Continent in search of additional means and improved methods of instruction ; he visited Rome as the centre of the Western Church. On his return, the kings of the south would fain have kept him among them, but he remained true to his home at York, and took up again his interrupted task of teaching. What his learning was, and his zeal in collecting the means of study, may be gathered from the abridged list of the books in his possession at the time when he retired from active life, which his pupil and successor and biographer, Alcuin, has left us. There were writings of Roman historians, philosophers, and poets ; the philosophical writings of Aristotle ; treatises on grammar ; the works of his countrymen, Aldhelm, Bede, and Willibrord ; and, best of all, a goodly collection of the fathers,—Basil, Athanasius, Chrysostom, Hilary, Ambrose, Augustine, Jerome, Leo, Gregory, and others. They were so numerous that he had built a library for them.

On Ecgbert's death, the popular voice designated Albert, who, like Ecgbert, was of the royal race, as his successor in the archbishopric. He became archbishop, and abundantly proved the wisdom of the choice. Alcuin tells us how, like a good shepherd, he fed his flock with the food of the Divine Word ; how he guarded the lambs from the wolf, and bore on his shoulders the sheep that had gone astray. He did not allow the manifold affairs of his high position to curtail his study of the Scriptures. He boldly rebuked vice, whether in the person of commoner, earl, or king.

For ten years he retained the headship of the school along with the archbishopric. He then determined to resign both, and to retire into private life in the monastery. His two favourite pupils succeeded him, Eanbald as archbishop, Alcuin as head of the cathedral school. And Alcuin is by far the most prominent figure in the educational progress of the Western world in those times.

Alcuin was born about the year of Bede's death, or seven years before that event, if the later date of 742 A.D. be accepted for the year of his death. He was educated under Albert at York, and became, as we have seen, Albert's successor. He was already famous for his learning, not in England only, but on the Continent ; so much so, that when he went to Rome to obtain the pall for Eanbald of York, Albert's successor in the archbishopric, Charlemagne persuaded him to take charge of the education of his sons, with all the educational affairs of his vast empire. Alcuin received the consent of his own king and the archbishop before accepting Charlemagne's offer ; and he became the master of the palatine or court school at Paris, and Minister of Education for the Franks. One of his first cares was to remedy a specially evil result of the anarchy which had for so many years prevailed in the countries which Charlemagne had at last brought to something like order. The copies of the Scriptures and of service books had in many places disappeared altogether ; in other places there were very inferior and incorrect copies, made by ignorant hands. Alcuin examined some of the best manuscripts, and then had them copied in large numbers, and the copies were sent out to cathedrals and important churches and abbeys, where they were still further multiplied. When this great work was accomplished, Alcuin set about furnishing the empire with the means of acquiring secular knowledge. He did not find in all France, and of course not in Germany, any such libraries as he had left in several places in England. He obtained permission from Charlemagne to send over some of his own pupils to England to copy the chief treasures in the library at York, which he knew so well.[1] And thus Saxon England gave to France—and in a less degree to Germany—the learning which it had itself derived from Theodore and Hadrian in the years preceding the birth of Bede. Theodore landed in England in 668 A.D., and found England in a state of ignorance ; and in less than a hundred and twenty years his work had borne such fruit that Englishmen were at the head

---

[1] A fuller statement of Alcuin's unique work and position will be found in *Alcuin of York*, G. F. Browne, 1908.

of learning in the Western world. We have seen how important a part Northumbria played in the pioneer work at Canterbury in the person of Benedict Biscop.

If we were to pass on to consider what the Christian world of Europe and of England owed—and still owes —to Alcuin for his labours in liturgiology, in church music, in details of Eucharistic Services, in the dominant use of the Psalms in services and especially in daily private life, a book might well be written on this branch alone of the flowers and fruits that the School of York produced for the Christian world in great abundance and of a high degree of excellence.

The Northumbrians were also—and no more fitting conclusion could be found for remarks on the state of England in the seventh and eighth centuries—at the head of missionary enterprise in Europe. It would appear that they caught the mission fever from the Irish, and with their practical instinct they made their work solid and stable, built on foundations sure and strong. The Irish, on the other hand, for the most part did not settle down and solidify, except when they found themselves among a solid people, as at St. Gall, and then they were absorbed, and continued to be an element of great value.

A Northumbrian noble, born in 639, thirteen years after the first conversion of Northumbria, so that his parents had certainly been pagans, was moved by his love of study and his zeal for learning, left his native country, and went to Ireland to profit by the teaching of learned men there, of whom there were many. It was a fashion in those very early days of Anglo-Saxon Christianity to go to Ireland for purposes of study and devotion.[1] Egbert, to retain that spelling

---

[1] *St. Aldhelm of Malmesbury*, G. F Browne, passim.

to avoid confusion with Ecgbert the Northumbrian
prelate, was only twenty years of age when he went
to Ireland in the year 659, five years before the Synod
of Whitby, and therefore at a time when the Irish
(Scotic) influence was very strong in Northumbria,
and there was much coming and going between the
two islands. He took with him Ceadda, afterwards St.
Chad, and several others. In course of time he caught
the zeal for missions which had been strong in Ireland
for a long time. Columban and Gall had left Ireland
together in 585, twelve years before Augustine brought
Christianity to the Anglo-Saxons, and had gone to the
country which we now call Switzerland, Columban
pushing on thirty years later to Bobio, or Bobbio,
which became a place famous in Irish and Anglo-
Saxon literature.

Egbert determined to lead a party from Ireland, in
687, just a hundred years after Columban and Gall
went, but not to follow in their steps. He thought of
the pagan peoples in the north of the great territory
which was known as Germania, who were the cousins
of Angles and Saxons and Jutes, and he desired to
take to them the blessings of the pure and wholesome
religion which was spreading so fast in the Angle-land.
If he could not accomplish that, he would go on to
Rome, to the thresholds of the blessed Apostles and
Martyrs, the twin chiefs of the Apostles, Peter and
Paul; or, as the early Irish ritual books put it, Paul
and Peter, following Eusebius, as did the old Slavonic
ritual books.

He was not to carry out either plan. The violence
of storms and the warnings of visions forced him to
remain in Ireland ; but in the year 690 he sent out
Willibrord, whom he had brought from Ripon, with

eleven companions, to Frisia, large part of which has been washed away since, leaving only the present Holland. Willibrord had great success. He was admitted to very friendly relations with the powerful Mayor of the Palace, Pepin d'Heristal, who conquered the Frisians, and by Pepin's son Charles Martel who saved Europe from the Saracens by the great battle of Tours. When Charles Martel's son Pepin le Bref was born, Willibrord was invited to perform the ceremony of baptism. The fort and city now known as Utrecht were given to Willibrord and he became Archbishop there, dying at an advanced age about the time of Bede's death. Pope Sergius had given him the name Clemens. Wilfrith of York, under whose tuition Willibrord had been in his early years at Ripon, had at one stage of his fitful career been cast upon the shores of Frisia, and had converted multitudes of pagans there.

Two Saxon monks, Hewald the white and Hewald the black, had got through to Saxony and preached Christianity there. They were martyred near Cologne, in the year 695. The Friesland mission pushed its work even into Prussia, and with fair success ; but political changes broke up the mission for a time. Winfrid of Crediton, a monk of Exeter, joined Willibrord at Utrecht about the year 716. He preached in Hesse and in Friesland. In 723 he was consecrated by Gregory II as missionary bishop of the Germans east of the Rhine, under the name of Boniface. For thirty years he laboured in this vast and dangerous sphere, keeping up a constant correspondence with the Pope, to whom he wrote with a frankness which few correspondents of popes have used. He held the great archiepiscopal see of Mainz, and was martyred at length in the year 755 at Dockum, in East Friesland. He was succeeded at Mainz by Lul, a monk from Malmesbury, who had studied at Jarrow.   Both Boniface and Lul owed much to Bede, whose works they used.[1]

It is much to the credit of our Anglo-Saxon ancestors that these great missionaries developed remarkable powers of statesmanship and had an instinctive skill in dealing with important civil and military authorities which enabled them to exercise large influence in the highest quarters.   Englishmen had the ear of Pepin d'Heristal, Charles Martel, Pepin le Bref, Charlemagne, the four generations of men from father to son who created mediæval Europe.   The three Englishmen were, Willibrord named Clemens, Winfrid named Boniface, and Alcuin.   It was in concert with Boniface and the Pope that Pepin le Bref emerged from his mayoralty and dukedom and became King of the Franks.   Alcuin played his part in concert with Charlemagne in the course which led Karl from kingship to empire.   From the year 690 to the year 804, the only years in which those four rulers had not a powerful Englishman always at hand were the years between 755, the martyrdom of Boniface, and 782 when Karl persuaded Alcuin of York to become his chief adviser, especially in educational affairs, but as a matter of fact in affairs of all kinds.   It adds much to the interest of this, that the last of the three advisers wrote the life of the first of the three, and that on the ground of relationship.   Alcuin tells us that Willibrord was the son of Wilgils, who lived a religious life with his wife and all his house, and eventually lived a solitary life on the promontory between the sea and the Humber, no doubt the present Spurn Point.   The great men of the realm gave Wilgils some small neigh-

[1] See *Boniface of Crediton*, G. F. Browne, pages 229 etc.

bouring properties that he might build a church. Here he collected a congregation of servants of God, and " his descendants to this day hold the property by title of his sanctuary, of whom I am the least in merit and the last in order. I who write this book of the history of the most holy father and greatest teacher Willibrord, succeeded to the government of that small cell by legitimate degrees of descent." It is unnecessary to dwell upon the interest of that statement, quite apart from its extrene interest as an evidence of the near kinship of Willibrord and Alcuin.

CHAPTER XVIII

ANGLO-SAXON ART

Art work in gems and precious metals—Silks—Pictures—Geography—Sculptured stones—Classes of objects—Churchyards—Classes of surface ornamentation—The human figure—The tree of life—The interlacements—Dragonesque interlacements—Irish examples—Caledonian Picts—The Lindisfarne Gospels—Comparison with the Book of Kells.

IT seems impossible to part with our Northumbrian ancestors without saying something of their successful study of art, for which they evidently had an instinctive love and a racial aptitude.

We have seen in what glowing terms Eddi describes the ornamentation of the Church of Ripon. He rings the changes on gold and silver and purple and jewels ; a purple altar cloth inwoven with gold ; the Four Gospels in purest gold, on purpled parchment, illuminated ; a case to contain the Four Gospels which he had ordered the setters of gems to construct of the purest gold and most precious jewels. This splendid collection of the gospels was no doubt suggested to his mind by the fact that on his earliest visit to Rome, while yet a layman, he had gone first to the church of the monastery of St. Andrew, had there seen on the high altar a Gospel-book, and had prayed that he might have grace to teach the Gospel to the races at home. Later on, Eddi tells how Bishop Acca enriched Wilfrith's church at Hexham with gold and silver and jewels and purple and silk, with a splendour which no words could describe. We shall see how the workmen at Wilfrith's early home at Lindisfarne carried out Wilfrith's idea of splendour in the covers of their own Lindisfarne gospel-books.

Skilled workmanship in the precious metals, and in the setting of gems, continued to be in large demand in England. Examples are to be found in the museums. We have among other such treasures in the British Museum the gold ring of King Ethelwulf, Alfred's father ; and in the Bodleian collection there is Alfred's own jewel, of gold and enamel, with its open-work gallery of inscription, ✠ *Aelfred mec heht gewyrcan*, *Alfred made work me*.

The inscription of Ethelwulf's ring, in gold letters on a niello ground, is ✠ Ethelwulf R, the cross, in each case, being of four equal arms. These two beautiful works of art have two close connections with one another, palæographical and ornamental, besides the natural fact that the W is in each case a double capital V On Ethelwulf's ring the HE is one bindletter, the second upright of the H forming the upright of the E. The use of bind-letters occurs three times in the Alfred jewel. The second upright of the M forms the upright of E, the second upright of the first H forms the upright of E as on Ethelwulf's ring, and the second upright of the second H is crossed at the top and so the bind-letter HT is formed. It is a curious fact, often illustrated in early Welsh rude inscriptions on stones, but startling on a beautiful piece of gold work like this, that the T of Ethelwulf is upside down. The other close connection, in ornament, is typical of a long continuity. A plant stem springs from a central root and divides the field in two. In the Ethelwulf ring, the upper part of which is triangular, two birds' heads come together at the top, one on each side, and the bodies and wings and tails of the birds swell out and occupy the lower parts of the triangle. In the Alfred jewel, which is almond-shaped, the point downwards, highly ornamental floral ornament takes the place of the birds' heads, and symmetrical foliage occupies the lower part on either side. The socket into which the pointer of ivory or precious wood fitted, which still has its rivet, is another example of continuity of type. It is the snout of a very carefully executed dragon's head.

The natural and rapidly increasing demand for crosses pectoral and processional, for reliquaries, for lamps, for sacred vessels, for all the varied *ornamenta* of the altar, acted as a perpetual stimulus to the development of beauty in design and skill in the execution of works in gold and silver and gems. Plates 7 and 8 show us simple and very early examples of gold work and silver work.

Robes of silk, magnificently ornamented, have always had a great vogue, in West and East alike. The sight of the Prelate of the Order of St. Michael and St. George, moving in procession down the aisle of St. Paul's in this present year of grace, is a sufficient indication of the continuance of the vogue. How strongly such magnificence appealed to our earliest Christian ancestors is shown by the fact mentioned on page 124, that the Northumbrian king and his councillors gave a considerable area of land to Benedict Biscop for two royal *pallia* made entirely of silk and worked in an incomparable manner. There was no lack of continuity in this respect among our ancestors.

Pictorial art had from the very first a strong appeal to the Anglo-Saxon instinct. A picture of the Saviour, and a processional cross, were the first Christian appeals to the eyes of those who became the first English converts. It is difficult for us to realise the vast importance of pictorial representations of the details of the Christian story, in an age when scarcely anyone outside the ministry could read at all, and when the gospels were open books to those only who could read and understand Latin. We have seen how completely Biscop and Wilfrith realised this value of pictures, and how fully they acted upon it. The taste for pictorial representation did not end with the Christian story. Geographical representations fetched an even larger price than royal *pallia*, as we have seen on page 124.

Among the principal remains of Anglo-Saxon Art which we possess, the sculptural stones rank high. Generalising from the specimens of the art of stone-carving which have come down to us through all the vicissitudes of war, vandalism, neglect, and decay, England must have been in many parts a great treasure house of art when the Normans came and dealt destruction. The occupying of the surfaces of squared or cylindrical shafts with ornament had been carried in the earliest Christian times to a high pitch of excellence. The excellence would seem to have disappeared under the Danish invasions, and to have been replaced by a dullness and rudeness which speak eloquently of the dearth and death of the religious fervour which had spiritualised the work of the early carvers. Northumbria was the land of origin of the highest art ; the lands of the Mercians, who like the Northumbrians were Angles, cannot have been much behind Northumbria ; and in the land of the West Saxons we still have a considerable number of bold examples of the

surface ornament of the earliest Christian times in
England.

There were two main classes of objects of worked
stone to which the art of surface ornamentation could
be freely applied in the early times of English Christianity. The one was the shafts of standing crosses
and the bases on which the shafts stood. The other
was the solid stones, resembling the lower part of
standing cross-shafts of large section, which the
itinerant priest set up at each place of which he took
possession as a Christian centre. The stone marked
the place where he would come on his rounds for
preaching and baptising. It served as the altar on
which he would place the small consecrated portable
altar he carried with him for celebrating the sacred
mysteries. We have a graphic account of Bishop
Wilfrith, about the year 667, taking with him, from
his home at Ripon in Northumbria, a party of workmen, carpenters and stonecutters, and setting up
memorials at his halting-places as he traversed the
thinly populated lands of the Mercian Angles. So
far as the standing crosses are concerned, we know
that in the year 709 they set up in Somerset and Wilts
seven stone crosses, all perfect in William of Malmesbury's time, say 1130, one at each of the seven places
where the body of Aldhelm rested for the night on its
fifty miles' journey from Doulton in Somerset to
Malmesbury in Wilts. The practice of setting up great
stone crosses beautifully sculptured must have become
usual before such crosses could be erected in such
numbers for one occasion. If the crosses of which
there are remains at two likely villages in North
Wilts are, as I believe them to be, examples of these
seven Aldhelm crosses, the memorials when complete

must have been magnificent. There are some six feet of the shaft at Littleton Drew, with remains of an inscription in very bold Latin capitals. The small fragments at Colerne have lacertine interlacements of perfect delicacy of design and workmanship. The magnificent high-crosses in the market-place at Sandbach in Cheshire are a noble relic of antiquity. At least as noble, and in higher art, are the great standing crosses at Ruthwell in Dumfries and Bewcastle in Cumberland.

The sculptured cross of Christ and the sculptured altar, at the place where the itinerant priest took his stand, would naturally be the centre for the burial of the faithful departed. It would thence be surrounded by a ring or more probably a square of rude stone walls. When in the course of time a church came to be built, a place would naturally be selected within the walls where the foundations would not disturb the bodies of the dead, and where the building would not prevent the rays of the sun from playing upon the place of their burial. The extreme north of the enclosure would alone meet those conditions, and there the church was built centrally. This accounts for the churchyard cross in very ancient churchyards being opposite the south door of entrance of the church, and being at the centre of the churchyard. It accounts also for the traditional objection on really ancient sites to burying on the north side of the church, which was originally beyond the consecrated area. The ceremony for the consecration of a cemetery in Ecgbert's Pontifical of the first half of the eighth century completely carries out these suggestions, especially as regards the square shape and the altar at the central point of the cemetery. From this it follows that if on a really early site the church is in the centre of the churchyard and there is no feeling against burying on the north side, the building of the earliest church and the earliest enclosure of the churchyard were simultaneous. The church and churchyard of Ilam in Staffordshire afford an excellent example of the earlier arrangement, the growth of the cemetery to begin with, and the erection of the first church later.[1]

We have seen that Bishop Wilfrith took about with him in Mercia—his own large possessions were chiefly in the county of Northampton—skilled workers in stone, whose business it would be to shape and ornament the crosses and the altars at the successive preaching centres. We shall see that there still remain examples in the district of his visit.

There were three styles of art for such purposes as those here described. One, which very soon lost the wonderful perfection of its very earliest time in this country, was the representation of the figures of Our Lord and His Saints, and important personages. We have this type of art in perfection on the Bewcastle[2] and Ruthwell[3] crosses, in Cumberland and Dumfries respectively, where the figure of Our Lord is of very striking dignity, somewhat lessened by the loss of the right hand, which was raised in blessing. The period of this Art was very short ; it may be doubted whether it had any real continuity beyond the generation which designed and executed the two examples named, presumably foreigners of Græco-Byzantine and Near-East training.

A second style of art represented arabesques of

[1] See my *Sculptured Stones of Ilam*, Bell and Sons.
[2] Pages 78, 175 and Plate 4.
[3] Pages 79, 178, and Plate 15.

flowers and tendrils and stems, with fruit in the
tendrils and birds and other creatures feeding on the
fruits, a veritable tree of life. At Bewcastle and Ruthwell these trees of life run up the edges of the shaft. We
must again trace this second style to a Græco-Byzantine or Near-Eastern (arabesque) origin. The ivory
chair of Archbishop Maximianus (546–556) at Ravenna,
in the Church of S. Vitale, is practically covered with
examples of just the tree of life which we find at
Bewcastle and Ruthwell. The inspiration of those
crosses, and probably the sculptors, came from
Ravenna or from some part of Lombardy, perhaps
Brescia. It is evident that this style of ornamental
foliage arabesque, with or without living creatures, is
suited equally for vertical and horizontal application.
It does not present the difficulty in drawing which the
forms of living creatures present, and the remains
which we possess show that it was generally popular
with our ancestors, and at many periods was creditably
designed and executed, at some periods with exquisite
skill. The symbolism of this style of religious ornamentation may carry us in one or all of three directions.
It may suggest the general feature of the Garden of
Eden, " every tree that is pleasant to the eye and good
for food," or the special feature of the tree " in the
midst of the garden, the tree of life," the *lignum vitæ*
of the Vulgate, so apt a subject for the shaft of the
cross of which it was a forecast ; or it may symbolise
the Kingdom of Heaven, growing on and on from a
minute grain till it becomes the greatest among herbs,
a tree such that " the birds of the air come and lodge
in the branches thereof." And considering the remarkable popularity which the Song of Songs attained and
maintained among our early Anglian ancestors, the

presence of little quadrupeds makes it natural to see some reference to that great song of love, " take us the foxes, the little foxes, that spoil the vines, for our vines have tender grapes." The Oriental origin of this type of ornament, which got such hold upon the Anglian mind, renders this reference specially probable.

There remains a third style, which may be described in one word, interlacement. This style affords scope for quite endless variations. The most subtle, the most delicate, the most elegant results can be attained. The predominant characteristic of this style, as carried out in early England, Ireland, and Caledonia, is the endlessness, the infinity, of the designs. Passing ever alternately under and over itself, one endless band— or the superposition of two endless bands—fills panels of surface with perpetual interlacements, forming now the circumference—skilfully broken—now the diameter of a circle and then passing on to form another like combination, till the whole panel is occupied in a beautiful maze by the endless band. It is a symbol of eternity.

This style subdivides into two. The one is the interlacement of one band, or of two, sometimes representing merely a piece of basketwork, sometimes producing the patterns described in the previous paragraph. The other is the interlacement of the bodies and limbs of lacertine creatures and serpentine quadrupeds. We may deal with the two styles separately. Figure 2 on Plate 17 is an illustration of the effectiveness and subtlety of this development of the main idea of the interlacement of bands. This and the other panels on Plate 17 are from the collection of great standing crosses at Kells in Ireland, the monastery made famous for ever by its production of the Book of Kells, referred to on page 321. The actual panels on the stones do not present at all the same clearness as the illustrations, or anything like it. Each panel has cost a good deal of labour in its interpretation. Rubbings were taken, the interlacements outlined after much study on the spot of the stone and of the rubbing, and then photographed down to their present size. The great reduction in scale has obliterated the roughnesses of my outlines of the interlacements.

It may be mentioned incidentally that all of these three panels produce a beautiful effect in embroidery, say of gold thread on yellow-cream silk. Many of the patterns from sculptured stones are being wrought in schools of art-work, in embroidery, and in wood and metal.

While the west side of the Bewcastle shaft on Plate 4 gives us beautiful examples of the human form in high relief, and, incidentally, the earliest original piece of Anglo-Saxon prose in existence, the south side, on Plate 18, carries us further into the art which was locally continuous. There are three panels of interlacement, two of them very simple, the lowest an effective example of the interlacements of a double band. There is also a sundial, in accordance with very early custom in connection with Saxon churches. And there are two panels of foliage ornament of the tree-of-life character. These two panels are of fundamental interest. They give us original examples of the two kinds of tree of life, the upper springing from one root, the other from two. We have examples of the development of both of these two kinds, the latter especially giving rise to patterns of beautiful interlacement of the details of the two trees, an art which received its highest development in the exquisite cross of Bishop Acca of Hexham, now in the dorter at Durham. The single tree of life shown on Plate 16 can be seen on the edge of the shaft on Plate 18. There is in the dorter at Durham a considerable portion of a very early Anglian cross-shaft, Plate 16, said to be a part of Ethelwold's cross, the whole cross having been standing, and known as St. Ethelwold's, up to and beyond the time of the Reformation with its terrible destruction of the priceless things of early art. The upper and lower panels are of ordinary interlacement, the lower resembling the panel at the foot of the Bewcastle shaft on Plate 18. The central panel is a battered example of the interlacement of two dragonesque creatures, the tail and hind-leg and fore-leg of each being conspicuous. Considering the special beauty of Ethelwold's cross, as mentioned at page 318, we cannot say that these panels justify the traditional assignment of this fragment. But it may be that there was something specially beautiful in the contemporary form of the cross when complete. This suggestion falls in with the original statement that the upper part of the cross was blown off in a gale of wind, and a skilful workman invented a method of fastening it on again by the use of molten lead.

Figures 1 and 3 on Plate 17 are apt illustrations of two kinds of lacertine or dragonesque interlacements. The panel shown in Figure 1 presented considerable difficulties in the way of interpretation. It is probably correct, with one exception due to a natural difficulty, the difficulty of being sure whether a dragon's tongue is projecting from his mouth, or another dragon's tail is being held in his mouth. If we name the two heads at the top of the panel A and B, from left to right, and the two at the bottom C and D, it would appear that what is drawn as a tail in A's mouth must be meant for A's tongue. With that correction, it will be seen that the panel is analysed thus :—

A's tail is in D's mouth. A's tongue ends in a fish-tail at the back of D's head. B's fish-tail crosses C's neck. C's tail, after a long journey all over the panel, is developed into a head in C's own mouth. D's tail is in B's mouth.

In the panel shown in Figure 3, the crest, neck, fore-leg, body, hind-leg, and tail, of each of the four dragons are used as interlacing bands, passing alternately under and over. This is an unusually non-subtle arrangement, but it is very effective. There is a Celtic quaintness about these two figures.

Figure 2 on Plate 17 is an example of the higher style of the art of interlacements. It is not in the highest style, for the interlacing bands do not form alternately diameters and circumferences, nor do they form alternately circumferences of outer and inner circles. But this is in considerable part due to the fact that eight out of nine of the circle systems are at the edges of the panel, and thus the bands have to be continually turning back instead of going straight on towards another circle system. We have in the public street of Stapleford, Notts, a cylindrical pillar with fifteen of these circle systems, and there the law of alternate circumference and diameter, and alternate inner and outer circumference, is most skilfully observed.

The figure under discussion is Irish. There are many such examples in Ireland, at Monasterboice, Termonfechin, and other centres of early remains. In the Pictish parts of Scotland there is a great abundance of elaborate examples ; while on the Scottish side of Caledonia there is very little indeed of this elaborate art of interlacement. The probability is that frequent invasions killed old schools of art and introduced new styles, so far as England was concerned, while the freedom of Ireland and Caledonia from such disturbances and destructions left the artistic mind free to study and to develop to its higher possibilities the attractive art, which was their chief style of ornamentation. A similar consideration explains the scarcity—even in Northumbria—of complete monuments with this style of ornament in England, as compared with Ireland and Caledonia.

The emphasis on the Pictish (eastern) parts of Caledonia as compared with the Scottish (western) parts can scarcely mean anything other than a continuance of the art which so much struck the Roman soldiery, the art of painting on the bodies of the Picts the figures of animals and other decorations. The sculptured stones which are so numerous in the Pictish lands, and some of them so magnificent, carry elaborate interlacements in the highest style, forming the head and arms and shaft and centre of large crosses in high relief on great erect flat stones. And not elaborate interlacements only but horses and hounds and deer and many kinds of symbolic ornaments. They must be the application to stone monuments of the art originally painted on the naked body of the Pict, an art so striking that the Roman soldiers of Stilicho A.D. 399 paused in the midst of battle to study the figures on the bodies of the fallen foe. Stilicho had with him in his invasion of Caledonia a martial poet, Claudian. Claudian has made the fact and character of the Pictish art immortal. He shows us the Roman soldier, wondering,

Perlegit exsangues Picto moriente figuras.

We, too, stand and wonder, as we gaze at these very same figures wrought in relief on stone, either at isolated places in Perthshire and Forfar and Kincardine and up to Elgin, or in the great group at Meigle, once the royal residence of the Pictish kings of the southeast of Caledonia.

There are, as has been said above, a considerable number of early pre-Conquest sculptures on the faces of cross-shafts in the West Saxon and British parts of Wilts and Somerset and Devon. The dragonesque style is the prevailing type there. At Colerne, Dolton, Ramsbury, Rowberrow, West Camel, examples are to be found. At Gloucester, too, there is a very fine example of involved dragons. Bearing in mind Harold's Dragon Standard in the Bayeux worsted-work, and the Dragon Standard of Wales, it is tempting to imagine that the pairs of interlaced dragons found on one early stone after another in those parts had some relation to the tug-of-war when Bret dragon met West Saxon dragon. At West Camel, one of the finest of the dragonesque stones, there is a very unusual combination of a panel of interlacing tendrils springing successively from a central stem on the principle of foliage ornament. This same feature is found on the massive shaft at Littleton Drew in North Wilts, the ornamentation of which is, so far as I know, unique.[1]

In the long wanderings of the monks of Lindisfarne

Figures of the stones mentioned here are to be found in a chapter on the subject which I contributed to the *Memorials of Old Wilts*, Bemrose and Sons, 1906.

with St. Cuthbert's coffin after the destruction of the monastery by the Danes, they carried with them two great treasures of art, Ethelwold's stone cross and the Lindisfarne Gospels.   The cross was erected by Bishop Ethelwold in his lifetime, and was so exquisitely ornamented with the best art of the period, 724–740, that they could not bear to leave it behind them.   What that art was we can learn with certainty from the Lindisfarne Gospels.

A passage inserted at the end of the Gospel of St. Matthew tells us how this beautiful book was built up.   " Eadfrith bishop of the church of Lindisfarne [698 to 721] he wrote this book at first for God and the holy Cuthbert and all the saints that are in the island and Ethelwold the bishop of Lindisfarne island he made it firm outside and bound it as he well could.   Bilfrith the anchorite wrought in smith's work the ornaments that were on the outside with gold and gems and silver overlaid a treasure without deceit.   And Aldred the presbyter unworthy and most miserable glossed it in English."   We may be sure that Aldred wrote this passage.   The glorious cover, with its gold and jewels, has completely disappeared.   The book itself is in the British Museum.

Plate 19, showing the ornamental page at the beginning of the Gospel of St. Luke, gives us good examples of the interlacements of endless bands and the entanglements of dragonesque interlacements.

The interlacements of a double band which run into all the beautifully formed cross in the centre is a remarkable piece of work.   It is a serious matter to follow with the eye these interlacements, with their alternate crossings under and over. The number of these crossings is uncountable, and they never fail to observe the law of alternation. We may well wonder at the skill shown in this design; but the skill in execution, with such instruments and pigments and inks as they had then, seems more wonderful still. The eyesight and the manual firmness of draughtsmanship of our ancestors must have been supremely good. There are cases elsewhere in which spirals like watch-springs seem to the modern eye to come to a mere blur in the centre, while the application of magnifying power reveals the spiral still working smaller and smaller in what seems to our unaided eye to be a mere blur of paint. Notice should be taken of the rule of endless continuity as worked out by the two light-coloured edges of the dark land which enclosed the whole magnificent work. They play off at the centres of the ends and sides to form the outlines of the throat and crest of the pairs of dragons' heads.

The six inset rectangular panels give four different examples of the involvement of quadruped dragons, in some of the panels biting their own bodies, in others biting each other's bodies. The long necks and powerful fore-quarters and hind-quarters are conspicuous in the four corner panels, with crests and tails to form the finer entanglements. The panel in the bottom left-hand corner best shows the usual and curiously expressive manner of indicating a joint as a spiral spring. The entanglements of birds in the four projecting corners are well worth study. It will be seen that the outline of the body and the tapering tail of the bird form double bands for the interlacing entanglements.

The diamond-shaped panels of key pattern are another expression of endlessness. The remainder of the background is in colour which photography shows as nearly black.

The only connection with Irish ornamentation in this splended piece of work is found in the four whorls in the centre of the leaf.

Plate 20 shows another of the leaves of the Lindisfarne Gospels. This is one of the most splendid things of the kind ever done, so far as our sadly limited examples of the perished splendours of illumination of those " dark " ages carries us.

Our study of the dragonesque interlacements in the central circle and the five horse-shoes of the cross is greatly aided by the fact that in each case there are two pairs of dragons painted in two different colours. They have long necks and bodies, with crests and tails that provide hampering interlacements, and two fore-legs, and two hind-legs ; thus each has seven members. The skill with which the patterns are worked into continuity at the five narrow necks connecting the central circle and the five horse-shoes should be specially noticed.

The parts outside the cross are greatly enriched by the introduction of gracefully shaped birds with painted wings. These are specially well shown in the right-hand lower corner. The birds have necks, and beaks that grasp in some cases their own neck, in other cases the bodies of serpentine quadrupeds. The birds have legs of a different colour, and the outline of their bodies and their tapering tails provide entangling interlacements. The lacertine quadrupeds have crests, and a fore-leg and two bold and well-drawn hind-legs, and a tail. The eight birds in the lowest corner, four in a row above and four in a row below, with their free-sweeping tails, form a wonderful picture in the colours of the original.

The projecting corner-pieces are full of minute interlacements which the small scale of the plate fails to show.

The whole is Anglo-Saxon work, not Irish. The basic motives are similar, or come from the same source or from cognate sources, but the working out of the motives is Anglian, not Celtic.

To study the stately illuminated pages of the Lindisfarne Gospels, and then to pass immediately to the study of the Irish Book of Kells, is to pass from order to chaos. Splendid as that Book is in design and colouring, there is lacking almost throughout the evidence of a master mind, intent upon securing balance and producing an effect of perfect continuity and equilibrium. There are endless pieces of beautiful pattern ; but not so arranged as to give harmony to the page. Some of the great collection of patterns on a leaf are spoiled by the presence of human faces and profiles, alike queer without being quaint, and mostly ugly. There are fifteen such profiles on one ornamental leaf, in three panels of five each. On another leaf there are fifteen or sixteen human forms, many of them in pairs, with their legs ridiculously used for interlacements. On one splendid page there is enclosed in a corner of the splendours a curious scene, two cats lying down facing one another. Standing on each cat is a rat. Between the cats there are two rats, biting at what must be meant for a wafer. All that would have been impossible at Lindisfarne. Anglian Art strikes the same sound note as Anglian history. Our ancestors were men of dignity.

And so we take leave of our Anglian forefathers, at the time when they were the leaders of the Western world in divine and secular learning and in missionary and political work. In so regarding them and rejoicing in them, we would fain shut out of our thoughts the terrible breakdown that the early future had in store for them.

INDEX